Gender Voices

Gender Voices

David Graddol and Joan Swann

Basil Blackwell

First published 1989

Basil Blackwell Ltd
108 Cowley Road, Oxford, OX4 1JF, UK

Basil Blackwell Inc.
3 Cambridge Center,
Cambridge, MA 02142, USA

British Library Cataloguing in Publication Data

A CIP catalogue record for this book is available
from the British Library

Library of Congress Cataloging in Publication Data

Graddol, David.
  Gender voices / David Graddol and Joan Swann.
    p.   cm.
  Includes index.
  ISBN 0-631-13733-5—ISBN 0-631-13734-3 (pbk.)
  1. Language and languages—Sex differences. I. Swann, Joan.
II. Title.
P120.S48G73 1990
306.4′4—dc20
                                              89-32368
                                              CIP

Typeset in 10 on 12pt Baskerville
by Footnote Graphics, Warminster, Wiltshire
Printed in Great Britain by The Camelot Press Ltd., Southampton

Contents

Acknowledgements

Our ideas for this book developed over the several years we have spent contributing to courses and carrying out research on language and communication at the Open University. We are grateful to colleagues at the Open University, who have always been ready to discuss ideas and provide critical comment.

Many people have given us useful comments on earlier drafts of chapters. In particular, we would like to thank Jenny Cheshire (Birkbeck College, London); Barbara Mayor, Neil Mercer and Will Swann (Open University); and Peter Trudgill (University of Essex).

For providing information and sharing their ideas on Esperanto and other artificial languages we are grateful to John Brownlee (Secretary, Esperanto Asocio de Britujo), Anna Brennan (Editor, *Sekso kaj Egaleco*), Marjorie Boulton, Daphne Lister, Reto Rosetti, Rasjidah St John and Alec Venture. We should also like to thank Robin Schneider of Esso UK; Roger Pauli and Marion Butler of Stuart Crystal; Diane Taylor (freelance training consultant); Jackie Hughes (Deputy Headteacher in Birmingham LEA); and John Pettit of the Equality Working Group in the School of Education, Open University, for providing us with information for the case studies in chapter 7.

Finally, we must thank Philip Carpenter from Basil Blackwell for his encouragement and unending patience.

The authors and publishers are grateful to the *Daily Mirror* for kind permission to reproduce the cartoons on pages 1 and 70. Text on pages 169–70 from the 1988 series of Electrolux 'Lifestyle' press advertising reproduced by permission of Electrolux Domestic Appliances.

1

Introduction

Andy Capp by Reg Smythe, *Daily Mirror*, 11 October 1982

'If the women in your street tend to yak over the garden hedge, do what they do in Meikleour, Perthshire – grow big hedges. The Meikleour beech hedge has a trimmed height of 85 ft. Mind you, it was planted in 1746, so you may have to wait a bit for some peace and quiet.'   (*The Pint Size Guinness Book of Records*, no. 4 High Society)

'Her voice was ever soft, gentle and low, an excellent thing in woman.'   (Shakespeare, *King Lear*, V iii)

'Mr Rex Winsbury wrote in the Financial Times with a bitchiness which made me forget he was a man.'   (*Guardian*, 1980)

'Do you not know I am a woman? When I think, I must speak.'
(Shakespeare, *As You Like It*, III ii)

'There can be no doubt that women exercise a great and universal

influence on linguistic development through their instinctive shrink-
ing from coarse and gross expressions and their preference for refined
and (in certain spheres) veiled and indirect expressions... Men will
certainly with great justice object that there is a danger of the
language becoming insipid if we are always to content ourselves with
women's expressions.'

(O. Jesperson, *Language: its nature, development and origin (1922)*)

The Study of Language and Gender

Stereotypes of women's and men's speech are plentiful and they
seem to have an extremely long history. They reflect popular images
of women's and men's language, perpetuated through proverbs,
jokes, journalism, literature and even by serious language scholars.
One of the striking features of these stereotypes is the way they
rarely favour women, who are consistently portrayed as chatter-
boxes, endless gossips or strident nags patiently endured or kept in
check by strong and silent men.

The fact that such persistent and well-developed images exist
suggests that this is a sensitive aspect of relationships between men
and women which will repay further study. And it is only reasonable
to wonder whether there is a grain of truth in the idea that women's
speech and use of language are, in systematic ways, different from
those of men. If it proves to be the case, then further questions are
raised, such as *why* such differences should exist. And does it
particularly matter? Can the allegations put forward by some
feminists be supported – that language is itself sexist and that
popular images serve both to denigrate and control the speech of
women? These are some of the issues that we are concerned with in
this book. In reviewing the answers that various scholars and writers
have given to such questions we will provide not only a survey of the
way women and men differ in their language habits but also an
exploration of the links between language and the stucture of
society, of how the way women and men speak ultimately affects
their position in society, their economic and political achievements,
and even their personalities and perceived identities.

Language and gender is an unusual and exciting area of research
which has enjoyed a phenomenal growth in the last decade or so.
One of the standard bibliographies (Thorne et al., 1983) lists the
work of over 1,000 authors and the number has grown considerably

since this list was compiled. Many universities and colleges offer courses in the subject and it is now a regular topic in textbooks and conferences on linguistics, sociology, women's studies and others. Alongside this academic activity, there have been the more practically oriented activities of researchers, journalists, feminists and writers of letters to the media who wish to bring about a change in women's and men's use of language, and in the language itself. And, of course, there has been the corresponding literature from people who resist such attempts at change. Language and gender has, then, both an academic and a popular appeal. It holds out the promise not only of advancing linguistic and social theory, but also of providing a social critique and a programme of political action aimed at reducing sexual inequality.

The popularity of the field, both within the academic community and the wider public, has not been entirely to its advantage. Its sheer diversity has made the development of a common theoretical perspective extremely difficult. And language and gender studies have been regarded with some suspicion by those who detect a bandwagon or who regard the field as just too fashionable; and by others who fear that some researchers' links with the women's movement and with identifiable political commitments prevent their work from being academically respectable. Such controversy routinely surrounds research which attempts to explain how society works, maintains its stability and permits change, but is nonetheless a reminder of the need for careful examination of any research which purports to link language with women's oppression. It is all too easy, in this as in other fields, to allow political sympathies to get in the way of intellectual rigour.

The present book attempts to provide a compact and readable introduction to the field of language and gender, dealing with both local and larger theoretical issues. We have tried to show how some important ideas in linguistics, psychology and feminist thought illuminate the role of language in establishing and regulating gender divisions, and we explore some of the possibilities for individual and social change. The 'voices' of the book's title are hence both literal speaking voices and figurative ones – the collection of opinions and positions held by those in the field.

The Nature of Language

Difficulties in defining the term *language* present the first obstacle to understanding the various claims made about the role of language in constructing gender divisions. The literature is filled with many lively debates, between writers of differing political persuasions and those with differing disciplinary backgrounds, and it is difficult to decide which conflicts of opinion have substance and which arise from different uses of the word language and from different understandings of what language is. It is not difficult to see why there exists such a problem of definition. Language, like gravity, is one of those things with which everyone is familiar but few can adequately describe and explain. This is a surprising fact considering the intimate part that it plays in our lives, but people have less privileged access to many of their own mental processes than they often imagine. Perhaps this is one reason why there are many popular conceptions and misconceptions about language, how it works, and how it affects people. But if there is a danger in taking language for granted, there is an equal danger of mystification. It is all too easy to talk about language in ways which make it appear a complex, mysterious and paradoxical thing which is beyond the understanding of non-specialists.

Both the authors of this book have a background and training in linguistics and take the view that, although complex, language can be described in a methodical and scientific manner. Our approach has been to adopt a traditional linguistic framework where possible, and to explain how competing ideas depart from this. In linguistics, for example, a clear distinction is usually made between the idea of language as a social phenomenon and the speech of an individual person. There also exists an orthodoxy that language is a specific human faculty, which can be distinguished from both animal communication and other kinds of human behaviour. Both these distinctions make a good starting point for any discussion of language and gender. The remainder of this introduction outlines these, and other preliminary notions, which we assume in later chapters.

Language is Personal

There exists a whole sub-discipline, *psycholinguistics*, that is concerned with discovering the individual mental processes involved in speech production and comprehension. In a cognitive sense, language is very much a private matter; it is said to be the vehicle of our internal thoughts and (some would say) desires. But our language is also an important part of our personal and social identity; our linguistic habits reflect our individual biographies and experiences. In all these ways, our language is our individual property.

Language is Social

Simultaneously, a language has an existence outside of ourselves; it pre-exists and continues when we are gone; it is much larger than us, embracing words and grammatical structures of which we are unaware. Language, in this sense, seems to be a public resource, like the water supply, that services a speech community and provides for the communication between individuals needed for social maintenance. The parallel with a public utility goes further. Many people seem to accept that some municipal authority, and not they themselves, has responsibility for the maintenance and upkeep of the language; for determining what is and what is not acceptable or grammatical; what should (or should not) be published and disseminated. Those who use words and structures that are not officially condoned are sometimes accused of 'polluting' this community resource.

The Saussurean Model

This tension between the personal and the social belongs to a long western tradition of language study but the distinction is particularly associated with the name of Ferdinand de Saussure, a Swiss linguist working at the beginning of this century. Following Saussure, the object of linguistic study is often taken to be the social, rather than the personal, facts of language. A 'language' is usually thought of as being an abstract system: a vocabulary and set of grammatical rules which govern how words may be combined to produce sentences. The concept of a system is more technical than it first appears, since it suggests that the elements that make it up are connected together in some specific manner. Saussure argued that the individual elements which made up a language system (the words of a language, say) did not have any meaning in an absolute sense, but could be defined in terms of their *relation* to one another. That is, the meaning of a word like *woman* cannot be defined without describing its opposition to other words such as *man* or *girl*. Furthermore, the relationship between a particular word and its meaning is essentially an arbitrary one. In order to understand such words, a listener must be party to what Saussure called the 'social contract' which bound all members of a speech community. The terms of this contract have evolved over many years and cannot be changed by any individual speaker, only through collective action.

These two Saussurean ideas – that of viewing language as an abstract system and that of the social contract – are still extremely influential among linguists. Some linguists, including the well-known grammarian Noam Chomsky, have gone so far as to claim that *language use*, being an aspect of individual behaviour, is of no linguistic interest. In this book, however, we are concerned with language in all its variety: in the character of men's and women's voices; in their patterns of interruption in conversation; in differences in accent as well as in certain aspects of vocabulary. At some points in this discussion it will be apparent that the crude equations *language system = a social abstraction and language use = individual behaviour* cannot easily be sustained. Many aspects of conversational behaviour, for example, are undoubtedly features of language use, but they are nevertheless institutionalized and socially recognizable behaviours. They seem to be part of a social contract rather than the idiosyncratic speech behaviour of an individual.

The Semiotic Approach

The phenomena we've just described are all closely associated with language, even if one is unsure of their precise status, but verbal language is only one of many ways in which people communicate their gender identity and recognize someone else's. We communicate with body gesture, with repertoires and rituals of action, by the clothes we wear, with graphic images and all manner of cultural practices. We can refer to all of these as 'signifying practices'; as well as communicating ideas they communicate much about the identity, ambitions and attitudes of the communicator. Whether it is a matter of a man holding open a door for a woman, or a woman serving a man with an extra egg for breakfast, such signifying practices can all be regarded as 'languages' of a kind, and there is at least one analytical tradition – that of *semiotics* or *semiology* – that provides a framework which embraces them all. Such semiotic systems are rough and ready ones compared with verbal language but, according to semiologists, the way in which they work and in which we understand them is very similar to the processes involved in language comprehension. For example, we can regard repertoires of action as a Saussurean system – a set of elements whose meaning is determined by a system of oppositions. Hence, part of the meaning of a 'skirt' is through its contrast with 'trousers', just as the word *woman* is opposed to *man* in the linguistic system. Saussure, and semiologists, regard both words and cultural practices as *signs* whose meanings are essentially arbitrary, a matter of social convention. The semiotic notion of a language is much wider in scope than is normally found in linguistics, but it is one employed by many writers in the language and gender literature. While the chief concern of this book is language in its more conventional (and restricted) sense, we shall draw on semiotics in chapter 2 and chapter 6.

These conceptual distinctions provide essential background for the discussions of research in later chapters, where it will be clear that however broad – or narrow – a view of language one wishes to take, it is essentially the *continuity* between both language as an individual and a social possession, and between verbal and other forms of human communication that allows language to play a major part in the construction and reproduction of culture – including gender divisions.

The Nature of Gender and the Gendered Nature of Society

The word *gender* can also give rise to misunderstanding, particularly when used in connection with language. *Gender* is used as a technical linguistic term relating to the grammatical categories of words in certain languages; we use the term in this specialist sense in chapters 3 and 5. Elsewhere *gender* is used in its more everyday sense to refer to a social distinction between masculine and feminine. In this sense it can be distinguished from the term *sex*, which relates to the biological and by and large binary distinction between male and female.

The opening words of Simone de Beauvoir's historic book *The Second Sex* capture the essential characteristic of gender: 'One is not born, but rather becomes, a woman.' Gender is a socially rather than a biologically constructed attribute – people are not born with but rather learn the behaviours and attitudes appropriate to their sex. During the last decade of research, it has become clear that gender is a very complex category. Theories are still being developed which try to grapple with this complexity but they share the idea that gender, unlike sex, is a continuous variable. A person can be more or less 'feminine' and more or less 'masculine'. Furthermore, a man can display 'feminine' characteristics just as a woman may demonstrate 'masculine' ones.

When we refer to society as being 'gendered' we mean that gender represents an important division in our society (and probably all human societies). Whether one is male or female is not just a biological fact, it assigns one to membership of one of two social groups. A great many consequences – social, economic and political – flow from this membership. Women and men, girls and boys, are treated in systematically different ways (by both women and men); they have different experiences at school, at work and at home; they do different things and different things are expected of them. In other words, women and men have different life experiences to an extent that cannot be satisfactorily explained by simple biological differences between the sexes. Furthermore, these differences between women and men seem such a natural and obvious part of our existence that we are usually unaware of their full extent. The way we talk is one of these all-pervasive and unobtrusive aspects of gender behaviour.

Gender is much more than a psychological attribute. It involves a person's sexuality, which has both a private and public dimension, and must always be understood in the context of particular, and changing, social relations between men and women.

The Relation Between Language and Gender

The two substantive words in the phrase 'language and gender' are linked by a small, unobtrusive word which gives little clue as to the precise nature of the relationship between the two. But it is this relationship which is most at stake. In exactly what way is language related to gender and vice versa? We have said that we wish to go beyond a catalogue of sex differences in language behaviour to explore why there should be such differences, and what social functions they serve. This book, if you like, is about the 'and'.

There are, broadly speaking, three kinds of relationship which can, and have been, put forward. First, there is the view that language merely *reflects* social divisions and inequalities; second, the position that such divisions and inequalities are actually *created* through sexist linguistic behaviour; and third, a view that argues that both processes apply, and that any full account of language and gender must explore the tension and interplay between the two.

Language Reflects Gender Divisions

Linguistic differences are merely a reflection of social differences, and as long as society views women and men as different – and unequal – then differences in the language of women and men will persist. (Coates, 1986, p. vi)

The view that linguistic behaviour merely reflects social processes is far from being a straightforward one. In chapter 3, for example, we discuss research on accent and dialect that shows how the language variety one speaks owes much to the patterns of interaction in a community, to the people one routinely talks to and to the status relationship one has with them. All these things are structured by social and economic processes that have little to do with language. In some communities, women have looser and more dispersed contacts with other people than men do (because of a conventional sexual division of labour, demographic patterns, and so on). Sociolinguistic theories have become adept at explaining why language usage is sensitive to patterns of living and patterns of interaction. In these ways one can say that certain sex differences in language behaviour are a side effect of the systematically different social experiences of women and men.

But certain kinds of speech may be regarded as socially appropriate for a particular sex, and may be learned by children just as they learn other kinds of gender appropriate behaviour. Men may swear and speak roughly, whilst women are more polite. We examine such claims in later chapters, but it can be argued that such sex differences in speech reflect different concepts of masculinity and femininity whose origins lie outside of language.

Language Creates Gender Divisions

Language helps form the limits of our reality. It is our means of ordering, classifying and manipulating the world . . . Having learnt the language of a patriarchal society we have also learnt to classify and manage the world in accordance with patriarchal order and to preclude many possibilities for alternative ways of making sense of the world. (Spender, 1985, p. 3)

The second position suggests that language does not function simply as a mirror of society. Rather, it is strongly implicated in the construction and maintenance of social divisions and inequalities. In learning important linguistic distinctions, speakers are also learning the distinctions regarded as important in their culture: they are learning to see their social and physical environment in one way rather than another. The way language is used in the media, or people's unreflective habits of speech, may project a biased evalua- tion of women and men and of female and male characteristics and thus come to define the expected social roles of men and women. Hence the position is a determinist one, suggesting that our individual lives and personalities are shaped by our language and by the discourses we engage in. This view has enjoyed some popularity – particularly, as we shall see in chapters 5 and 6, amongst radical feminists and some anthropological linguists.

There is an Interplay Between Language and Social Structure

Talk works to create and maintain sex-stereotyping and male dominance. Our speech not only reflects our place in culture and society but also helps to create that place. (Sally McConnell-Ginet, 1983, p. 69)

Our own view is that there is truth in both of the positions outlined above. Such a synthesis is not simply a compromise between the idea that language reflects and the opposing one that it creates gender divisions and inequalities. By suggesting that linguistic and social practices are mutually supportive, it suggests a stronger mechanism, that single causes will be more difficult to identify and change more difficult to effect. This position draws attention to the way language is part of a greater social jig-saw: we sometimes need to step outside linguistic analysis to see how a linguistic feature supports some other non-linguistic mechanism in sustaining gender divisions. For example, it can be argued that language helps reproduce traditional concepts of 'femininity' and 'masculinity' but to understand why such traditional concepts are oppressive to women requires social theories that have little to do with language. This is a debate we take up again in chapter 6.

In these various ways language has been implicated in the mechanisms that lead to gender divisions and, more specifically, those that support social inequalities between the sexes. In this book, we explore the specific arguments that have been put forward. The next four chapters examine the role played by various aspects of language and speech. In each case the treament largely reflects the theoretical approaches current in each research area. The last two chapters of the book are rather different. Chapter 6 examines the kind of general social theories that have been provided to explain the role of language in social reproduction, discussing further the ideas we have outlined here. In chapter 7 we look at various practical measures that have been taken, or proposed, for intervening in the social processes described in earlier chapters.

2

The Voice of Authority

'I don't care how many women you make love to in this room,' she lashed, scarcely recognising the high pitched voice as her own.

'Don't expect me to apologise for it.' His resonant voice had gone slightly hard.

'I hate you!' There was an unmistakable tremor in her voice.

'Kate.' His voice was incredibly low and deep, his eyes dark and sensuous. He had never spoken her name before and the speaking of it made her aware of the deep, slightly grating timbre of his voice. It was the kind of voice suited to him, holding the gritty deeps of his nature.

Rachel gave a husky laugh.

'Love you?', he grated. 'Of course I love you.'

'What *is* love?', she sighed.

Lyle, she croaked, and was unaware that her voice came out as a wordless whisper.

He gave his gravelly laugh.

Such a torrent of tenderness and passion was in his voice, she closed her lovely eyes and offered him her mouth.

'I felt the same way,' Gay faltered.

His roaming hands pressed her curves to the hard contours of his length.

'Giles,' she groaned breathlessly. 'Oh God, Giles!'

(Lines from Mills and Boon)

'The voice of the natural is a voice in favour of the status quo.'

(J. Sturrock, *Structuralism and Since*, 1980)

Introduction

Popular stereotypes portray men as loud voiced and women as softly spoken; men as deeper pitched, and women as lighter and higher pitched. Like other stereotypes of male and female speech, those that refer to qualities of the voice are both rich and well known. Descriptions of voices in popular fiction, for example, include many aspects of voice quality, as we can see in the lines taken from typical Mills and Boon romances above.

Such stereotypes raise issues which are familiar to researchers in gender behaviour. One is the question of accuracy: how many of these stereotypical voice qualities actually exist? Unfortunately, research in this area is partial. There are many studies which report facts about the pitch of men's and women's voices but there is very little evidence about some of the more interesting and subtle aspects of voice quality which are more difficult to categorize, such as 'breathiness' and 'harshness'.

That male and female voices differ, however, is not in doubt. Most people can easily tell whether a voice belongs to a man or woman. But why should men's and women's voices be so different? This apparently simple question has a rather complicated answer. It may seem self-evident that characteristics such as pitch of voice have a biological basis. Just as men are thought of as being somewhat bigger and more powerful than women, so their voices are heard as being louder and lower in pitch. Indeed, many, if not all, gender differences in voice are commonly imagined to arise from such physical sex differences. But such gender differences can also be seen as just one of many ways in which voices carry systematic information about the identity of a speaker. It is possible to tell from someone's accent, for instance, things about their social, ethnic and geographical background (we return to this in chapter 3) and their voices often indicate also their emotional state and attitude to others.

These systematic properties of the voice have one of two possible causes. Accent is obviously a learned and social characteristic, but a nasal quality of voice due to a cold, or a hoarse voice due to laryngitis has a medical and ultimately physical cause. Voice characteristics which have a physical origin may nevertheless carry social meaning, since certain characteristics of voice may indicate particular life styles: the rough voice of a habitual smoker, or a thick voice the morning after a late party. In this way, the study of voices brings us round to a very familiar debate in the social sciences about the social construction of behaviour. To what extent are voice characteristics socially learned and to what extent are they biologically determined? And what social meanings become attached to them? These are the questions which we deal with in this chapter.

The Physical Basis of the Voice

One way of explaining why people's voices sound as they do is to describe the mechanics of voice production. Figure 2.1 is an outline diagram of the kind you will find in any medical or phonetics textbook. It shows the interior parts of the mouth and throat down to the voice-box or *larynx*. Collectively, these parts of the anatomy are called the *vocal tract*. When you breathe out, air passes from the lungs to the cavities of the mouth via the wind-pipe, and escapes eventually through the lips or nostrils. In normal breathing, this air-flow is free and unrestricted but when you speak you interfere with this air-stream in various ways. First, the air passes through a muscular constriction at the top of the wind-pipe which is formed by the *vocal folds* (also known as *vocal cords*). These behave rather like a pair of lips. In order to cough, you close them completely, shutting off the air-flow and then releasing it under pressure. When you talk, though, you bring the vocal folds together until the air causes them to vibrate – exactly like blowing a raspberry with your real lips. A coarse, buzzing sound is thus injected into the vocal cavities. These cavities – in the throat, mouth and nose, give rise to resonances (called *formants*) which give a characteristically speech-like quality to the noise that emerges from the mouth. These resonances, however, reflect the shape and size of the cavities, just as the sound you produce by tapping a glass depends on its shape and air volume.

The sense of the pitch of a person's voice comes from two separate aspects of this process of voice production. The most important is probably the basic rate of vibration of the vocal folds (the *fundamental frequency*). This depends on the length and thickness of the vocal folds. If you gently stretch a rubber band between your fingers and twang it, then you will find that a shorter or thinner band will twang at a higher pitch than a longer or thicker one. Just so with the vocal folds. A person with long and thick folds would

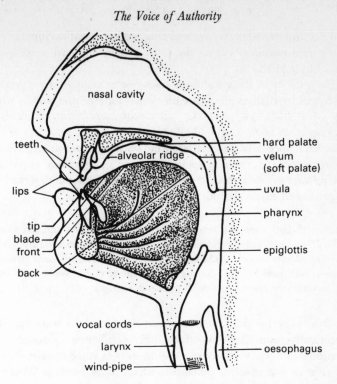

Figure 2.1 The human vocal tract

normally be capable of speaking at a lower pitch than someone with smaller ones. The impression of pitch which comes from this vibration is, however, often fused with the perception of another aspect of voice – the resonant structure (i.e. the formants). Resonances arise because the buzz of the vocal folds is a rich and complex sound, containing many higher frequencies (*harmonics*) in addition to the fundamental frequency. A large and long vocal cavity will emphasize the lower pitched of these extra components and give the impression of a richer and, perhaps, lower pitched voice.

Strictly speaking, the size of the vocal cavities affect a voice's *timbre* rather than its pitch, but the two impressions are frequently difficult for a listener to disentangle. The important point is that both aspects of perceived pitch depend on physical characteristics of the vocal tract: the one reflects the mass and length of the vocal folds and the other reflects the size and length of the vocal cavities. Hence you would normally expect the pitch of someone's voice to reflect their physical size.

The activity of the vocal folds gives rise to many other aspects of voice quality besides pitch. Breathy voice, for example, occurs when the vocal folds do not make full closure when they vibrate; in whisper there is no vocal fold vibration at all, so the sense of pitch in whispered speech comes entirely from vocal tract resonance effects.

Big people are generally assumed to have a larger vocal apparatus and a lower pitched voice. Accounts given in textbooks designed for linguists and medical students claim this explicitly:

A tall, well-built man will tend to have a long vocal tract and large vocal folds. His voice quality will reflect the length of his vocal tract by having correspondingly low ranges of formant frequencies, and his voice dynamic features will indicate the dimensions and mass of his vocal folds by a correspondingly low frequency. (Laver and Trudgill, 1979, pp. 7–8)

In fact, very few studies have been conducted to test this idea empirically, and those that have offer conflicting evidence. The relationship between body size and aspects of voice certainly holds for animals but it seems difficult to establish for humans. There is, however, some evidence that voice qualities are inherited characteristics. The voices of Siamese twins are more similar than those of non-identical twins, for instance. In one experiment (Gedda et al., 1960), identical twins were unable to distinguish recordings of their own voices from those of their twins. In a medical study, Luchsinger and Arnold (1965) approached the question from a different point of view, by tracing the types of singing voices of patients' ancestors. They found, for example, that in the case of one famous tenor, all male ancestors had tenor voices while female ancestors were mezzo-soprano. They were able to show that the distribution of voice types through the generations showed the pattern which would be predicted by genetic inheritance.

What people inherit is not just a particular size and shape of vocal apparatus but also a disposition towards certain patterns of hormonal secretion which affect the voice. In fact, the size of the larynx in men depends in large measure on the release of those hormones that give rise to secondary sexual characteristics in adolescence. Various studies (e.g. Vuorenkoski et al., 1978) have shown that boys' voices drop in pitch about an octave at about the same time as they develop pubic hair. Pedersen et al. (1984) demonstrated that this change in voice was directly connected with hormonal activity by taking 48 boys from the Copenhagen Boys' Choir and measuring androgen blood content and the size of their testicles. It was found that the pitch of voice of boys of different ages was closely correlated with their testis volume and androgen levels.

Women's voices also are affected by hormonal, or related, activity. Women patients given hormone treatment (such as ana-bolic steroids) usually find their pitch gets lower (Damste, 1964, 1965), but women also reportedly experience changes in voice quality during menstruation and pregnancy. Flach et al. (1968) found that most of a group of professional singers they studied reported pre- and inter-menstrual voice changes of which the majority were described as 'disadvantageous'; whilst two thirds of singers experienced 'positive voice changes' during pregnancy. Perello (1962) suggested that the reason for 'premenstrual dys-phony' was a thickening of the mucus which normally lubricates the vocal folds. Since vocal fold action is essentially a mechanical one, such changes can have a dramatic effect on voice pitch and quality. It may, however, be a reflection of social attitudes to menstruation and pregnancy that the effects of the former were perceived negatively and those of the latter positively.

Such reports seem to provide evidence that a person's voice is created in a complex manner by physical and biological phenomena which are beyond voluntary control. This, however, is not quite as clear-cut as it appears. A person's physiological make up can be affected by certain kinds of deliberate and voluntary behaviour. For example, changes in voice quality are claimed to occur when people become sexually aroused – a change in mucosal lubrication gives rise to a breathiness or huskiness of tone. In fact, there exists a tradition that too much sex will affect your voice. Singers, in particular, are often advised to avoid sexual activity unless their voices are already low.

I always remember being told by one of the world's great male singers that his life involved him in great sacrifices. Making love affected his voice. Smoking didn't, drinking didn't – just the act of copulation enjoyed even three days before a performance. He earned £500 every time he trod the boards. Few people can be faced with such a poignant choice so often, would you say? (Morgan, 1965, 'London Diary', *New Statesman*, 61, 15. 1. 65. p. 71. Cited in Laver, 1975, p. 308)

Bettina Jonic, who trains singers and actors at the Royal Opera House, claims 'At Covent Garden I can always tell what a tenor has been doing the night before. They always have difficulty with the top notes'. Jonic offers the advice of a famous Italian voice coach: 'tenors and sopranos never during a performance run, baritones once or twice a week, and low voices every night' (*Guardian*, 31. 3. 84).

Accounts such as these may embody a fair amount of folk-wisdom, which is no more than a polite way of saying that they make certain sexist and stereotypical assumptions. There is, however, an important point to be made, which is that human social activities may have an effect on human physiology. It is a similar argument to one occasionally made to explain differences in size and strength between men and women: are some of the measured differences due to differences in nutrition, training and experience?

The Evidence for Social Learning of the Voice

The evidence that a person's voice is an inherited characteristic which reflects the vocal anatomy of its owner is strong, and it might therefore seem downright cranky to argue that men's and women's voices are socially learned. There is, however, a point of view which argues that sex differences in voice are much more social in origin than is usually supposed. Dale Spender has claimed:

It has been found that males tend to have lower pitched voices than females. But it has also been found that this difference cannot be explained by anatomy. If males do not speak in high pitched voices, it is not usually because they are unable to do so. The reason is more likely to be because there are penalties. Males with high pitched voices are often the subject of ridicule. And what is considered the right pitch for males varies from country to country. (Spender, 1978, p. 19)

Spender does not fully discuss the argument and, indeed, seriously weakens her case when she writes elsewhere 'despite some evidence, I am not convinced that the voices of women are more highly pitched than men's' (Spender, 1985, p. 40). Spender's cavalier treatment of the issue is unfortunate, since it makes it too easy to dismiss the argument itself as an unserious one. The social argument need not attempt deny the physical evidence in this way; it simply suggests that is another side to the story.

Each person can vary the pitch of his or her own voice over a considerable range. Using the analogy we made earlier with rubber bands, you will find that the pitch at which they twang depends not only on their length and thickness, but also on how much they have been stretched. The vocal cords can also be tensed in various ways by the muscles within and around the larynx. This is the main, but not the sole, method of altering the pitch of one's voice. Another is to vary breath pressure – this is why the pitch of someone's voice tends to go up when they shout. When anyone talks, their pitch fluctuates from moment to moment – they might use a rising intonation, for instance, to ask a question. When people talk to young children or animals they often use a higher pitch of voice throughout. What is surprising is that despite the way people's voices vary very rapidly, one still gets a strong impression of the overall average pitch of their voice. In fact, we have shown in experiments (Graddol, 1983) that listeners are extremely sensitive to the *average* pitch of a speaker's voice.

Figure 2.2 shows the average rate of vocal cord vibration (i.e. the fundamental frequency, which is the main determinant of the sense of pitch) in 27 members of staff at the Open University. The unit of frequency used is the *Hertz* (one Hertz is one cycle of vibration per second). In musical terms, for comparison, Middle C is usually 261 Hz. A simple doubling of the frequency raises the perceived pitch by one octave, and halving the frequency lowers perceived pitch by a similar interval. It can be seen from Figure 2.2 that average speaking pitch varies from person to person but that in spite of this variation there is a clear gap between men and women. In other words, women and men can easily be distinguished according to the average pitch of their voice.

This much is hardly surprising – it accords with the everyday experience that it is easy to tell from someone's voice whether they are a man or a woman. Figure 2.2 tells only part of the story, however. When the whole of the pitch range used by individuals (Figure 2.3) is examined two new facts emerge. First, that the pitch ranges of men and women overlap considerably. Second, that people vary considerably in the extent of their pitch range; some speak in a rather monotonous way whilst others are much more lively and more expressive. Put together, these facts suggest that men and

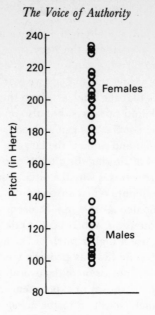

Figure 2.2 The average speaking pitch of a sample of men and women

women could, if they wished, use similar pitch ranges and hence adopt a similar average speaking pitch. To do this, men would have to restrict themselves to the upper part of their ranges, while women would have to avoid their upper ranges.

This argument is based on the observation of the pitch ranges actually used by men and women. There is evidence, however, that people customarily use only a small part of the range that their vocal organs are capable of. Infants demonstrate this vocal potential in a remarkable way. Fairbanks (1942) made gramophone recordings of hunger wails produced by his infant son during the first nine months of life and he found that the boy's pitch ranged from 63 Hz to 2631 Hz – a span which encompasses the singing ranges of both bass and soprano. There have also been several stories of professional singers who, through special training techniques, have achieved prodigious vocal ranges. Luchsinger and Dubois (1956) described the voice of Jennifer Johnson who boasted a range similar to that of Fairbanks' infant (from 65 Hz to 2794 Hz, well over five octaves).

Evidence of this kind undermines the claim that the difference in voice pitch between men and women is a simple and inevitable

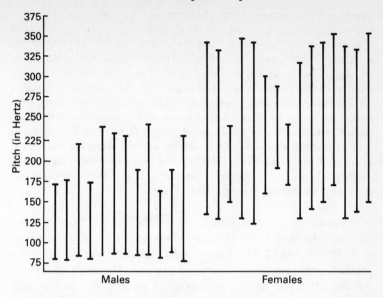

Figure 2.3 The extent to which the pitch ranges of men and women overlap

consequence of their different vocal anatomy but it hardly supports Dale Spender's claim that sex differences are socially constructed. It is one thing to argue that there is no absolute physiological bar which prevents men and women speaking at the same pitch and quite another to argue that they avoid doing so for social reasons. It might simply be that whilst possible it is rather difficult and uncomfortable for a man to speak in a high pitched voice or for women to restrict themselves to their lower ranges.

As it happens it is well known that men can, with a little practice and motivation, converse in a falsetto voice for extended periods and without apparent difficulty. Various drag artists routinely do so. Dustin Hoffman very successfully played the part of a woman in the film *Tootsie*. There are cases, also, of adult men whose voices are unusually high in pitch. Greene, the author of a standard medical text on the human voice describes several men whose voices appear not to have broken. Charles was typical:

Charles, a young man of eighteen years, was in his first year at university and had come under criticism from his tutor for his unintelligible speech, especially when reading aloud. He had speech therapy as a child for an articulation disorder and stammer ... His voice had never broken. When his parents were interviewed by the speech therapist and were asked what they felt about Charles' voice, his mother said it sounded all right to her; it was his stammer she was worried about. The father disagreed with her and positively agreed with the speech therapist that Charles' voice was girlish. An Edinburgh Masking Instrument [which prevents the patient from hearing his own voice] was obtained for use with stammers and it was tried out with Charles. A totally unexpected result was achieved; Charles spoke without stammer and in a deep, masculine voice ... When the masker was switched off and he heard his voice he immediately reverted to falsetto and was not to be caught out again by this ruse. It was decided to refer him for psychiatric treatment. (Greene, 1980, p. 244)

What demands attention here is not just the fact that Charles' voice appears to be unbroken (in strictly physiological terms it obviously *has* broken), but that his use of abnormally high pitch was regarded as a psychological rather than a medical problem. Documented cases of this kind demonstrate that psychological motivation would be sufficient to eradicate the difference in pitch between women and men.

It seems that, in practice, the opposite is true: men seem to be under some kind of social or psychological pressure to make their voices sound as different as possible from women (and, perhaps, vice versa). In fact it is not immediately obvious whether one sex plays a greater role than the other. In our own study which we referred to above (Graddol and Swann, 1983), we came to a surprising conclusion. The pitch at which men spoke seemed to reflect their physical size, whilst there was no relationship between women's voices and their size. Whilst this might suggest that men are using their 'natural' voices and women distorting theirs, a moment's thought will demonstrate that this cannot be true. The comparison shows that people can place their voice ranges somewhat flexibly. For some reason, the men and women in our study were adopting different strategies. Men's voices reflected their physical size because they used the lower limits of their pitch range and adopted intonation patterns which were more monotonous than women's; women by contrast, were more variable in their use of voice, both in the sense of using more expressive intonation and in differences between individual women. Such differences seem to indicate that pitch of voice carries social meanings and that men and women try to communicate different social images.

Our study pointed to an area of interest, but did not provide much in the way of explanation. The evidence that people learn to speak with gender appropriate voices comes from two principal sources. First, there are studies from different parts of the world which show that pitch and voice quality are culturally variable. Second, there is evidence that girls' and boys' voices can be distinguished well before their vocal apparatus becomes differentiated in adolescence.

Cross-cultural Evidence

Sir Duncan Gibb (1869) was one of the first to observe that men spoke with different voice qualities and pitches in different countries:

The voices of the natives [of India, who appeared to be generally male] are ... generally soft and plaintive, and very feminine ... not so very powerful as the shrill, the natives always sing in falsetto ... the compass of the voice is small, hardly above the octave. (Gibb, 1869)

In contrast 'Negros have the power of uttering bass notes in a low and grave tone.' What is interesting about Gibb's extraordinary and anecdotal observations is his willingness to see the 'character of the voice' as a combination of physiological and learned characteristics. 'Negros' suffered, it seems, from a peculiar deficiency shared by many non-Europeans – a 'pendency of the epiglottis' which, together with the position of the ventricles was 'unfavourable to intensity and gravity of sound'. The Tartars' larynx was judged, from the descriptions of voice given by travellers alone, to be 'well developed', 'prominent in the neck', 'the vocal cords, consequently, are long and powerful, surmounted most probably by capricious ventricles.' Nevertheless – and this is where Gibb's account becomes interesting for us – local culture and habits were also said to affect the voice. The hill tribes in India 'from the habit of always calling to each other from hill to hill, have contracted a habit of loud speaking'. The 'American Negro' had developed a nasal twang 'derived by imitation from his master'.

Gibb also noted that men and women differed in voice less in some cultures than others and he linked these observations with comments on the social position of women. Thus:

In Tartary, the women lead a very independent life, riding out on horseback at pleasure, and visiting each other from tent to tent ... The Tartar woman presents in her bearing and manners a power and force well in accordance with her active life and nomad habits, and her attire augments the effect of her masculine, haughty mien. The voice of the Tartar woman is not inferior to that of men, in power, at any rate, if we may judge from the behaviour of an innkeeper's wife, who for her obstinacy received a formidable box on the ear from her husband, which sent her into a corner, screaming at the pitch of her voice. (Cited in Gibb, 1869, p. 249)

More recent, and rather more scientific, studies have shown that the average pitch of voice does indeed vary from country to country. One of the most impressive was that reported by Majewski et al. (1972) who found the average speaking pitch of 103 Polish men to be 137.6 Hz whereas that of a comparable (though much smaller) group of American men was 118.9 Hz. Difference in physical size was eliminated as a contributing factor, since no relationship between height, weight and speaking pitch was found amongst the Polish males. (Such evidence is interesting in connection with our earlier discussion.) As further evidence in favour of a cross-cultural explanation, the authors point out that the measures for the Polish men are similar to those obtained from American samples in earlier studies in the 1940s. In addition to Majewski's study, there is further tentative evidence from Loveday (1981) who examined the average pitch of voice used by Japanese and (British) English female and male speakers, finding a considerable discrepancy between Japanese men and women (women sometimes reaching heights of 400 Hz, for example) which did not occur between English speakers.

One of the besetting problems of data of this kind is that alternative explanations can often be provided. The difference in average pitch may simply reflect the different intonational patterns used in different languages, for instance. We have shown (Graddol, 1986) that when people read two different kinds of text in the *same* language it can have a dramatic effect on the average pitch of their voices. Another possible explanation is that there are systematic differences in body build between different ethnic groups. Average height is known to vary, for example, not just from one country to another but even between social classes in a developed country such as Britain. Even the data which show the magnitude of the sex difference within cultures does not escape this problem, since physical sex differences may also be variable (this may be a function of the better nutrition given to males in many parts of the world, including the developed countries). It should be said that these problems are not altogether insurmountable – it would be helpful to have data taken from bilingual and multilingual speakers, for example.

Pre-adolescent Children

Several researchers have shown that it is possible to tell the sex of a young child from their voice long before puberty. Such differences, it is alleged, must be socially acquired. A classic instance of the social adaptation of pitch of voice was reported by Philip Lieberman who observed that infants who had reached the babbling stage varied the pitch of their babbling according to whether the father or the mother was present. Alone in the cot, a 10 month old boy babbled to himself at 430 Hz, but dropped to 390 Hz when playing with his mother, and further dropped to 340 Hz when with his father. Similarly, a 13 month old girl varied between 390 and 290 Hz depending on whether she was interacting with her mother or father. Crying in both children was at a higher pitch and was not affected by the presence of adults (Lieberman, 1976). It has been argued that this shows children are sensitive to the fact that fathers speak with a lower pitched voice than mothers and that the children, who are able to adjust the pitch of their voices, learn later to adopt permanently the gender appropriate pitch level.

Although this report has achieved some importance in the literature on the acquisition of gender appropriate speech, it must be admitted that the evidence is pretty anecdotal. Only two infants were observed and no-one else seems to have reported similar findings. Furthermore, it is difficult to provide a coherent explanation in the light of findings by other researchers that pre-adolescent boys tend to have *higher* pitched voices than girls (as measured in terms of fundamental frequency of vocal cord vibration) right until their voices break.

One such study was reported by Sachs, Lieberman and Erickson (1973). Although they found that boys tended to have higher fundamental frequencies than girls (this is associated with higher muscular tension and activity) they did find that boys had significantly lower vocal tract resonance (which we earlier described as a contributory factor in perceived pitch). Since the sex difference could not be explained by physical difference in size the researchers argued that children learned to adjust the effective length of their vocal tract by adopting gender appropriate muscular postures (known as *articulatory settings*).

In conclusion, although there are a large number of research papers which report evidence of the social adaptation of pitch and voice quality, there are very few indeed which are not flawed in some way, are not contradicted by other researchers, or are not amenable to alternative interpretations. The lack of solid evidence is by no means proof that no social adaptation goes on. It may simply illustrate the difficulty of trying to isolate the contribution of social factors where several factors interact. Average pitch of voice seems to be partly a function of vocal anatomy, partly of environmental factors such as excessive smoking or drinking, partly a reflection of the intonation patterns of the speaker's language or dialect, and partly a result of social adaptation.

There is limited evidence that what is regarded as socially desirable in a voice varies from culture to culture. Maxine Hong Kingston gives us an example of contrasting ideas of 'feminine' voice quality in her autobiographical book *The Woman Warrior*:

Normal Chinese women's voices are strong and bossy. We American-Chinese girls had to whisper to make ourselves American-feminine. (Kingston, 1976, p. 172)

Recent research supports the notion that cultural ideals vary. Valentine and St Damian (1988), for example, contrasted the way ideal male and female voice types for radio presenters were perceived in Mexico and the United States. The concluded:

Comparison of the ideal male voice types revealed that ideal male vocal delivery was somewhat low in pitch and somewhat slow in delivery. Both ideal voice types were additionally described as firm, cheerful, well-modulated, and careful in enunciation. However, the ideal Mexican male was expected to use greater volume and take more care with diction than was his United States counterpart.

The ideal female voice types in Mexico and the United States were similarly described as soft in volume, medium to somewhat slow in rate of delivery, and careful in enunciation. However, the ideal Mexican female voice was additionally expected to sound delicate and sensual. (Valentine and St Damian, 1988, p. 300)

It would be surprising if people did not use their voices to project a culturally desirable image. Other parts of the human body which have been endowed with social significance are manipulated, groomed or decorated before being presented in public. We know that voices are socially significant, we know humans have the capacity to alter their voice; it would be strange indeed if the voice was not subject to socially motivated adaptations. But even if people do not, in fact, manipulate their voices (either consciously or unconsciously) to create social images, the voices they use may still be endowed with immense social meaning. In the remainder of this chapter we will examine the independent evidence that relates to such social meaning.

The Social Meaning of Men's and Women's Voices

We will look briefly at the three most popular ways of describing the meaning of voice qualities. These are the sociobiological, the social psychological and what we have called the sociopolitical.

Sociobiological Explanations

Studies of animal behaviour by ethologists show that in many species the male has a louder and deeper pitched vocalization than the female. Such differences are thought to have resulted from selective breeding caused by the twin evolutionary pressures of 'sexual selection' and the general 'struggle for life'. For example, male toads have deeper pitched croaks than females, and it has been shown that female toads seek out as mates the males with the deepest croak (Fairchild, 1981). This is thought to be because the depth of croak indicates the size and vigour of the male animal. In other species, though, the low pitched vocalizations of the male have developed not as a means of attracting females but as a means of intimidating rival males, and setting up male dominance hierarchies. The male of one species of bird-of-paradise, for instance, has developed a remarkable vocal tract which is many times longer than the bird itself and which is coiled like an intestine under the skin. Mary Clench, who has made a special study of this species, suggests that 'the tracheal elongations of birds-of-paradise serve to lower the pitch of, and amplify, their vocalisations' (Clench, 1978, p. 428). The vocal displays are part of a striking mating ritual which sets up a male dominance hierarchy and ensures that only one male gains access to any female who appears (Lecroy, 1981).

Amongst our human ancestors, the male voice is thought by some to have played a similar role. Darwin supposed that most distinctive male characteristics, including the facts that man is 'taller, heavier, and stronger than woman ... more hairy and his voice has a different and more powerful tone' emerged through what he called the 'law of battle', namely, the fight between men for women:

> With savages, for instance the Australians, the women are the constant cause of war both between members of the same tribe and between distinct tribes... With some of the North American Indians, the contest is reduced to a system... It has ever been the custom among these people for the men to wrestle for any woman to whom they are attached; and, of course, the strongest party always carries off the prize... There can be no doubt that the greater size and strength of man, in comparison with woman, together with ... his greater courage and pugnacity, are all due in chief part to inheritance from his half-human ancestors. These characters would, however, have been preserved or even augmented during the long ages of man's savagery, by the success of the strongest and boldest men, both in the general struggle for life and in their contests for wives. (Darwin, 1874, pp. 556–8)

Support for this idea that male vocalizations are designed to be aggressive and threatening comes from Ohala (1983, 1984) who observed that there was a remarkable similarity in the vocalizations used in competitive encounters by a very wide range of species including birds and mammals:

> The sounds made by a confident aggressor or dominant individual are low pitched and often harsh, whereas those of a submissive or subordinate individual are high pitched and tone like. The dog's threatening growl and submissive whine are familiar examples of this pattern which I will henceforth refer to as the 'frequency code'. (Ohala, 1983, p. 7)

The 'frequency code', claimed Ohala, is a universally used and innately recognized method of signalling dominance and aggression. When animals fight, it will usually be the larger one who wins. Hence antagonists can avoid injury if actual contact is avoided and if the competition displaced and made symbolic. Animals use a variety of means to indicate (and exaggerate) their body size: dogs erect their hair, cats arch their backs, birds extend their wings and so on. Ohala continues:

The pitch of voice can also indirectly convey an impression of the size of the vocalizer since there is a correlation (an inverse one) between the rate of vibration of the vocal cords (or the syringeal membranes) and overall body mass... Moreover, the more massive and thick the vibrating mass, the more likely it is that secondary modes of vibration will be set up in it and in that way give rise to irregular vibratory patterns and thus harsh voice quality. The individual that intends to prevail in the contest – initially both competitors may – will try to convey his largeness (even if it is a bluff) by producing the lowest-pitched and harshest vocalization he is capable of. The individual who wants to capitulate will attempt to appear small and non-threatening and will therefore emit as high-pitched and tone-like a cry as possible. (Ohala, 1983, p. 8)

Ohala suggested that a further reason why a high pitched voice appears submissive and subordinate may be because it imitates the cry of an infant which triggers an instinctive taboo against the harming of offspring. Ohala's proposal was intended specifically to explain the origins of the human male voice. He suggested that since the lowering of men's voices appeared at puberty, it may serve a similar evolutionary function to other secondary sexual features:

Growth of hair at the perimeter of the face of males, as with so many other primate species, increases the apparent size of the head and thus enhances the visual effectiveness of a threat display. The enlargement of the vocal anatomy gives the male a lower-pitched voice and lower resonances which, according to the frequency code, also indirectly enhance his apparent size. It would seem plausible, then, that the dimorphic aspects of the vocal apparatus serve to improve the male's ability to protect the family unit, i.e., that they are adaptations to the sex specific role of the human male (in earlier days, if not at the present stage of human society). This is consistent with current ethological speculation on the factors leading to sexual di-morphism and with the role played by adult males in other primate groups. (Ohala, 1983, p. 13)

Men's larger larynx is thus likened to the large proboscis of the elephant seal, which lowers the pitch of its call and increases its 'success of maintaining a harem in the face of competition from other males'.

So it seems from studies of animals that the low pitched, male voice has developed in order to sound aggressive and dominant. This aggression was directed at other males rather than females, but it is noteworthy that the evolutionary story is one in which women are anyway given a submissive and subordinate role. The details vary according to which evolutionary mechanism is thought to have been responsible, but the stories are mutually compatible. If the lower pitched voice arose through the mechanism of sexual selection, then this could only occur in an environment where men were promiscuous and fought or intimidated other men for access to women. If it arose through the 'struggle for life' then there must have existed a society in which there was an inescapable division of labour; and in which men roamed the world battling with the men of other tribes and engaging in other dangerous pursuits while the women devoted themselves to child-rearing and domestic labour. Sex differences in our ancestors' voices, according to the evolutionary explanations, reflected and helped maintain their primitive pattern of labour and sexual relationships.

Some people certainly believe that men's voices have very similar functions today – to help get a mate and to dominate over other males. Luchsinger and Arnold, in a classic medical text on the human voice, suggest that these attributes of the male voice are lost in old age:

At this age the voice no longer serves for physical attraction as it does in the young male who is about to found a family and to strive for their care. Likewise, the senile voice is no longer suitable for the militant leadership of assembled males, be it in army barracks or in executive offices of industrial enterprises. (Luchsinger and Arnold, 1965, p. 137. Cited in Laver, 1975, p. 304)

Although the majority of ethological accounts of the human voice focus on the male, rather than the female, there have been one or two attempts to explain female vocal behaviour in such terms. Whispery voice, which is an extreme form of breathy voice, carries particular associations, Laver suggests:

the use by some popular female singers and film actresses of whispery voice ... simulates the effect on phonatory quality of the change in consistency of the mucal lining of the larynx which takes place during sexual arousal. (Laver, 1975, p. 298)

Henton and Bladon (1985), discovered that female speakers in two

British accents consistently used a more breathy voice quality than men in ordinary speech. They noted that breathiness was an inefficient mode of voice production which had various 'communicative limitations' and continued:

It may not be too speculative to assume a physiological basis for the association between breathiness and arousal... This is not to say that British women using a breathy voice are actually aroused; rather that they imitate the voice quality associated with arousal. If a woman can manage to *sound* as though she is sexually aroused, she may be regarded as more desirable or with greater approbation by a male interlocutor than if she speaks with an ordinary modal voice. At an ethological level, breathy voice may be seen as a part of the courtship display ritual, as important as bodily adornment and gesture. A breathy woman can be regarded as using her paralinguistic tools to maximize her chances of her achieving her goals, linguistic or otherwise. (Henton and Bladon, 1985, p. 226)

Although explanations of human behaviour in terms of atavistic animal behaviour seem popular in some quarters, there are several reasons for caution. Such sociobiological accounts often make unwarranted assumptions about the similarities between humans and other animals and may be guilty of trying to justify and legitimate some of the more sexist and oppressive aspects of human behaviour as 'natural', and instinctive. When the evolutionary and ethological explanations require us to make assumptions about the biological inevitability of a certain prehistoric sexual division of labour and human sexuality, both of which have complex social dimensions, we may become particularly uncomfortable. Both the social psychological and the sociopolitical explanations of the meaning of female and male voices reject the sociobiological one for these reasons.

Social Psychological Explanations

We can say with some confidence that biological explanations of social meaning can provide no more than a dangerous 'grain of truth'. Such explanations are, for example, extremely partial. It seems intuitively correct to suppose that loud voices can be threatening, today as in prehistory, but the ordinary speaking voice is not exactly a frightening or screaming one. If the male speaking voice carries such conviction, authority and sexual attractiveness it must do so by a subtler method than through brute strength, or even through its symbolic representation.

Ohala, whose idea about the universal pitch code we have already discussed, showed in experiments that listeners hear lower pitched voices as more confident and dominant than higher pitched ones (Carleton and Ohala, 1980) and argued that this supported his ethological explanation. The finding, however, fits well with a range of experiments by social psychologists which show that listeners make complex responses to men's and women's voices. Higher pitched voices are heard as less competent (Brown et al., 1973) or even less truthful and generally less 'potent' (Apple et al., 1979). Such characteristics seem to be components in more general perceptions of 'masculine' and 'feminine'. Coleman (1973) played recordings of 20 women's and men's voices to a panel of listeners and he asked them to rate each speaker's 'masculinity' and 'femininity' on a single scale. He found that when people made such judgements they seemed to be mainly influenced by the pitch of the speaker's voice. (See figure 2.4)

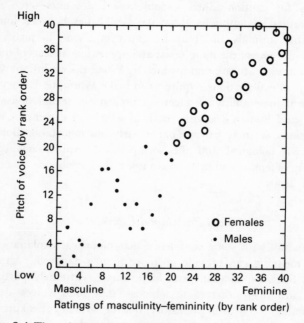

Figure 2.4 The relationship between speaking pitch and perceptions of masculinity–femininity

Coleman thought of gender as a psychological attribute which formed a continuum from very masculine to very feminine. A man might possess certain feminine characteristics just as a woman might possess masculine ones. Such a model of gender is a great deal more sophisticated than a two way division which sees all males as masculine and all females as feminine, but it has the disadvantage that it assumes that anyone who is high on masculinity must also be low on femininity. More recent work on the psychology of gender uses separate masculinity and femininity scales. Hence a person can be simultaneously 'aggressive' (judged to be a masculine trait) and 'affectionate' (seen to be more socially desirable in a woman). A person who possessed both masculine and feminine traits in this way is referred to as *androgynous*. This model of gender provides a more complex psychological space on to which people can map other people's gender identities. Since evaluations of a person's gender identity also depend on whether they are identified as male or female, the space is not strictly two-dimensional but contains two overlapping rectangles. Figure 2.5 shows this schematically.

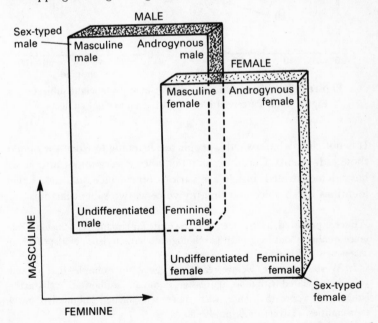

Figure 2.5 A schematic representation of the multi-dimensional nature of gender identity

Smith (1985) tried to find out whether listeners can locate speakers in such a space on the basis of their voices. He asked a large group of people to evaluate themselves on standard rating scales for attributes which were considered stereotypically 'masculine' and 'feminine'. He then selected the four men and four women who had located themselves in the extreme corners of the gender rectangle. He was able to show that listeners' evaluations of speech samples corresponded roughly with the speakers' own self-evaluations (figure 2.6).

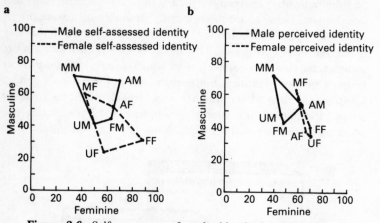

Figure 2.6a Self-assessment of gender identity by eight subjects
Figure 2.6b Perceived identity of the same eight subjects.

It is not clear what, exactly, people are listening to when they make these judgements. Certainly, pitch of voice is very important, as we have demonstrated, but so are various other voice qualities. Laver identifies harsh voice and breathy voice as two salient factors;

We seem prepared, as listeners, to draw quite far reaching conclusions from voice quality about long-term psychological characteristics of a speaker, in assessments of personality.

In Western culture, we are ready to believe, for example, that a harsh voice is correlated with more aggressive, dominant, authoritative characteristics, and a breathy voice with more self-effacing, submissive, meek personalities. (Laver, 1968, pp. 49–50)

Such studies demonstrate that rather complex gender images are projected through the voice and are interpreted by listeners. Furthermore, when you look more closely at what these dimensions of 'masculinity' and 'femininity' are, they turn out to be based on socially stereotypical features such as 'aggression', 'dominance', as opposed to 'affectionate', 'submissive' and so on.

Sociopolitical Explanations

Feminists have often claimed that the appearance of naturalness which surrounds so many aspects of gender has important political implications. If certain characteristics – such as the sexual division of labour – appear to based on 'natural' (i.e. biologically determined) qualities, then such social arrangements may be seen as inevitable and beyond sensible questioning.

Vocal images are interesting in this respect. Even if one accepts that many differences in voice quality between the sexes are consequent upon evolutionary history and anatomical make-up, it does not follow that the meanings which these voice qualities have acquired are as biologically determined as the voice qualities themselves. In any form of symbolic communication the relationship between a perceived entity (or signifier, to use the term adopted in semiotics) and the meaning which is attributed to it (the signified) is essentially a matter of social convention. A flower is a product of nature and its form and colour can be explained in botanical and evolutionary terms. Nevertheless, the meanings people attach to particular kinds of flower – a rose which signifies love or a poppy which signifies remembrance – are not created by natural history but by human history and social convention. It is thus to be expected that a single species will acquire different meanings in different cultures and at different times (a poppy signified forgetfulness in classical times, for instance) and such meanings will be susceptible to redefinition.

So, it has been argued, with the meanings attached to the human voice. The linguist, Debbie Cameron, suggests there is no intrinsic reason why women's voices are heard to be lacking in authority:

It is inconceivable that these judgements have anything to do with pitch. If men talked in higher pitches than women, low voices would be said to lack in authority... Linguistic sex-differences act simply as a badge of female-ness, and are valued negatively quite irrespective of their substance.

Explaining that women's high pitch is learned/can be authoritative/is really very pleasing to the ear will have no effect on the irrational process by which everything 'female' is pejorated, whether it actually reflects women's behaviour or not. (Cameron, 1985, p. 54)

Cameron is here invoking the Saussurean doctrine of the 'arbitrariness of the sign' which we described in chapter 1. This suggests that there should be no intrinsic reason why breathiness symbolizes female sexual availability, or why low pitch signals authority. In principle, such meanings could be changed through concerted social effort. It is, after all, exactly such semiotic engineering which the advertising and propaganda industry is constantly engaged in. A decade ago, the drinking of lager in England was seen as effeminate, but has been transformed into a macho activity by the brewing industry (who played upon its different connotations in Scotland and Australia). Cameron is pessimistic about the chances of such attitudinal change with regard to the voice, and rightly so, but she probably underestimates the complexity of the problem in two respects.

First, the meanings of different voice qualities are *not* entirely arbitrary or conventional. In the case of animal communication, for example, low pitch is not *symbolic* of largeness but is *indicative* of it – just as a human footprint in the sand is indicative rather than symbolic of the passage of a human being. Certain voice qualities in humans besides pitch are also indicative as we have shown – nasality is indicative of a head cold, breathy voice of sexual arousal. However, as we have also argued, such voice qualities may be produced intentionally and have acquired more complex connotations. The singer who adopts a soft, breathy voice is projecting an image of sexual interest and availability rather than experiencing or simulating sexual arousal in the recording studio. But the symbolic nature of such gestures can be obscured in unreflective reasoning because of the inherent 'grain of truth'. Because breathy voice can indicate sexual arousal, it does not mean that all instances of breathy voice are indicative in this way.

Although in principle one might imagine a feminist utopia in which high rather than low pitch was heard as authoritative, this would be extremely hard to achieve whilst the world is filled with child voices, large growling dogs and so on. What might be much more successful is an attempt to evaluate these meanings differently

– to undermine the tyranny of the voice by making aggression and dominance less attractive social features. This, of course, is precisely a part of the programme of the women's movement.

There is a second way in which Cameron underestimates the role of the voice. It is not sufficient to observe that high pitch, wide pitch variation, breathy voice, and so on have certain meanings in western culture without also noting how this complex of meanings fits squarely with the wider set of ideas denoted by femininity and masculinity. Through their vocal behaviour, women are not just perceived to be 'feminine'and men 'masculine': the validity and legitimacy of these complex stereotypes is also confirmed. Women are heard to be 'naturally' submissive, weaker, less reliable and more suited to domestic work than to the rigours of public life. Men, on the other hand, are heard to be dominant, aggressive, competent, authoritative – attributes which are daily denied to women by their voices.

Vocal gender images are not just abstract, mental things. They can directly affect the lives of individuals, their job opportunities and their relationships with other people. High pitch and low pitch may not just signal femininity and masculinity but may also have deeply rooted sexual connotations. This fits with the notion we reported earlier, that sexual activity has long term effects on voice quality. Havelock Ellis, an influential British sexologist in the early twentieth century who played an important role in the development of post-Victorian views on female sexuality illustrated the wider implications of such ideas:

Delaunay remarks that while a bass need not fear any kind of sexual or other excess so far as his voice is concerned, a tenor must be extremely careful and temperate. Among prostitutes, it may be added, the evolution of the voice and of the larynx tends to take a masculine direction. This fact, which is fairly obvious, has been accurately investigated at Genoa by Professor Masini, who finds that among 50 prostitutes 29 showed in a high degree the deep masculine voice ... only six of the 50 showed a normal larynx; while of 20 presumably honest women only 2 showed the ample masculine larynx. (Cited in Ellis, 1896, p. 237)

This supposedly scientific report betrays its social values. The situation today may not have greatly changed. Breathiness may be flirtingly suggestive of sexual availability, but socially acceptable in a woman if associated with a high pitch that connotes a lack of sexual experience. High pitch in a man may, on the other hand, offend against traditional views of male sexuality. Ellis himself possessed a high pitched voice and once tried to explain away the embarrassment by suggesting that this was 'remarkably common in men of intellectual ability ... possibly be due to a slight paralysis of the vocal cords' (see Grosskurth, 1980, p. 266).

It does seem to us that sexuality forms an important dimension in dominant images of male and female voices, though we can only speculate on what, exactly, is involved. Nevertheless, it seems that whilst a man can aspire to a voice quality which attracts many socially desirable connotations (bigness, sexually experienced, and authoritative) a woman will be faced with compromises. The vocal attributes which signal authority and competence, for example, conflict with those that signal desirable features of femininity and female sexuality. Margaret Thatcher provides a now well-known example of how social attitudes to voices can affect a woman's career. In her early days as British prime minister her voice was considered a liability to the public image which her advisers wished to project. Gordon Reece, a TV producer called in to advise on TV interview techniques, is reported to have remarked that:

The selling of Margaret Thatcher had been put back two years by the mass broadcasting of Prime Minister's Question Time as she had to be at her shrillest to be heard over the din. (Wapshott and Brock, p. 170. Cited in Atkinson, 1984, p. 115)

The solution decided upon was a programme of voice training to make her voice sound more in keeping with the image of a powerful and competent politician:

Under the guidance of a tutor from the National Theatre, she underwent a training programme which included special humming exercises aimed at lowering the pitch level at which she formerly spoke. From tape recordings of speeches made before and after receiving tuition a marked difference can be clearly heard. When these are played through an electronic pitch analyser, it emerges that she achieved a reduction in pitch of 46 Hz, a figure which is almost half the average difference in pitch between male and female voices. (Atkinson, 1984, p. 113)

It may be that the sacrifice in perceived femininity that such a training implies is a small one for a woman in her position to make, or it may be that it can be countered through careful attention to dress and appearance. However, it is not just Margaret Thatcher who experiences such problems, but practically any woman who has to speak in public. In the media, TV and radio producers are notoriously circumspect about using women for 'serious' work, such as news bulletins. It was many years before female news readers and continuity announcers were heard, and when they were, only 'suitable' voice qualities were selected. Producers play a much more active role than might be suspected in such matters. We know how difficult it can be to persuade BBC producers who make Open University programmes to let women provide commentaries or voice-overs, for example. The insistence on low pitched voices for serious presenters may be one way in which the association between authority, competence and certain kinds of low pitched voice qualities are perpetuated and it actively prevents other kinds of voice from playing such a role. In other areas of the media, more conventional programming values still apply. We ourselves know of cases in the recording studio where a producer has encouraged a man to adopt 'a more aggressive, harder edge' to his voice and a woman to 'soften her tone' in order to conform to expected vocal contrasts. Producers vary in the reasons they give for choosing the voices they do, but the end results seem the same.

The majority of women are not actors and politicians, but discrimination of this kind goes on in much humbler occupations. Women often have jobs in which they deal with the general public, and employers will take into account the public's expectations and reactions to the voices of their telephonists, receptionists and secretaries. Even advertisments for shop assistants and till operators in supermarkets routinely make requirements about voice and speech. Women whose voices conform to received qualities of manner and clarity have an advantage over those with voices perceived as unfeminine.

Conclusion

In this chapter we have shown that many apparently natural aspects of men's and women's voices cannot be explained simply in terms of anotomical differences between the sexes but are acquired as speakers learn cultural norms of feminine and masculine behaviour.

We have also reviewed some of the arguments that establish a line of connection between men's and women's voices and their different life experiences; between, for example, the pitch of a man's voice and the wider employment opportunities available to men; between breathiness in a woman's voice and the treatment of women as sexual objects, and so on. Characteristics of voice take on a wider and perhaps more sinister significance through the demonstration that they form part of the social mechanism that maintains gender inequality. Employment and sexuality are two clear examples of the political importance of vocal gender images, but it must be admitted that the complex and wider relationship between voice and gender inequality is still poorly understood. Better understood and more extensively researched is the closely associated area of pronunciation and accent which we investigate in the next chapter.

3

Accents of Femininity? Gender Differences in Language Use

Introduction

In 1665 the French writer Rochefort described the language of the Carib Indians, who lived in the Lesser Antilles in the West Indies:

the men have a great many expressions peculiar to them, which the women understand but never pronounce themselves. On the other hand, the women have words and phrases which the men never use, or they would be laughed to scorn. Thus it happens that in their conversations it often seems as if the women had another language than the men.

Rochefort gives a local explanation for these differences:

When the Caribs came to occupy the islands, these were occupied by an Arawak tribe which they exterminated completely, with the exception of the women, whom they married in order to populate the country. Now, these women kept their own language and taught it to their daughters... But though the boys understand the speech of their mothers and sisters, they nevertheless follow their fathers and brothers and conform to their speech from the age of five or six. (Cited Jespersen, 1922, p. 237)

We shall never know whether an invasion and subsequent slaughter of half the population is the correct explanation for the linguistic differences found by Rochefort, and other Europeans who mixed with the Carib community, but the idea that women and men might actually use different languages naturally provoked a great deal of interest – and the Carib Indians have become something of a classic case in accounts of sex differences in language use. Despite this interest, it does not seem as if the Carib male and female speech varieties were actually distinct enough to count as two separate languages. In 1922 Otto Jespersen re-examined Rochefort's data and found that distinct male and female forms accounted for only about one tenth of the vocabulary items he had recorded.

While the Caribs have often been seen as one of the most extreme examples of women and men using different language varieties, it is likely that some form of sex difference will be found in any language. Those differences that have been recorded occur at all linguistic levels: they include, for instance, use of different words, grammatical differences and pronunciation differences. In some cases such differences are categorical – men use one form and women another. In other instances they are a matter of degree – women use some feature more than men, or vice versa.

Sex-exclusive Differences and Differences of Degree

In some languages, an obligatory (grammatical) distinction is made between female and male speakers. For instance, Edward Sapir (1929) reports that in Yana, an American Indian language, most words have distinct male and female forms. 'Male' forms are used exclusively by males speaking to other males, whereas 'female' forms are used by females speaking to other females, males speaking to females or females speaking to males. Sapir's examples include those in table 3.1.

Table 3.1   Some examples of female and male forms of speech in Yana

Female form*	Male form	Meaning
sigāk‘a	sigāga	quail
cūc^u	cūcu	dog, horse
dāx^a	dāha	river
t‘ūs^i	t‘ūsi	he does
t‘ūsi	t‘usi’i	he will do

Source – Sapir, 1929, pp. 208 and 210

Other languages show similar pronunciation differences – though these are not always so extensive as in Yana. In another American Indian language, Koasati, differences are restricted to certain verb forms, for instance those in table 3.2.

Table 3.2 Some examples of female and male verb forms in Koasati

Female form*	Male form	Meaning
lakawčîn	lakawčî·s	don't lift it!
lakawwîl	lakawwís	I am lifting it
lakáwwilit	lakáwwilič	I lifted it

Source – Haas, 1944, p. 229.

Note: these spellings are the linguists' attempts to represent accurately in graphic form the speech of the communities they studied.

Mary Haas (1944), from whose study of Koasati these examples are taken, notes that such differences are retained by older speakers, but tend to be dying out amongst young people. Differences in vocabulary, grammatical forms or pronunciation have been found in other American Indian languages, in the Eskimo language spoken in Baffin Land, in Chukchee, spoken in Eastern Siberia, in Thai and so on. (Some of these examples are discussed in Haas, 1944, and Furfey, 1944. For a more recent account see Trudgill, 1983a.) These differences form part of the grammar of a language: it is a grammatical rule that female speakers use one form and male speakers another. It's also worth noting that, at least in Yana and Koasati, there is no taboo on a speaker using a form associated with the other sex. For instance, in recounting a story a narrator will use sex-appropriate forms when quoting speech from male and female characters; and a mother may correct her son if he uses the inappropriate female form.

Furfey, in an early review of 'women's and men's language', argues that the very existence of sex-differentiated forms implies:

some consciousness of men and women as different categories of human beings. Furthermore, at least at some period in the history of language, this distinction must have been regarded as being of a certain consequence; for it would seem to be a general truth that the great categories of grammar are not based on distinctions regarded by the speakers as trivial. (Furfey, 1944, p. 222)

Furfey later suggests (albeit tentatively) that 'language sometimes serves as a tool of sex dominance.' (1944, p. 223). Beyond this very general level, few satisfactory explanations were offered for sex-differentiated forms in language. Sapir writes (of Yana):

> Possibly the reduced female forms constitute a conventionalised symbolism of the less considered or ceremonious status of women in the community. Men, in dealing with men, speak fully and deliberately; where women are concerned, one prefers a clipped style of utterance! (Sapir, 1944, p. 212).

But the scope of this explanation is, at best, limited – it is not possible to account for Haas's Koasati examples in terms of 'reduced' female forms.

While the work we've been discussing has focused on non-European languages, it's worth noting that grammatical rules that make explicit the sex of a speaker occur in some European languages too. French, for instance, does not have 'male' and 'female' forms like American Indian languages, but it does have a system of *grammatical gender*. This means that all nouns are assigned to the category 'masculine' or 'feminine' (see table 3.3). Whether a noun is masculine or feminine affects the form of other parts of speech, such as pronouns and adjectives which take a masculine or feminine form depending on the gender of the noun they are referring to. In words for women and men, grammatical gender largely corresponds to sex (though there are exceptions – see chapter 5). The sex of the person speaking, being spoken to or spoken about often needs to be made explicit.

Table 3.3　Masculine and feminine forms in French

Feminine form	Masculine form	Meaning
Je suis heureuse	Je suis heureux	I (feminine/masculine) am happy
Tu es belle	Tu es beau	You (feminine/masculine) are beautiful
Elle s'est assise	Il s'est assis	She/he sat down

Grammatical rules can be regarded as categorical; a female speaker always uses the female form unless she is, for some reason, taking on the part of a male. Similarly, a male speaker always uses the male form. This is not to say that such rules are immutable. Like other aspects of language they are subject to change, as we saw in the case of Koasati. However, many differences between women's and men's speech do not operate as grammatical rules: they can be regarded rather as statistical tendencies. In this case, all other things being equal, women will tend to use some forms more often, and others less often than men – but there is no hard and fast rule that designates certain forms as 'female' and others as 'male'. Such differences between women's and men's speech probably occur in most languages, but much of the evidence we have comes from studies of English.

English, like other languages, is inherently variable. Differences are found not just between female and male speakers but between speakers from different regions, middle-class and working-class speakers, older and younger speakers and so on. Individual speakers will also vary their speech in different contexts – depending, for instance, on whether they are in a relaxed and informal setting (such as chatting to friends at home) or speaking more formally (as in a job interview). In an early study of this sort of variation in language use, John Fisher (1958) investigated the speech of 24 children of primary school age in New England. Fisher restricted his investigation to the pronunciation of the *-ing* ending in words such as *running*, *coming* and *fishing*. In New England speech (as in other varieties of British and American English) the *-ing* ending may be pronounced 'ing' (as in the word *ring*) or 'in' (often represented in writing as *runnin'* or *fishin'*). Fisher discovered systematic differences in his informants' use of these two pronunications: he found that all speakers used both types of pronunication, but differed in how often they used each form; furthermore the context in which they spoke affected how often each form was selected. The 'ing' form was used more often by girls than by boys; amongst boys it was used more often by a 'model' pupil than by a mischievous one; middle-class children also used the 'ing' form more than working-class children; and this pronunciation occurred more frequently in more formal or stressful situations. The overall picture obtained by Fisher was of a more prestigious pronunciation, 'ing', contrasting with a less prestigious 'in', and with girls more often adopting the prestigious pronunciation.

Such systematic patterning of language use in a community has been the subject of investigation by *sociolinguists*. Researchers carrying out a sociolinguistic study identify certain linguistic features (such as the *-ing* example above) that are used variably in a community and that they take as indicators of different varieties or styles of language. Any type of linguistic feature could be selected for study (since the use of particular words, syntactic structures or pronunciations could all vary within a community). In practice, however, sociolinguistic studies of English most frequently have recourse to pronunciation features – partly because speakers tend to be less self-conscious in their use of such features, and partly because even fairly short extracts of speech can provide sufficient examples for statistical analysis. Features of language that are used variably within a community are termed *sociolinguistic variables*. In the remainder of this chapter we examine the kinds of accent differences which have been found using sociolinguistic techniques and then investigate the various explanations which have been provided for these and other differences between the language varieties used by women and men.

Social Stratification Studies

In the 1960s the American linguist William Labov carried out a survey of the speech of New York city. He interviewed a random sample of the population and tried also to elicit a range of speaking styles in his informants – from casual conversation, through a more formal interview, to various reading styles. Labov suggested that this range of styles showed a progressive increase in formality, and also in the degree of attention speakers paid to their speech. Labov, like Fisher, identified an interaction between speakers' social background and the formality of their speaking style. Particular pronunciations were especially associated with higher-class speakers, and all speakers increased their usage of these 'prestige' pronunciations in their more formal styles. It seemed that although different groups of speakers might *use* different pronunciations, they all conformed to a pronunciation *hierarchy* with the same prestige forms at the top and vernacular forms at the bottom. Labov felt that the women in his sample were more sensitive to the prestige pattern since, for some sociolinguistic variables, they showed a more extreme shift towards the use of prestige forms in their formal speaking styles. Labov also suggested that New York women were the prime motivators for *changes* in pronunciation. This New York study is reported in Labov 1966. The 'sex difference' findings are also discussed in Labov 1972a.

A tendency for women to use more prestige linguistic features than men from similar social backgrounds has now been reported in several studies carried out in (particularly western) communities. Reports of American studies can be found in Shuy (1970) and Wolfram (1969). Macauley (1978) reports similar findings from Glasgow. As an illustration both of the methods employed in such work and some of its findings we can look at a well-known study carried out by Peter Trudgill in Norwich (and reported in detail in Trudgill, 1974).

Trudgill studied the speech of a sample of the inhabitants of Norwich in the late 1960s. Overall, he interviewed 50 adults and ten school children (aged 10–20). This sample was constructed so as to be as representative as possible of the population of Norwich in terms of social categories such as age, type of occupation and level of education. Half the sample was female and half male. Trudgill allocated his informants a social class position on the basis of several factors (including occupation, education, salary and housing locality). Men were rated according to their own occupation and salary, married women according to those of their husbands, and children and unmarried women according to those of their fathers. An exception to this rule was made in the case of a few women whose occupation and salary level were higher than their husbands' or fathers'. These women were rated in their own right. As in Labov's New York study, Trudgill obtained several different speaking styles from his informants, ranging from casual conversation through an interview style to a series of reading styles. Like Labov, Trudgill assumed these styles increased progressively in terms both of their formality and the degree of attention paid to speech.

Within the samples of speech he collected, Trudgill examined the distribution of several sociolinguistic variables. The majority were pronunciation features, such as the *-ing* ending analysed in John Fisher's study; the pronunciation of the *t* sound in words such as *bet* and *better*; and the *a* sound in *name*, *mail*, *plane* etc. Most of Trudgill's sociolinguistic variables showed similar patterns of distribution to those found by Labov in New York: the use of certain pronunciations was associated with higher socioeconomic status and also with more formal speaking styles. As a general rule, women used these prestige forms more often than men from the same social class background, and this pattern occurred across the different speech styles.

Trudgill also found an interesting relationship between sex differences in language and linguistic change. One of the pronunciation features he studied was the variable *o* (as in the words *top*, *grog* and *lorry*). He found that middle-class women used a prestige pronunciation of this sound more frequently than middle-class men (the expected pattern) but that working-class men used a pronunciation similar to the prestige form more frequently than working-class women (a trend in the opposite direction). Trudgill's explanation for this is that working-class men are changing this feature of pronunciation to correspond more closely to a form used in the local (vernacular) accent of Suffolk. It so happens that this alternative vernacular form is similar to the prestige form used most frequently by middle-class women. On the basis of his own work and that of other researchers such as Labov, Trudgill (1983a) suggests that men are more active in promoting linguistic change when this involves the use of new vernacular forms, but that women are in the vanguard of change towards new prestige forms.

Sociolinguistic surveys such as those carried out by Labov and Trudgill have mapped out patterns or trends in the way different social groups use language in different contexts – but such trends are very general. Trudgill's Norwich study identified some linguistic features whose pattern of variation was not so clear-cut as the more classic examples. Even the more clear-cut patterns, however, conceal irregularities. Table 3.4 shows the distribution of different pronunciations of the *-ing* variable.

At first glance the table seems extremely complicated, and in fact when representing such data diagrammatically (as a chart or histogram) it's usual to show only part of the information, or to simplify this. Such partiality or simplification also tends to make the patterns neater. Nevertheless, using this table, comparisons can be made between the speech of women and men from different social class backgrounds and in different speaking styles – and it's clear that the *-ing* variable shows the overall trends described above. Women, on the whole, obtain *lower* scores than men from the same social class speaking in the same style – they are using proportionately *fewer* vernacular 'in' pronunciations. There are, however,

Table 3.4 Percentage of 'in' pronunciations used by women and men in Norwich

Class		Style			
		More formal <- - - - - - - - - - -> Less formal			
		Word list style*	Reading passage style*	Formal interview style	Casual style
Middle-middle-class	Men	0	0	4	31
	Women	0	0	0	0
Lower-middle-class	Men	0	20	27	17
	Women	0	0	3	67
Upper-working-class	Men	0	18	81	95
	Women	11	13	68	77
Middle-working-class	Men	24	43	91	97
	Women	20	46	81	88
Lower-working-class	Men	66	100	100	100
	Women	17	54	97	100

Source – Trudgill, 1974, p. 94.
Note: these are two of Trudgill's 'reading styles'. In early sociolinguistic studies it was assumed that reading a word list counted as a more formal style than reading a continuous passage.

some deviations from the overall pattern: lower-middle-class women use the 'in' pronunciation much more frequently than lower-middle-class men in their casual styles, for instance (they score 67, whereas men score only 17). Also, in many cases, differences between women and men are small (5% or less) or non-existent. Since Trudgill did not carry out any statistical analysis of the distribution of the variables he analysed, it is not possible to say whether the differences between women and men are greater than could be expected to occur by chance. Trudgill concedes this point, but is still confident in the validity of the patterns he obtains because different variables produced similar results. The assumption seems reasonable, but it confirms the fact that this kind of sociolinguistic survey detects only very general patterns.

Some Initial Interpretations

Trudgill (1974) argues that women use high prestige varieties of language more often than men partly because they are more status conscious and more sensitive to the social significance of language. He gives two reasons for this: women's social position is less secure than men's (and usually subordinate); and whereas men can be rated by their occupation and earning power – or by what they *do* – women are more likely to be rated by their appearance. Trudgill also argues that working-class speech has connotations of masculinity which make it more attractive to men. These masculine connotations may derive from the association of working-class life – and therefore speech – with 'toughness'. These early interpretations were highly speculative. In a more recent discussion of linguistic sex differences, Trudgill (1983b) considers a far wider range of possible explanations, but still seems sympathetic to those we have outlined.

There is some support for the association of working-class speech with masculinity since, in addition to collecting samples of speech from his informants, Trudgill also asked them to listen to a number of words that were pronounced differently (with more prestigious or more vernacular pronunciations). His informants had to say which of these pronunciations they used. Trudgill could then compare the pronunciation his informants claimed they used with their actual pronunciations. While many informants reported their speaking styles accurately, some 'over-reported' (i.e. claimed to use prestige forms when they didn't) and some 'under-reported' (i.e. claimed to use vernacular forms when they actually used more prestige pronunciations). It was more often women who 'over-reported' and men who 'under-reported'. As an example of this, we can look at how Trudgill's informants reported their pronunciation of the variable *er* (the vowel sound in words such as *ear, here* and *idea*). In Norwich the

Table 3.5 Norwich informants' reporting of their pronunciation of 'er'

	% under-reporting	% over-reporting	% accurate
Women	14	68	18
Men	50	22	28

Source – adapted from Trudgill, 1972, p. 187.

vernacular pronunciation is rather like the vowel sound in *air* and *hair*. Table 3.5 shows Trudgill's results for this variable.

Trudgill argues that these and similar results substantiate a claim made earlier by Labov: that working-class vernacular forms of speech themselves enjoy a kind of prestige, termed *covert prestige* to distinguish it from the more conventional *overt* prestige associated with high status varieties of speech. There are certain attractions in the use of vernacular forms (which is why working-class speakers retain these forms rather than moving towards middle-class speech) and these appeal more to male than to female speakers.

Criticisms of Social Stratification Studies

Labov's and Trudgill's studies were attempts to find systematic patterns in the variable use of language and they were breaking new ground. Earlier work on language variation carried out by dialect-ologists had concentrated on how language varied from one region to another. The methods used by traditional dialectologists were not suited to recording and analysing the speech of socially mobile urban communities – and the language of these communities was, therefore, somewhat neglected. What was new about the urban stratification studies was the way they handled language that varied both socially and stylistically. But these newer studies also had limitations that have attracted criticism. We shall concentrate here on criticisms that are particularly relevant to the issue of language and gender.

Women and class Social stratification studies took class as their basic social division: comparisons were made between the language use of women and men belonging to the same social class. Such comparisons are only valid if all speakers have been appropriately classified – if women and men classified as, say, working class do in fact occupy the same social position.

In Trudgill's Norwich study, different criteria were used to assign women and men to a social class. Women were classified partly on the basis of their relationship to someone else – a husband or father – whereas men were classified in their own right. This was not some strange perversity – it has been common in sociological studies to classify women according to their husband's socioeconomic status, although this method has not been without criticism. Anne Oakley and Robin Oakley (1979) note that it assumes the main unit of social stratification is the family or household; that the status of the (male) 'head of household' determines the family's social position; and that women's social position is, therefore, dependent upon that of the men to whom they are attached. But Oakley and Oakley also point out that, in households where both partners are economically active, a high proportion of women would be assigned to a *different* social class from their husbands on the basis of their own occupations. Hence the assumptions traditionally made in social surveys *may* lead to the distortion of findings relating to sex differences in language use. Deborah Cameron comments on this problem:

Although the distortion may not be very great, it is possible that stratification methods which assign women to classes according to their husbands' occupation distort the picture. The differences between men and women may partly reflect the fact that if one used other criteria for the stratification – educational attainment for instance – married couples might not turn out to be parallel at all. (Cameron, 1985, p. 51).

It is not possible to say with any certainty whether the methods used by sociolinguistic researchers introduced a systematic distortion into their analyses. Trudgill has noted (1988, personal communication) that most women in his sample, if classified in their own right, would have come out with a *lower* social class position than their husbands. However, Cameron's criticisms do point to a genuine problem in sociological (and therefore sociolinguistic) research. This problem is often thought of as 'how to classify women' – but it could more accurately be seen as how to allocate women and men to social groupings in such a way that comparisons can be made between them.

The solution is by no means obvious. One might argue that, where people live in traditional family units, some sort of index *for the family* best represents the social position of its members (although this would suggest assigning a composite 'family score' to both women and men, rather than classifying men independently and women as a 'social appendage'). While this might work for traditional communities, in contemporary Britain – where there is a greater variety of living arrangements – it is likely that an alternative method of classification would be needed to represent women's and men's social positions. But the use of identical criteria (such as occupation or level of education) to allocate women and men to a social class position could introduce another kind of distortion: given their different social roles, there is no reason to assume the same criteria will always be appropriate to women and to men. For a general discussion of these and similar problems, see Abbott and Sapsford (1987).

Explanations of women's speech   According to many feminists, men are often regarded as the 'norm' in social scientific research. When women's and men's behaviour differs, women's behaviour is treated as deviant and in need of explanation. This tendency occurs also in linguistics. Jespersen's (1922) book on *Language: its nature, development and origins* contains a chapter entitled 'The Woman', which seeks to explain women's linguistic habits – but nowhere is there a comparable chapter entitled 'The Man'. In the 1940s and 1950s dialectologists often restricted their study of regional dialects to the language of male speakers (for a discussion of the nature of this bias in dialectology see Coates, 1986). Labov, in his 1966 study of New York speech, did include male and female speakers in his sample, but he devotes relatively little space to sex differences. Such interpretations as he suggests seem concerned to explain how (and why) women differ from men, rather than vice versa.

Trudgill makes an advance on this position – in his Norwich study he attempts to explain the speech both of women and of men. But his explanations have come in for criticism, much of it directed at his argument that women's use of prestige pronunciations derives from their 'status consciousness' (see, for instance, Cameron and Coates, 1985; Cameron, 1985; Spender, 1985). Trudgill's theory is important, not least because it has reached a comparatively wide audience through his introductory book *Sociolinguistics*. Such a theory requires independent evidence, but the only source cited in support of it is a survey carried out in Greenwich and Hertford in 1950 (reported in Martin, 1954). This early study appears to be the sole basis for the 'status consciousness' interpretation of women's speech, so it's worth looking at its findings in some detail. Martin was interested in comparing people's position in the social hierarchy with their perceptions of their social class. He allocated his subjects an occupation status on the basis of their own occupation, in the case of men and unmarried women living away from their parents, or their husband's or father's occupation in the case of all other women. He was, of course, making the assumption that women occupy the same social position as their husbands or fathers, and we have already pointed out that there are problems with this assumption. Martin then asked his subjects to say which social class they belonged to. Most manual workers called themselves 'working class' and most non-manual workers called themselves 'middle-class' – but there were two 'deviant' groups (manual workers whose self-identification was middle class and non-manual workers whose self-identification was working class). Of these 'deviant' groups, the first (which we can call Group A) contained more than twice as many women as men, whereas the second (Group B) contained more men than women, as we see in table 3.6.

Table 3.6   Percentage of women and men in 'deviant' groups in Martin's study

Groups	*% Women*	*% Men*
A (Manual workers claiming to be middle class)	68	32
B (Non-manual workers claiming to be working class)	42	58

Source – Martin, 1954, p. 57.

Martin interprets this sex difference in terms of women's status consciousness:

women, it seems, are considerably more disposed than men to upgrade themselves into the middle-class and less likely to allocate themselves to the working-class – a finding which confirms the common observation that status consciousness is more pronounced among women. (Martin, 1954, p. 58)

Martin then contradicts this interpretation within three or four pages. He reports that Group A and Group B people have a different conception of the class system. For Group A people, 'middle class' often refers to 'everyone who works for a living'; it includes manual workers – but tends to exclude professional people, who are thought of as 'upper class'; the term 'working class' is reserved for those much lower down the social scale, who are 'living on the borders of poverty'. Group B people, on the other hand, classify many white collar workers among the 'working class', and reserve the term 'middle class' for people occupying professional or managerial positions. Rather than 'upgrading' (or 'downgrading') themselves as individuals, members of Group A and Group B are drawing class boundaries at different points: they have different perceptions of 'working class' and 'middle class'. Group A members identify with others occupying a similar social position to themselves and show no more social ambition for themselves or their children than those who identify themselves as working class.

In their more recent study of women and class, Pamela Abbott and Roger Sapsford (1987) point out that while people are willing to allocate themselves to a social class position (normally working class or middle class) the basis on which this allocation is made is not clear. People may take into account factors other than their own or their husband's employment, and women and men may take different factors into account. Furthermore, while some researchers have found that women, more often than men, 'uprate' their class position relative to the researchers' classification, not all studies have replicated this finding (see, for instance, Runciman, 1964). In Abbott and Sapsford's study differences between women and men were very slight. Approximately 28 per cent men and 31 per cent women 'uprated' their social class positions (for women, results were similar whether they were classified according to their own, or the head of household's occupation). In comparing Abbott and Sapsford's results with those of Martin, it must be borne in mind that Abbott and Sapsford's data come from a survey of all parts of the UK, including Scotland, Wales and Northern Ireland, and that these data were collected more than 30 years after Martin's. It is likely that the attitudes and aspirations of women and men have changed considerably during that time.

Martin's work offers little support for Trudgill's 'status consciousness' theory of women's speech. The theory does, however, *require* some additional evidence: it cannot be derived from the linguistic data alone. Women who consistently use more prestige patterns are no more status-conscious than men assigned to a higher social class position; and the fact that some speakers 'under-report' or 'over-report' their use of prestige pronunciations could be interpreted as a difference in level of social ambition. Trudgill also suggests that women's 'status consciousness' may be associated with the fact that they are judged 'by their appearance' more than men. This is an interesting hypothesis, which he does not develop any further. However, it does not tell us why a woman's appearance needs to be a relatively high status one.

The status consciousness explanation thus has several weaknesses. On the other hand, Trudgill's second main explanation of sex differences – that working class speech has connotations of masculinity – has received support from other research. We shall consider later studies that have examined the connotations both of working class and middle class speech.

Bias within the interview   Cameron (1985) criticizes sociolinguistic surveys because they have often used only male interviewers. Social psychologists (see for instance Giles, 1973 and Giles et al., 1973) have shown that people change their speech depending on the person they are talking to. Labov recognized this in his research on the speech of the Black community in New York. He used Black interviewers to elicit 'representative' examples of Black vernacular English (see the introduction to Labov 1972b). Cameron argues that a male interviewer may well have a different effect on male and female speakers, and may find it harder to elicit examples of vernacular speech from women.

The issue of the 'interviewer bias' is far from resolved. Trudgill (1983b, p. 162) suggests such criticisms are weakened by the fact that sex differences in the expected direction have been found in research using both male and female interviewers. However, to investigate this 'bias' thoroughly one would need to take into account not only the sex of the interviewer, but whether their own speech differed for female and male informants. For instance, if both male and female interviewers used prestige forms to their women informants, they might expect to get more prestige variants back.

Bias within the interview may affect more than the selection of the interviewer. In many studies the questions asked have a distinctly masculine flavour. Labov's 1966 study (which also used two male interviewers) is one of the worst examples of this. Questions designed to elicit a discussion of 'common sense' and 'success' relate these concepts to men: 'I'd like to ask you to define something. A successful man. What is a successful man?'. Two reading passages used to obtain samples of formal speech are also particularly male-oriented. Both are meant to be accounts by teenage boys – the first of life 'when I was nine or ten' and the second of a Saturday night out. 'When I was nine or ten' discusses the street games played by boys, and the various antics of the narrator's first dog. It ends: 'I suppose it's the same thing with most of us: your first dog is like your first girl. She's more trouble than she's worth, but you can't seem to forget her.' The 'Saturday night' text tells how the narrator, Joseph, took a girl out for the evening. Its theme is 'the teenager's ... exasperation at the foibles and inconsistencies of the girls he dates' (Labov, 1966, p. 95): 'She used her sweet-and-sour tone of voice, like ketchup mixed with tomato sauce'; 'When Mary starts to sound humorous, that's bad: merry hell is sure to break loose.'

The most striking example of masculine bias comes at an early point in the interview, when Labov's speakers are asked questions about 'folklore' (this is one source of speakers' casual styles). Here, entirely different questions are asked of men and women. Men are asked questions about fights when they were boys, and about terms for different ethnic groups, terms for girls and ('if the informant's temperament seems to permit') for a girl's sex organs. Women are asked about childhood signs and expressions (such as crossing the fingers to indicate that what one was saying didn't really count), skipping rhymes and clapping games. With the best will in the world, it seems unlikely that a discussion of skipping rhymes could induce the rapport of two men talking about smutty words.

The stylistic continuum   A more general criticism has been made of the notion of a single continuum of style ranging from an informal, vernacular variety to a formal prestige variety in which more attention is paid to speech. This now seems at least to be over-simplified, and has been qualified by other researchers. The assumption that speakers pay more attention to speech in their more formal styles seems to have been made largely on intuitive grounds, and there is evidence that this does not hold good for all speakers. The notion that language varies along a *single* continuum is also questionable: it is likely that language relates to several aspects of a speaker's identity – and so varies along several different dimensions. We shall consider some evidence for this below.

Alternative Accounts of Female and Male Speech

Social stratification studies have identified a relationship between speakers' membership of social groups and their use of certain linguistic features. Some researchers have also tried to account for the motivation that might lead speakers to adopt a particular language variety (e.g. Trudgill's claim that men hold vernacular speech in 'covert prestige'). We shall now look at some more recent studies that have attempted to explore what motivates women and men to adopt different ways of speaking.

Social Psychological Explanations

Just as listeners seem to make judgements about speakers on the basis of voice quality (see chapter 2), so evidence from social psychology suggests there may be rewards for speakers who adopt particular language varieties. A series of studies carried out in Britain by Howard Giles and his associates found that *RP*, or *Received Pronunciation* (the non-localized middle class accent that has also been referred to as 'Oxford English' or 'BBC English'), was judged as having high prestige. We might expect this on common-sense grounds, as well as on the basis of Trudgill's work in Norwich and other similar studies. Giles also found, however, that an RP-accented speaker was judged as being more intelligent, self-confident and generally more competent than a speaker with a regional accent. On the other hand, there were rewards for speakers with certain regional accents too. Such accents were regarded as more socially attractive (for example more trustworthy, sincere, likeable and persuasive) than RP (see Giles and Powesland, 1975 for an account of this work). Giles' early studies used only male speakers. They give some support to Trudgill's argument that, while there are accepted prestige forms in a speech community, male speakers at least may also feel an opposing 'pull' towards vernacular varieties.

An association between working-class speech and *masculinity* was found in a study by John Edwards (1979). This study also gives us more information about female speakers. Edwards recorded the speaking voices of 40 ten year old girls and boys, 20 of whom came from working class and 20 from middle class backgrounds. Edwards asked adults to listen to his recordings, and to say whether each child was male or female. Although the children's voices had not broken, adults were more often than not able to identify their sex correctly. But when mistakes were made, working class girls tended to be misidentified as boys, and middle class boys misidentified as girls. A second panel of adult listeners rated the working-class voices as lower, rougher and more masculine – and the middle-class voices, correspondingly, as higher, smoother and more feminine.

A study of listeners' ratings of women's speech (Olwen Elyan et al., 1978) indicated that RP provides some of the same advantages and disadvantages for female as for male speakers: RP-speaking women, like men, are judged to be more intelligent, competent and so forth, but also less sincere and likeable than women with a local (northern) accent. Elyan et al. also suggest, however, that a prestige RP accent can confer additional benefits on female speakers. RP speech was rated as being more feminine than northern-accented speech, but also high on certain characteristics stereotypically associated with masculinity (such as independence and adventurousness). This may sound contradictory, but as chapter 2 pointed out, people may possess both stereotypically feminine *and* masculine attributes. Such individuals are referred to as *psychologically androgynous*. Elyan et al. suggest that, in Britain, female RP-accented speech may be the 'voice of perceived androgyny'.

More work will be needed to corroborate Elyan et al.'s findings: one would need to check, for instance, whether male RP speakers were also rated as more androgynous than their local-accented counterparts. However these social psychological studies do show that a system of rewards (and, by analogy, forfeits) attends the use of different speech varieties. This system may operate differently for women and men, contributing to women's greater use of prestige features of language and men's preference for vernacular forms.

Social Networks and Patterns of Interaction

Social psychologists have measured people's attitudes to language varieties; other researchers have concentrated on the mechanisms by which particular dialects or accents are maintained in a community.

In the 1970s, Leslie Milroy carried out an investigation into language use in Belfast (Milroy, 1980). Her aim was to identify factors that supported the use of local vernacular forms of speech. Unlike the social stratification studies discussed above, which are based on the speech of a random sample of people, Milroy examined the speech of pre-existing social groups within three working class communities: Ballymacarrett, the Hammer and the Clonard. She approached someone in each community as a 'friend of a friend' and asked to be introduced to relatives, neighbours and workmates with whom that person had ties. In this way she established contact with a network of speakers with whom she could meet and talk.

The three communities were all working class, but they differed in some respects. In Ballymacarrett the men tended to work in the local shipyard. They also associated socially with workmates and others from the local community. Women travelled outside to work and many younger women had left the community. The population of the Hammer was in the process of being dispersed to the suburbs and to city flats and maisonettes. Former inhabitants still visited the Hammer regularly but the normal interaction patterns of the community had been disrupted. In the Clonard there was high male unemployment and men moved in a relatively wide area, with fewer local ties than in Ballymacarrett. There was, however, high employment among the women studied, and many of the younger women worked together and had close ties in the community.

Milroy wanted to measure how closely integrated people were within the community. She allocated each speaker a 'network score' that varied according to how many local ties they had (someone who had relatives in the community, who worked alongside others in the community and associated with them during leisure hours would obtain a higher network score than a person who worked and mixed with others outside the community). As might be expected Bally-macarrett men had high network scores – much higher than Ballymacarrett women. In the Clonard this sex difference was slightly reversed, mainly because of very high network scores obtained by younger Clonard women.

Milroy identified a number of sounds that were pronounced variably, and analysed how the different forms of pronunciation were distributed within each community. Overall, she found the expected pattern of sex differentiation, with women using fewer vernacular forms than men. This general finding, however, con-

cealed some important differences between areas. Sex differentiation
was particularly strong in Ballymacarrett. In the Hammer, differences were less extreme, but still as expected. Older Clonard women
and men also showed this pattern – but it was reversed amongst
younger Clonard women and men. The differences between women
and men seemed to be related to network scores. Milroy claims that
close-knit networks support the use of local vernacular forms. She
also suggests that networks influence language use more consistently
in traditional working class communities such as Ballymacarrett,
where there is stricter sex-segregation and men have several close,
local ties.

Milroy also found some *differences* in the way sociolinguistic
variables were related to network scores. Speakers with high
network scores used more vernacular pronunciations of the variable
a (as in *hat*) and *th* (as in *mother*). This relationship occurred for
both women and men, but it was stronger for women. On the other
hand, it was only men with high network scores who used more
vernacular pronunciations of the variable *u* (as in *pull*). Milroy
concludes that while the overall pattern is for close-knit networks to
be associated with more vernacular forms of speech, this differs
slightly for women and men. Some sociolinguistic variables are a
sign of integration into the community for both women and men;
others only for men.

Milroy's findings receive support from two studies of adolescent
speech, one carried out by William Labov in New York and the
other by Jenny Cheshire in Reading in the UK. Labov (1972b)
investigated the speech of male adolescent gangs in New York.
Prominent and central members of these gangs regularly used
certain 'gang-like' vernacular forms of language. More peripheral
members used these features less systematically. Cheshire (1982)
studied the speech of two groups of adolescent boys and one group of
girls whom she met in adventure playgrounds in Reading. She was
interested in their use of standard and nonstandard grammatical
features (for example, whether some said *I ain't got one* or *I haven't
got one*). Cheshire found that the boys, overall, used more nonstandard grammatical features, as male speakers had done in earlier
social stratification studies. This general finding, however, obscured
other influences over girls' and boys' use of language. In the boys'
groups, nonstandard forms tended to be used more frequently by
those who were closely integrated within the group. Cheshire used

the term 'peer group status' to refer to the extent of a group member's integration. The relationship between the use of non-standard forms and peer group status was less regular and systematic than in Labov's study of New York gangs, which Cheshire attributes to the fact that Labov's gangs had a distinct identity (they had names such as 'the Jets' and 'the Cobras') and a close-knit hierarchical structure. The Reading groups, on the other hand, had a much more flexible and loose-knit structure. As in Milroy's study, it seemed that a close-knit cohesive group could encourage a more systematic use, among its members, of certain vernacular speech forms.

Cheshire's group of girls was even more loosely knit than the boys' groups: girls tended to pair off with 'best friends' but these friendships broke up and new friendship ties were formed. Cheshire could determine no clear differences of 'peer group status' between the girls in her study, and so was unable to compare this factor with the use of vernacular speech.

She could, however, measure adolescents' adherence to 'vernacular culture'. Vernacular culture did not refer to 'legitimate' youth culture, such as an interest in pop music, but to participation in more illicit activities such as swearing, fighting and petty crime. Cheshire divided the boys in her study into four groups, ranging from those who adhered most closely to the vernacular culture to those who were most distanced from it. Such fine discrimination was not possible with the girls, partly because they appeared less regularly in the playground and partly because they talked less about their exploits than the boys did. She divided the girls into two groups: 'bad girls' (those who showed some allegiance to vernacular culture) and 'good girls' (those who did not). She found that the use of certain nonstandard grammatical features was associated with an allegiance to vernacular culture for boys and girls; some features had this association only for boys; and others only for girls. Like Milroy's work in Belfast, Cheshire's study shows that it is not enough simply to look at sex differences in language without taking account of other social factors. She comments:

The main point that emerges from this analysis ... is not that girls are more susceptible to the more overt norms governing the use of standard English features (though this is certainly *to some extent* true), but that different linguistic features are used in different ways by boys and girls. (Cheshire, 1982, p. 110)

This work shows that simply totalling the variable usage of linguistic forms by women and men presents us with a very partial picture. To understand why sex differences occur one needs to look at the roles played by women and men in the community, whom they habitually interact with, and what might motivate them to adopt particular forms of speech. Some work carried out in other communities (and also in the 1970s) supports this conclusion.

Susan Gal studied the speech of Oberwart, a village in Austria. Oberwart is on the border between Austria and Hungary, and the inhabitants are bilingual in (Austrian) German and Hungarian. In bilingual communities, people do not always keep their two languages separate – they sometimes switch from one to the other during a conversation. In this community, Hungarian is associated with peasant status and German with worker status. The two languages have come to symbolize different sets of values: Hungarian symbolizes 'the old way of life, the old forms of prestige of the peasant community', whereas '[t]he world of schooling, of employment, and of material success is a totally German-speaking world. The language itself has come to symbolize the higher status of the worker and the prestige and money that can be acquired by wage work' (Gal, 1979, p. 106). Young women tend to prefer German irrespective of their social background. Gal claims this is because they prefer not to be associated with peasant life. The young women's life style will be affected by the men they marry, and a peasant wife works harder and under worse conditions than a worker's wife. According to the local marriage register, since the early 1960s peasant men have had to find wives outside the village. Since these women tend to be monolingual German speakers, this further promotes the use of German within the peasant community. Gal's account of sex differences is reported in Gal (1978). The whole study is reported in Gal (1979).

Patricia Nichols (1978) studied the speech of a rural Black community living on a river island in South Carolina. She obtained access to the community by volunteering to teach a weekly writing class (she already worked as an unpaid classroom assistant in a mainland school attended by children from the island). The speech of the island community formed a continuum of varieties ranging from an English-related Creole through a form of Black vernacular English to a regional standard English. Overall, island speech was moving closer to the standard, with young and middle-aged women leading this change. Young men, on the other hand, retained many Creole features. Older speakers of both sexes had similar speech on the island – but in a nearby mainland Black community older women retained more Creole features than did older men. Differences between young male and female speakers on the island were in the same direction as those identified by Labov and Trudgill (and other researchers). However, amongst older mainland speakers there was a trend in the opposite direction.

The communities' life styles might help explain these differences. The island community used to be largely self-contained, having little contact with mainland communities. At the time of Nichols's study people did travel off the island, but women and men had different kinds of contact with mainland communities. Men rarely had college training and tended to work in the construction industry, often alongside other island men. Women, at one time, had found jobs as domestic workers but had recently begun to work in commerce or, in a few cases, as school teachers; several young women had college training. In the nearby mainland community, older women worked locally as domestic labourers or seasonal farm workers. Older men held labouring jobs locally or in nearby towns. They tended to travel further afield than women to work and had wider contacts outside the community. Although Nichols did not use Lesley Milroy's concept of 'social network' her results, and her explanations, are similar to Milroy's Belfast study.

More recent studies have tended to confirm the fact that sex differences in language use can often be explained in terms of other social factors that interact with sex. Viv Edwards (1986) describes a British study of the speech of 45 young Black people living in Dudley in the West Midlands. The study examined the frequency with which the young people used features of 'Patois' (the term used by the local community for Black vernacular English). Edwards found that a high use of Patois features was associated with negative attitudes towards mainstream white society and with a high degree of integration into the Black community measured by means of a network score. There was also a sex difference in the expected direction, but this interacted with level of education: a higher educational level had no effect on young women's use of Patois, but decreased the use of Patois with young men. Edwards suggests the sex differences she found could be explained in terms of social networks. Her Dudley study:

draws attention to the normative influence which close-knit social groups can exert on their members and has the added advantage of showing that any differences between the young men and women in the sample can be explained in terms of different patterns of social networks associated with both sexes. (Edwards, 1986, p. 86)

We can point out in passing that this study, in addition to taking acount of other social factors that might 'explain' sex differences, also tried to remedy some of the limitations identified in earlier correlational studies. For example, different interviewers were used in an attempt to elicit a range of speech styles – but for all participants sessions were included with a Black interviewer of the same sex as themselves.

Gender Signals

The investigations which we have just described show how the use of certain linguistic features is associated with particular social network patterns. If such associations are recognized within a community they may provide a resource which members can use to advertise their social identity. The patterns which are observed may arise because people deliberately choose to speak in certain ways to signal their membership of a particular community, their gender, and other aspects of their social identity.

Milroy's work provides evidence of how such gender signalling may operate. We mentioned her finding that the relationship between sociolinguistic variables and network scores sometimes differed for women and men. In some cases, a linguistic feature could signal allegiance to a local working-class community and masculinity; in other cases, simply community allegiance. Cheshire's study of adolescent speech in Reading also showed that linguistic features were used in different ways by girls and boys. Milroy (1988) reports some later work carried out in Newcastle on Tyne, which offers further evidence that different sociolinguistic variables behave differently: some relate more closely to the sex of a speaker, others to class, or to style ... etc. This suggests that, potentially, speakers may use different features to signal different aspects of their social identity.

A study carried out by Derek Bickerton in Hawaii (Bickerton, 1980) provides an interesting account of gender signalling. Bickerton studied language use in a group of working-class men in Puhi, a plantation village, where a variety of Hawaiian Creole is spoken. He describes in detail the speech of two men, Vic and Sailor. Bickerton recorded speech in a variety of everyday settings, which he intuitively ranked on a scale ranging from more to less formal. There was some support for this ranking, as many of the sociolinguistic variables he analysed showed the expected distributions across these contexts (greater use of vernacular forms in informal contexts, more standard forms in formal contexts, much as in the studies carried out by Labov and Trudgill). Some variables, however, had different distribution patterns: they seemed to be affected by the sex of those present during the conversation, as well as by formality. For these variables, more vernacular forms were used in an all-male context with the interviewer present than in a mixed sex but less formal context with no outside interviewer. Bickerton argues that linguistic variables in this community do not vary along a single 'formality' continuum. There are at least two dimensions. Some vary along an 'in-group–out-group' dimension (when the presence of non-local speakers encourages more standard speech forms) and others along a 'macho–non-macho' dimension (when the presence of female speakers encourages the use – among men – of more standard forms). Other researchers have argued against Labov's and Trudgill's notion of a single stylistic continuum along which language varies. Gal (1979) found this could not account adequately for situational variation in Oberwart; and a study of language in the Caribbean (Le Page and Tabouret-Keller 1985) also found that language varies along several different dimensions. Le Page and Tabouret-Keller argue:

the individual creates for himself [*sic*] the patterns of his linguistic behaviour so as to resemble those of the group or groups with which from time to time he wishes to be identified, or so as to be unlike those from whom he wishes to be distinguished. (Le Page and Tabouret-Keller, 1985, p. 181)

This is not a specific reference to gender, but since gender is such an important social division in all cultures, it would be remarkable if it were not a part of the social identity which people demonstrate through their use of language. We have mentioned that, in addition to signalling gender *per se*, speakers also signal their aspirations, their adherence to a certain life style and their allegiance to other social groups. But many of these other factors will be related to gender. In any community there tends to be a contrast between the life styles associated with women and with men (peasant *versus* non-peasant status in Gal's Austrian village study, presence or absence of strong local ties and degree and type of education in the community studied by Nichols, etc.). To the extent that other aspects of social identity correlate with gender, any language behaviour which signals them will also, indirectly, be signalling gender. It will also contribute to a package of ideas about aspirations and activities which are appropriate to concepts of femininity or masculinity, current in a particular community.

Social identity is not a static and monolithic thing. Different aspects of a person's social identity may be emphasized by different features of speech (accent, voice quality, use of certain vocabulary, etc.) and these may vary from context to context. Howard Giles (1980) suggests that a woman and a man talking together could use features of accent to express solidarity and a common identity as members of a certain social group, and (simultaneously) pitch of voice, breathiness and intonation to signal their respective gender identities (Giles, 1980). Speakers' verbal messages may also be supported, or subverted, by non-verbal signs such as dress, posture and gesture.

Conclusion

We began this chapter by looking at early anthropological studies of differences in women's and men's language. Many of these differences were categorical – some forms were used exclusively by men and others exclusively by women. In this case, it seemed reasonable to interpret the differences purely in terms of gender as an important social division which finds expression in language use. This was the interpretation put forward by Furfey (1944) in his review of some anthropological studies. A similar type of explanation persisted in the social stratification studies carried out in America and Britain in the 1960s and early 1970s. Explanations were refined, but they were still related to qualities regarded as inherent in being female or male in our culture (women's greater status consciousness, for instance, and men's greater attraction to the covert prestige of working class speech). More recent studies have indicated that sex differences may occur incidentally, or as a by-product of women's and men's different patterns of interaction. In terms of a semiotic model, they are indexical of social organization.

Explanations deriving from social stratification studies were in some cases nothing more than an appeal to current prejudices, and more recent studies of social networks have provided a useful corrective to this. There is a danger, however, in going too far in the other direction. We have seen that where there exists an indexical association between language use and social divisions, language can also be used symbolically to signal membership of a social group, or acceptance of a set of values. The discussion of gender signalling shows that this may be a complex activity, in which different features have different associations, and that some associations may be particular to a given community.

In several respects, sex differences in the use of language varieties parallel those in voice quality. Social significance is visible in the interplay between the indexical and symbolic associations of different voices and of different language varieties. And evaluations of both aspects of speech involve complex notions of femininity and masculinity within which many individual attributes can be distinguished. Whereas voice qualities are particularly linked with biological notions of gender and sexuality, the study of language varieties introduces strong elements of class association, and of economic and social conditions that relate to gender divisions.

In the next chapter we move on to consider how women's and men's conversational styles may differ. Conversational features have traditionally been considered separately from the linguistic variables we have focused on in this chapter and different interpretations have often been made about their use.

4

Conversation: The Sexual Division of Labour

'There is an unequal distribution of work in conversation ... Women do support work while men are talking and it is the women who generally do active maintenance and continuation work in conversations.'
(P. M. Fishman, 'Interaction: the work women do' (1983))

Introduction

It may seem odd to view conversation as work. We often think of it as something casual, that people engage in spontaneously and without much conscious effect. However it has been argued that conversations need to be 'managed' by participants. Harvey Sacks and his associates (Sacks, Schegloff and Jefferson, 1974; Schegloff, 1972; Schegloff and Sacks, 1974) have shown that conversation is a structured activity: the talk has to be sequenced, effectively opened and brought to a close. Studies by Fishman, and others that we shall examine below, suggest that women and men habitually carry out different tasks in conversation management. This has been investigated not just as an end in itself but because an important function of conversation, and other forms of talk, is the establishment and maintenance of relationships between people. Through our talk with others we can pull rank, express intimacy or show respect; we can indicate cordiality or hostility. If women and men carry out different kinds of activities in conversation this will affect not only the local management of talk but also how women and men are able to relate to one another.

These are some of the topics we shall examine below, but first we look at a more basic issue: do men and women have differential access to talk itself?

Speaking and Silence

'It would be cheaper if we bought our own communications satellite . . '

Cartoon by 'Nibz', *Daily Mirror*

Women are often stereotyped as the 'overtalkative' sex. Cheris Kramarae surveyed peoples' attitudes towards female and male speech (in the USA) and found that 'gossip' and 'talk a lot' were frequently cited as characteristics of female speech. (This research is reported under Kramarae's original name, Kramer, 1977).

Prescriptions about female speech have often been designed to curb this loquacity. Bornstein (1978) analysed prescriptions in sources ranging from mediaeval 'courtesy' books to contemporary US etiquette manuals and magazines. Women, she found, were advised to speak little and temperately.

In contrast to the stereotype, many studies have now been carried out in Britain and the USA which show that, in a variety of contexts, it is men who talk more (see for instance Soskin and John, 1963;

Bernard, 1972; Swacker, 1975; Eakins and Eakins, 1976). These studies measured the amount of talk produced in a given context. They did not compare different types of talk. In a later study analysing talk in university committee meetings, Edelsky (1981) found that women could hold their own in 'collaboratively developed' informal talk, but not in the 'one person at a time' talk which is more common in formal meetings.

Talking in Class – An Illustration

Many studies of amount of talk have been carried out in educational contexts. These are worth looking at in a little more detail, since talking is thought by many to play a particularly important part in learning in the classroom:

The way into ideas, the way of making ideas truly one's own, is to be able to think them through, and the best way to do this for most people is to talk them through. Thus talking is not merely a way of conveying existing ideas to others; it is also a way by which we explore ideas, clarify them, and make them our own. Talking things over allows the sorting of ideas, and gives rapid and extensive practice towards the handling of ideas. (Marland, 1977, p. 129)

Since talk is thought to be so important, it would seem reasonable to suggest that all pupils should have equal access to it. Yet many studies of classroom interaction have shown that boys talk more than girls (see Elliott, 1974; Spender, 1982; French and French, 1984a; Sadker and Sadker, 1985). In Sadker and Sadker's study of over 100 classes, covering both arts and science subjects, boys spoke on average three times as much as girls – and this figure is by no means unusual.

Many explanations of such discrepancies have placed at least a measure of responsibility on the teacher. For instance, there is evidence that teachers pay more attention to boys, giving them both more disapproval and also more praise and encouragement (Clarricoates, 1983, discusses some of the evidence for this claim). Even a conscious aim to divide one's attention equally between girls and boys may be difficult to achieve; Spender (1982) found she spent, on average, only 38 per cent of her time interacting with girls in lessons she taught – even though her aim had been to spend an equal amount of time with pupils of both sexes, and her perceptions had been that she frequently spent more time with the girls. Whyte (1986) is slightly less pessimistic. She found British teachers involved in the Manchester based Girls Into Science and Technology project were able to devote an equal amount of time to girls and boys, but only with considerable effort.

Teachers may also reward the same behaviour in boys that they discourage in girls. For instance, Sadker and Sadker found that boys were eight times more likely than girls to call out answers, and that teachers accepted such answers from boys but reprimanded girls for calling out.

As this last finding demonstrates, boys are not simply passive recipients of increased levels of teacher attention, but may actively demand this. For instance, boys tend to be more disruptive than girls and are the focus of teachers' attempts to maintain control (Stanworth, 1981; Spender, 1982; Clarricoates, 1983). French and French's (1984a) detailed analysis of one of a series of primary school lessons they observed and recorded suggests that boys use various strategies to ensure greater participation – they may, for instance, simply contrive to have more interesting and noteworthy things to say, thus prompting the teacher to question them further.

Our own video analysis of discussions between a teacher and small groups of primary school children supports the claim that boys' greater participation in classroom talk comes about because of an interaction between the teacher's behaviour and that of the pupils. We found teachers were able to encourage boys through the use of very subtle cues such as eye gaze but also that talkative boys seemed to be able to operate successfully within very different teaching styles. When butting in was allowed, talkative boys butted in; when the teacher required pupils to raise their hands, boys managed to get their hands up fractionally earlier than girls, thus securing more speaking turns. We suspect that girls were also accomplices here. They could also 'read' the teacher's style and thus avoid participating in discussion (Swann and Graddol, 1988). Although researchers often talk of men (or boys) as 'dominating' talk this needn't mean there is a struggle to gain speaking turns. Both quiet and talkative participants (and teachers, in the case of classroom discussions) may play a part in ensuring male dominance.

In order to explain why girls and women are *perceived* as talkative, despite evidence to the contrary, Dale Spender has argued that a double standard is in operation in attitudes to talk. Just as teachers hold mistaken impressions of the amount of attention they pay girl and boy pupils, Spender claims our impressions of the amount spoken by males and females are systematically distorted:

A talkative female is one who talks about as often as a man. When females are seen to talk about HALF AS MUCH AS MALES, they are judged as dominating talk. (Spender, 1978, p. 19)

Aiding and Abetting: Gender and Other Factors

Although speaker sex has been associated with the amount of talk produced in many contexts, how much anyone talks on any occasion clearly depends upon a variety of factors. Personality and emotional state will be important, as will many other aspects of the speaker's social identity, such as whether they have higher or lower status than their interlocutor. The roles speakers play and the conversational goals they are pursuing will affect how talk is organized and how much each speaker contributes. In a classroom, boy pupils may talk more on average than girls, but it is the teacher (whether female or male) who does the most talking.

Leet-Pellegrini (1980) has studied amount of talk in relation to two speaker variables: sex and expertise. Her subjects were 140 US college students asked to discuss the negative effect of television violence on children. The students discussed this issue in pairs, some single sex and some mixed sex. All conversational partners were unacquainted with one another. In some pairs, neither partner was given additional information. In other pairs, one partner was allowed to read material discussing television and violence before beginning the conversation. This person was then considered to have expertise relative to their (uninformed) partner.

The opening section and closing section of each conversation were analysed. Leet-Pellegrini's measures included the amount of talk produced by each speaker and her results suggested that amount of talk was associated with both speaker sex and expertise. She found that men talked more than women; 'experts' talked more than 'non-experts'; and male 'experts' talked more than female 'experts', particularly in relation to female partners. The study provides evidence of one other factor that may affect the amount of talk someone produces – and that *interacts* with speaker sex, so that speakers who are both male and have 'expertise' tend to spend the most time talking. However, expertise in the kinds of subjects which mixed sex groups talk about may not be distributed equally between men and women: 'expertise' may not always be a factor which is independent of gender.

Amount of talk has been taken as an indicator of conversational dominance in many studies, but its function needs to be interpreted in context. Phillipsen (1975) carried out an ethnographic study of a working class neighbourhood in a US town and found that, in many situations, the men 'disvalued' speech as a way of presenting themselves. Speech was used to express solidarity (e.g. in the men's 'corner clubs') but in more formal contexts (such as when speaking to people outside the community) men often had recourse to an intermediary such as a local politician or an employer. Within the community, speech was not normally used to respond to an insult (unless this came from a member of one's peer group). Nor was it used to control a status inferior, such as a child. A non-verbal threat or physical punishment tended to be used on these occasions instead.

This study cannot be compared directly with work we have cited earlier. Phillipsen's research was based on long-term observation of a community. He did not measure the amount of talk produced in particular contexts, and nor does he tell us anything about the women's talk. We mention the study simply as an illustration of a general point that will crop up again in this chapter: particular linguistic features may be used for certain purposes and effects in conversation, but you cannot say that one feature always and unambiguously has the same function – nor that one function has always to be fulfilled by the same feature. To be able to understand the function of different aspects of a conversation one needs considerable knowledge of the context in which this takes place: in a context in which people routinely had recourse to physical violence, perhaps a dominant person could afford to be a man of few words.

Conversation Management

Several pieces of research carried out since the early 1970s have suggested that women and men (and girls and boys) have different interactional styles. 'Male' techniques, it is said, allow speakers to dominate conversation whereas 'female' techniques are more supportive. We shall look at four claims: that female speakers use more support indicators than males; that male speakers interrupt more than females; that, at least in single-sex interactions, male and female speakers have different ways of issuing directives to one another; and that female speakers use expressions conveying hesitancy and uncertainty more than males.

The Supporting Role

For conversations to take place at all conversational topics have to be introduced, pursued (or, of course, dropped) by the participants. However the US researcher Pamela Fishman, in a series of papers, suggests that topics have different survival rates depending upon whether they are introduced by women or men. Fishman tape-recorded several days of conversation in the homes of three couples, all white American, aged between 25 and 35 years and professionally oriented. We shall take two of Fishman's papers (Fishman 1978a and 1978b) as examples of her work.

Fishman gives an example of a 'successful' topic:
(M = man and F = woman)

M: What do you think your best weight is?
F: 95 he he heh Oh I'll say 92
M: I saw in the paper where Olga Korbut Korbut
F: Yeah
M: Went to see Dickie
F: You're kidding (*pause*) What for?
M: I don't know (*pause*)
F: I can just imagine what she would go to see Dick Nixon for. I don't get it (*pause*)
M: I think she's on a tour of the United States (*pause*)
F: Has he sat down and talked to her?
M: Shows the picture in the paper
(Adapted from Fishman, 1978a, p. 16A)

The conversation continues in much the same vein. The topic of Olga Korbut was introduced by the man but is supported and elaborated upon by his female conversational partner. Contrast this with the following 'unsuccessful' topic, introduced by a woman:

F: They have this many publications in women's studies received every month. It's one of these. In oth-

M: Uhm

F: In other words – about um (*pause*) well at this rate (*pause*) you know about (*pause*) two thousand a year

M: It's a lot

F: And Carol said that they found out that there were four hundred applications from graduate students doing PhDs in women's

M: { studies }
   { hmh   }

(Adapted from Fishman, 1978a, p. 16C)

Note: { } indicate the extent of overlapping speech.

Here, and for the remainder of this topic, the man gives very little conversational support, often producing only *minimal responses* (such as *mmh*).

This contrast in the level of support provided by women and men was characteristic of the conversations analysed by Fishman. For instance, whereas both women and men used minimal responses they used them differently. Men might give only a minimal response at the end of a woman's (lengthy) speaking turn, whereas women would insert *mmh*s, *yeah*s and *oh*s throughout the stream of men's talk, signalling their constant attention (Fishman, 1978b).

Women raised 62 per cent and men 38 per cent of all topics. However, whereas virtually all (28 out of 29) of the men's topics succeeded (they were followed up by the other speaker and became established) only 17 out of 47 of the women's topics were successful. Women used more attention-getting devices such as 'D'you know what?', and asked more questions. Fishman interpreted these as attempts to guarantee attention and a response. Fishman's work has received some support from other research, such as Hirschman (1974). Findings reported in Leet-Pellegrini's (1980) study were also compatible with Fishman's claim: women in this study used more 'assent terms' such as *yeah*, *right*, *that's true*, interpreted by Leet-Pellegrini as offering conversational support. These 'supporting' usages were also related to expertise: female 'experts' used more assent terms than male 'experts', and they used these more often with male than with female partners. Furthermore, 'uninformed' partners used more assent terms than 'experts' in all situations expect when a male 'non-expert' conversed with a female 'expert'.

An important feature of conversation is that speakers coordinate their talk so that (normally) one person is speaking at a time and speaking turns succeed one another relatively smoothly. It may seem obvious that people take turns at speaking but this is in fact an achievement requiring considerable skill. The gap between two speaking turns is often as little as a fraction of a second and to achieve such rapid transitions listeners need to predict when the current speaker is likely to finish speaking and a new turn can legitimately begin.

One model of turn-taking (Sacks et al., 1974) argues that speaking turns include *transition-relevance places* – points where a sequence is grammatically complete, and at which it might be reasonable for a turn to end. Since speaking turns may contain several transition-relevance places, however, listeners need to use additional cues such as the speaker's eye gaze, intonation and gesture to predict the point at which the turn is actually complete. Brief overlaps between successive speakers might be expected to occur in such a model, but larger overlaps, or interruptions, pose a problem as they suggest people may be misreading turn completion cues.

However, interruptions have also been seen as a sign of conversational dominance rather than interactional incompetence. For instance, not everyone is allowed to interrupt – children may be explicitly told not to by their parents. In some contexts, an interruption takes the conversation away from the previous speaker. It gives the perpetrator a turn and, quite possibly, allows the conversation to be directed towards a particular topic that they wish to pursue:

A: I do, to get that kind of kicks 'cos it's, you know, it's {going to
                                                              {Well I'm
B: sure you sit there with your orange juice ...
Note: { indicates the start of simultaneous speech.

Two American researchers, Don Zimmerman and Candace West, have argued that interruptions are not randomly distributed in conversation but that they are perpetrated more often by certain types of speaker than others (adults more than children; men more than women). In a study that has now become something of a classic, Zimmerman and West (1975) recorded (surreptitiously) brief two-person interactions between male speakers, female speakers and mixed-sex pairs. They distinguished two kinds of simultaneous speech: *overlaps* (one speaker talks over another, but begins speaking very close to a transition-relevance place); and *interruptions* (perpetrated before the word immediately preceding a transition-relevance place). Zimmerman and West also examined their speakers' use of *delayed minimal responses*. Minimal responses were categorized as 'delayed' when they did not immediately follow the previous speaker's turn. Such delayed responses were often succeeded by silences:

SPEAKER A:	introduces topic
	5-second silence
SPEAKER B:	um
	3-second silence
SPEAKER A:	continues

In single sex pairs overlaps and interruptions were distributed fairly evenly between speakers. In mixed-sex pairs, overlaps and interruptions were more frequent and they virtually all came from men. Women, in conversation with men, exhibited more silences than their partners. These silences tended to follow the man's overlap, interruption or delayed minimal response. Zimmerman and West argue that interruptions and delayed minimal responses are ways of controlling the conversation: minimal responses, for instance, normally indicate interest and attention, but delaying this signal may suggest a lack of interest or inattention.

In a more recent study (reported in West and Zimmerman, 1983), the researchers examined interactions between women and men in a laboratory setting. The sample of speakers for the earlier study had been non-random, and, in many cases, the speakers were acquainted with each other. West and Zimmerman wanted to see if their results held good for a random sample of people who were strangers to one another. Their sample consisted of male and female undergraduate students who were put into mixed-sex pairs and asked to 'relax and get to know one another' before embarking on a more formal discussion. The initial 'informal' conversations were analysed, and West and Zimmerman found that, in every couple, the man interrupted more often than the woman (the average was 75 per cent male interruptions to 25 per cent female). Men also began their interruptions much nearer the beginning of their partner's turn than did women. West and Zimmerman conclude that the gender of participants has important conversational consequences and that interruptions are one way in which power relations may be worked out.

Other studies carried out in different contexts have supported Zimmerman and West's findings. Esposito (1979) found similar patterns of interruption in pre-school children (aged 3.5–4.8 years); and in their faculty board study mentioned above Eakins and Eakins (1976) found men interrupted women more than vice versa.

Eakins and Eakins also suggest interruptions may be related to status – in their data, speakers with higher status in the university department interrupted more often than lower status speakers. But in a later study of doctor–patient interactions West (1984) found that female patients were interrupted by male doctors, but also that female doctors were interrupted by male patients. She concludes that sex constitutes a 'superordinate status' so that no matter what professional level a woman achieves she is still treated like a woman.

A British study by Beattie (1981, 1983) provides some counter evidence to this claim. In an analysis of talk in university tutorials he found a high level of interruptions, but these came as often from female as from male students. Beattie relates his findings to the dynamics of university tutorials, in which students' performance may contribute towards their assessment.

Unfortunately, it is difficult to make a direct comparison between these results and those of Zimmerman and West as the researchers used different criteria for interruptions. Beattie identified several different types of interruption, but his 'simple interruption' comes closest to Zimmerman and West's interruption category. In Beattie's study, a simple interruption occurs when the first speaker's turn is left incomplete.

A: ... so he (.) he gives the impression that he he wasn't able to train them
up. ⎧Now
B   ⎩He didn't try hard enough heh heh heh.
(Adapted from Beattie, 1983, p. 115)
Note: (.) indicates a brief pause.

Incompleteness is judged intuitively (taking into account both verbal and non-verbal cues). The judgement is made at the point when the first speaker stops speaking, not where the second speaker starts.

The example above would probably not be classified as an interruption by Zimmerman and West, since the second speaker comes in at a transition relevance place. On the other hand, it is possible that some of Zimmerman and West's interruptions would fail to satisfy Beattie's 'incompleteness' criterion. At least some of the differences between the two studies might therefore be accounted for by differences in definition. Although West and Zimmerman revised their definition of interruption in their 1983 study, this new definition does not affect the argument here.

Interruptions also pose certain problems of interpretation. Zimmerman and West saw them as signs of conversational dominance. Beattie (1983) notes they need not always fulfil this function, but still sees them as signs of competition for the floor. Like other conversational features, interruptions need to be interpreted in context. In many cases they do allow someone to butt in and take over the conversation, but in other contexts they do not appear rude and may even be supportive. For instance Kalcik (1975), in a study of women's consciousness-raising groups, found several examples of overlapping speech that helped develop a topic, and that seemed to indicate support rather than a take-over bid.

The two problems we have mentioned here – those of formal definition and interpretation – are not restricted to analyses of interruptions, but apply to all conversational features. We shall return to this point at the end of the chapter.

Rings and Slingshots: The Use of Directives

Much of the work we've looked at so far has examined the roles of women and men in mixed-sex discussions or conversations and has suggested various ways in which women may be at a disadvantage. In single-sex groups, different patterns emerge. It has often been suggested, for example, that women engage in a more collaborative and co-operative style of interaction whilst men are more aggressive and competitive.

Marjorie Harness Goodwin (1980) studied groups of working-class Black children, aged between eight and 13 and living in the same street in Philadelphia. Goodwin examines how talk is organized in single-sex groups in which the boys are making slingshots from coathangers and the girls rings from old bottle-tops. The boys tended to make slingshots in two competitive teams (reminiscent of boys' team games), each with a hierarchical organization. Leaders, or potential leaders, of a group established their position partly through their use of directives, which took the form of explicit (or 'aggravated', in Goodwin's terms) commands:

MICHAEL: Gimme the pliers!
POOCHIE: (*Gives pliers to Michael*)

MICHAEL: All right. Give me your hanger Tokay.
TOKAY: (*Gives hanger to Michael*)

HUEY: Get off my steps.
POOCHIE: (*Moves down*)

HUEY: Get away from here Gitty.
CHOPPER: (*Moves*)
(Goodwin, 1980, pp. 158–9)

Such comments could be accepted (by compliance) or rejected by direct refusals to comply:

MICHAEL: Get out of here Huey.
HUEY: I'm not gettin out of nowhere.
(Goodwin, 1980, p. 159)

The production of rings by the girls' group was not organized hierarchically and there was minimal negotiation of status. Directives took the form of proposals for a future activity rather than an explicit command. A 'we' form was often used, which included the speaker in the proposed activity:

SHARON: Let's go around Subs and Suds.

PAM: We could go around lookin for more bottles.

TERRY: Maybe we can slice them like that.

PAM: We gotta find some more bottles.
(Goodwin, 1980, pp. 165–6)

Since relations between the girls were more symmetrical, anyone in the group could make such proposals.

Goodwin suggests the use of different directive forms both arises from and constitutes different organizations within each group. She points out, however, that these are not uniquely male or female styles. For instance, girls can use 'aggravated' forms when the occasion demands:

NETTIE: Get out the way offa that – get off that lawn!
(in response to a boy from the neighbourhood walking on her lawn).

There is some evidence that women use a collaborative style of interaction in feminist discussion groups. Kalcik (1975) analysed stories (or 'personal narratives') recounted in a number of women's consciousness-raising groups in the USA. We mentioned earlier that Kalcik noted many instances of 'supportive' simultaneous speech in these groups. She also observed that women filled in gaps in a story for one another, and that frequently 'story chaining' occurred (in which several stories were added together to explore a theme). Kalcik argues that this often amounted to a 'group production' of a story.

   This sort of collaborative interaction has reinforced the view that women are more co-operative than men in conversation. Cameron (1985) suggests an alternative explanation, arguing that a co-operative style has been institutionalized in feminist gatherings:

In such gatherings it is conveyed to participants that they should not interrupt nor raise their voices to silence others, that solidarity should be expressed frequently, that women must give way to each other rather than competing for the floor, and so on. Long silences are tolerated.
   This style was worked out painstakingly to avoid advantaging relatively more 'articulate' (i.e. middle-class and educated) women. That it is a feminist and not a female norm is suggested by remarks my women informants have made to me about it:
'I had a lot of trouble not interrupting. I felt everyone was thinking I couldn't keep my mouth shut.'
'It struck me the minute we started, all the silence and letting people finish.'
   Although there are obvious political justifications for the 'feminist style' I am talking about, it is interesting that many feminists justify its peculiarities differently. They tell you it is a style that 'suits women better' or gets away from 'male ways of speaking'. In other words, though the history and anecdote of early second-wave feminism suggests a difficult and painful process of working out a suitable style, under considerable pressure from women who had not been trained to speak in public, this process has already been obliterated and the style has become naturalised. (Cameron, 1985, pp. 42–3)

The Language of Uncertainty

Robin Lakoff (1975) identified a set of features which she claimed occurred more frequently in women's speech than men's, and that could be referred to as 'women's language'. This language gave the impression that speakers were polite, tactful, hesitant and lacking in authority – and not particularly to be taken seriously. Lakoff's list of features includes: 'empty' adjectives like *divine, charming, cute*; question-intonation in statement contexts:

A: What's your name, dear?
B: Mary Smith?

tag-questions (a question tagged onto a declarative, of the form *isn't it?, wasn't he?, don't you?* – e.g. 'It's so hot, isn't it?'); the use of hedges, that might normally indicate someone's uncertainty – e.g. *sort of, kinda, you know, I guess ..., I wonder...* (See Lakoff, 1975, p. 53ff).

Lakoff's observations were based not on a formal study but on her intuitions about the language used in her own speech community. Many subsequent empirical studies have failed to substantiate her claims. Studies of tag-questions found these occurred as often in male as in female speech (e.g. Baumann, 1979; Dubois and Crouch, 1975). Furthermore, tag-questions do not always function as indicators of hesitancy or uncertainty.

Nor is it certain that the use in statements of a rising intonation (normally associated with questions) is more characteristic of female than male speakers. Brend (1975) suggests there are intonational differences in (US) women's and men's speech: that women use more patterns involving a rising intonation than men, and that women also use higher rises. However, a survey carried out amongst speakers of American English (Edelsky, 1979) found little support for this claim. In Carole Edelsky's study, students on a university campus were asked where they were born and what their favourite colour was, by interviewers claiming to be carrying out a survey for a university class. The majority of respondents, both female and male, used a falling intonation in the reply as in

Wash
ing
ton

The only pattern used more frequently by women than men was a 'rise-fall-rise' intonation:

This, however, was used more often by women only in response to a female interviewer. Edelsky also notes that the actual intonation patterns produced have to be interpreted in context. For instance, rising intonations need not indicate hesitancy. They could indicate surprise ('Is that all you want to know?').

Edelsky asked a group of listeners to rate different intonation patterns, and her findings here show that rising intonations are perceived as being more feminine. It may of course be that they are used more by women than by men in certain contexts, but as yet there is little direct evidence for this.

Janet Holmes (1986) studied the occurrence of *you know* in a large corpus of Australian English. She notes that *you know* fulfils a variety of different functions, often simultaneously. Its position in an utterance (e.g. whether it comes at the beginning or the end) contributes towards its meaning, as does its intonation pattern. *You know* is normally a filler − it allows speakers some time for 'forward planning'. Holmes found that it could also indicate either certainty (e.g. emphasizing a speaker's confidence) or uncertainty (e.g. acknowledging the need for qualification of a previous utterance). Holmes found no significant difference in the overall distribution of *you know* between women and men in her sample. But she did find that women more often used *you know* to express certainty, and men to express uncertainty (a direct contradiction of Lakoff's hypothesis). She also suggests the use of *you know* varies in different contexts: it is common in 'sustained narrative' and accounts of personal experience but not in stretches of discussion, argument, planning or talk where there is more frequent speaker change.

Holmes points to a recurring problem in analysing functional aspects of language: simply totalling instances of *you know* tells us nothing about its function (whether it is expressing uncertainty or not). On the other hand, identifying the function fulfilled by a particular expression is extraordinarily difficult and inevitably rests on a subjective assessment.

William O'Barr and Bowman Atkins (1980) set out to test

Lakoff's hypothesis by looking at the whole range of features she identified as being predominantly used by women. O'Barr and Atkins recorded over 150 hours of trials in a North Carolina superior criminal court in 1974. Almost all the lawyers they recorded were male, but of the witnesses roughly half were male and half female. Amongst the witnesses the researchers found occurrences of all Lakoff's 'women's features' mentioned above except tag-questions. However both men and women used these features and there was variation within both sex groups between individuals' frequency of use. They identified two factors associated with infrequent use of 'women's language': high social status (i.e. good education, middle class or professional background) and what they term 'status accorded by the court' (e.g. being called as an expert witness). They argue, therefore, that a better name for this style of speaking is 'powerless language'. In concluding this part of their study they suggest:

that the tendency for more women to speak powerless language and for men to speak less of it is due, at least in part, to the greater tendency of women to occupy relatively powerless social positions. What we have observed is a reflection in their speech behaviour of their social status. Similarly, for men, a greater tendency to use the more powerful variant (which we will term powerful language) may be linked to the fact that men much more often tend to occupy relatively powerful positions in society. (O'Barr and Atkins, 1980, p. 104)

Two points to bear in mind about this study are that O'Barr and Atkins totalled up occurrences of particular features of language – theirs was not a functional analysis; also that Lakoff herself had paved the way for their interpretation: 'I think that the decisive factor is less purely gender than power in the real world' (Lakoff, 1975, p. 57).

Perhaps the most detailed study of women's and men's use of indicators of tentativeness has been carried out by Bent Preisler (1986). Preisler suggests one needs to take into account the linguistic context in which 'tentativeness' features occur. For instance, tag-questions can only occur tagged on to a declarative (such as 'You play hockey, don't you?' or 'You don't play hockey, do you?'). Speakers who were asking a lot of questions couldn't be expected to produce a high number of tags. Preisler argues that a more appropriate measure of usage would be the percentage of tag-questions actually used in contexts where it was possible for these to occur.

Preisler analysed the speech of 48 speakers from Lancaster, in the North West of England. Half the speakers were male and half female, but Preisler also took account of age and socioeconomic status. His speakers came from two age groups: 20–25 and 45–50; and from three employment categories: managerial, clerical and manual workers. Speakers were put into groups of four, along with others of the same age and employment status. Of these groups, half were mixed sex, one quarter all-female and one quarter all-male. Groups were given controversial topics (e.g. whether corporal punishment of children should be prohibited by law) to discuss and, if possible, reach agreement on. Discussions ran for about 43 minutes. They were audio- and video-recorded and every other three minutes of talk was coded for analysis.

Preisler based his analysis on what he terms a 'communicative act' (a unit of analysis derived from a model of interaction proposed by Bales, 1970). This is a functional categorization. It distinguishes 12 types of act: 'seems friendly', 'dramatizes' and 'agrees' (classified as *positive reactions*); 'gives suggestion', 'gives opinion' and 'gives information' (classified as *attempted answers*); 'asks for information', 'asks for opinion' and 'asks for suggestion' (classified as *questions*); and 'disagrees', 'shows tension' and 'seems unfriendly' (classified as *negative reactions*). Allocating utterances to such functional categories is, of necessity, subjective but Preisler notes there was a high level of agreement between himself and other coders.

Preisler used his functional classification for two purposes. First, within each group he distinguished two types of speaker: those with a relatively high proportion of attempted answers were said to be 'task-oriented', and those with a relatively high proportion of other categories of act were said to have a 'socio-emotional' role. This provided Preisler with a measure of each speaker's interactional role: a further factor that might be related to their use of different linguistic forms.

'Communicative acts' also formed the basis of Preisler's linguistic analysis. He described how each category was realized, noting both linguistic features and various nonlinguistic signs such as posture and gesture. Thirty features were taken into account which are those 'generally acknowledged to have a bearing on the expression of tentativeness' (Preisler, 1986, p. 75), including many of those identified by Lakoff (such as use of tag-questions and hedges). In each case, Preisler noted the proportion of 'tentativeness features' that actually occurred in contexts where it was possible for them to occur (e.g. the proportion of declarative clauses that ended with a tag-question).

Overall, Preisler found that women did tend to use tentativeness signals more often than men, and that they did so in single-sex as well as mixed-sex groups:

For the corpus as a whole, we have seen consistent and statistically significant results representative of a female lead in compound modality, including tag questions with past tense form but not past tense reference ('That would be a good idea, wouldn't it'), tag questions after emphatically pronounced finite auxiliaries or finite *be* as main verb (e.g. 'That *is* cruel, isn't it'), hedges and modal verbs ('You shouldn't do that, really'; 'It might be fun, sort of'), hedges and modal adverbs in combination with *I think* ('I think you just sort of talk it out'; 'I think maybe you talk it out') – besides a marked female lead in the use of hedges in general.

Conversely, we have seen a consistent and statistically significant male lead in a feature of linguistic assertiveness: the use of the imperative in utterances functioning as suggestion, opinion or information ('If you want to take action, do it on the spot'). (Preisler, 1986, p. 284)

Tentativeness signals were also associated with interactional role – speakers falling within Preisler's 'socio-emotional' category used them more than 'task-oriented' speakers – but there was a stronger association with sex than with interactional role. Sex differences occurred in both age groups and all three employment statuses, though there were some differences in the patterns found in these different social groupings.

Although Preisler's study is probably the most detailed and thorough exploration of women's 'linguistic tentativeness', we feel it requires one or two qualifications. His initial classification of speech into 12 types of communicative act was quite reliable (since different coders agreed on this classification), but the system does seem to be a little too neat. Dividing up the functions of talk into four major categories, each with three subdivisions, undoubtedly provides for symmetry, but one might question whether such functions can reasonably be compressed into 12 tidy categories.

Preisler also concedes that his linguistic tentativeness features are really indicators of *potential* tentativeness. Some at least could indicate careful deliberation. Preisler justifies his interpretation because, in the contexts analysed, these features were usually associated with female speakers, and with 'socio-emotional' speakers: if 'pragmatic tentativeness is a natural characteristic of [socio-emotional] behaviour . . . linguistic tentativeness features which correlate with such behaviour must be regarded as expressive of pragmatic tentativeness' (Preisler, 1986, p. 76). Part of Preisler's explanation seems to be circular, since he claims 'socio-emotional' speakers use more tentativeness signals, but his interpretation of these signals as tentative relies on their association with 'socio-emotional' speakers. Given the possibility of alternative interpretations, Preisler's attribution of these features to women as *tentativeness signals* requires some further justification.

Preisler explains his results by suggesting women and men have developed certain 'sex-specific speech patterns' (Preisler, 1986, p. 288). Since usages in single-sex groups do not differ from those in mixed-sex groups, they cannot depend upon women being 'cowed' into submission by 'male chauvinists' but are more likely to be the institutionalized reflection of women's 'historical social insecurity'. Preisler relates this explanation to that offered by sociolinguists (such as Labov and Trudgill) for women's greater use of prestige pronunciations. The relative infrequency of tentativeness features in men's speech may also, he suggests, have similar roots to men's greater tendency to use vernacular forms of speech: 'it may be associated with "masculinity" and "toughness"' (Preisler, 1986, p. 292).

Women's Language? Some Qualifications

The studies we have discussed identify certain features of talk as women's speech and others as men's. Many of them go on to claim that features associated with men's speech allow them to dominate mixed-sex talk. Such findings and interpretations raise a number of problems:

● *formal identification*: we have mentioned disagreement between researchers over the identification of features such as interruptions. Many of the conversational features we have discussed pose similar problems of definition. Even measures of amount of talk will differ depending on whether one is concerned with the amount of time taken by each speaker, the number of words spoken, or turns taken, or some other measure.

● *functional interpretations*: in connection with interruptions and other features we have mentioned the difficulty of totalling occurrences of a linguistic feature and assuming that these all share the same conversational meaning or function. One linguistic feature may fulfil several functions, and the same function may be fulfilled by different linguistic features. One solution to this problem for some researchers has been to note down the function of each occurrence of a feature as part of their analysis. Such analyses are necessarily subjective. We have mentioned that people may operate a 'double standard' with regard to female and male speech, and this may affect researchers as much as anyone else. Janet Holmes argues that: 'one (female) person's feeble hedging may well be perceived as another (male) person's perspicacious qualification' (Holmes, 1986, p. 18). It is hard to say, in subjective categorizations, whether one is evaluating the speech or the speaker.

● *differences of degree*: as with the work discussed in the previous chapter, we are concerned here with linguistic features that are used more often by women or by men: the differences are not categorical. The features identified also vary across contexts – they may be found in some contexts and not others. Aggregating results from different studies to produce lists of 'women's' and 'men's' features results in a gross over-simplification.

Women's Language: Explanations

Given the qualifications we have expressed about comparing results from different studies, using different measures, any attempt at a comprehensive explanation of women's and men's styles needs to be approached with caution. Several have been offered, however, and it's worth considering their relative merits – how well do they account for the evidence we have discussed?

Gender Subcultures

Maltz and Borker (1982) suggest that women and men come from two 'sociolinguistic subcultures'. The rules of 'friendly interaction', they argue, are learnt between the ages of five and 15, when a large part of children's interaction with one another takes place in single-sex peer groups. Girls and boys adopt certain usages to signal their respective group membership and to differentiate themselves from the contrasting gender group. So far, this has some similarities with Preisler's explanation. However Maltz and Borker also argue that conversational features are differently interpreted by male and female speakers. For instance, to women minimal responses may mean 'I'm listening to you; please continue' whereas for men they have a stronger meaning, more akin to 'I agree with you', or at least 'I follow your argument so far'. Women therefore make greater use of minimal responses simply because they are listening more often than men are agreeing – but the differing interpretations can give rise to miscommunication between the sexes.

Maltz and Borker's explanation does not seem to us adequately to account for all the evidence we have considered. For instance, the girls in Goodwin's (1980) study tended not to use 'aggravated' directives in single-sex group activities, but could and did use these forms in other situations. There is no indication that, in these contexts, they were attributing different meanings to aggravated directives than boys would. Many conversational features are associated both with speaker sex *and* with factors (such as status) that might give rise to differences in power between speakers. And some features identified as 'women's language' have been found to be associated with status and power *rather* than with speaker sex.

Maltz and Borker's argument that girls and boys adopt certain conversational features as ways of signalling their adherence to their respective gender groups fits with explanations presented for accent differences in chapter 3, but requires a little expansion. As we have seen, it is not only in peer group talk that girls and boys use different interactional styles – this occurs also in formal contexts such as the classroom, and with the sanction, if not the encouragement, of the teacher. It is also unlikely that the learning of such social roles begins at five and ends at 15: children learn to behave as girls and boys before school age and adults are able to modify their behaviour in changing circumstances. Even when such limitations are taken into account, the subcultural model suggests that interactional styles used by women and men are simply different. It fails to take into account the fact that many of them operate to the advantage of men and are associated with a difference in power between men and women; that men can use certain conversational features to dominate mixed-sex talk.

Gender and Power

The argument that differences between men's and women's speech reflects power differences also requires further examination, as it seems to encompass several points. It might, for example, refer to the idea that women are a relatively powerless social group (i.e. that they have less power than men). In a statistical sense, there exist more powerful men than women according to any indicator of social power in our culture (e.g. economic power, political power). This is clearly not an accident but shows the workings of a widespread social process. In employment, for instance, women may find it more difficult to acquire the qualifications that are necessary to achieve powerful positions, but men may also do better than women with similar qualifications and experience. However, it is equally clear that many men are not particularly powerful in this respect. In any mixed-sex interaction, one would expect to find at least some men who are less powerful than other participants.

O'Barr and Atkins' explanation of 'women's' and 'men's' language in their courtroom study is compatible with this argument. They argue that status or power, rather than gender *per se*, explains the differences they observed. The association between power and gender is seen as indirect and has to do with nonlinguistic processes.

However, it has also been argued that powerlessness is an essential characteristic of femininity and the fact of being a man is sufficient to confer interactional power on a speaker. Some of the studies we have discussed suggest that women take less powerful roles in mixed-sex interactions irrespective of their occupational status relative to their male interlocutors. West (1984, p. 18) argued that gender operated as a superordinate status – it was able to intervene and override other indicators of social power such as professional status.

It is possible to reconcile the two positions. Although on any measure of social power (say, economic power) there would be a degree of overlap between women and men, people may arrange their lives so that the structural inequality between men and women is reproduced in individual interactions. A rich woman may still be financially dependent on a husband; an unemployed man may still be the boss in his own home. If this is the case, this may reinforce the impression that men are dominant. When it is relevant to be seen as a woman or a man (rather than, say, a doctor or a teacher) men would be expected to dominate the talk.

Gender and Politeness

So far, we have considered explanations that restrict themselves to women's and men's use of different conversational styles. But there have also been attempts to place the findings of interaction studies and those from studies of accent and dialect within a common framework.

One such framework is known as *politeness theory*. This suggests that participants in interactions normally avoid 'face threatening' acts which undermine the social position of an interlocutor. Various alternative definitions of politeness in speech have been offered. Lakoff, for example, suggested people were polite in order 'to reduce friction in personal interaction' (Lakoff, 1975, p. 64). More recent formulations have observed that the extent to which one may risk a face threatening act will depend, in part, on one's own vulnerability. Thus the use of politeness routines may reflect power relations between speakers. Gumperz suggests that politeness does not merely reflect, but also helps reproduce, social relations, claiming that it is 'basic to the production of social order and a pre-condition of human co-operation' (Gumperz, 1987, p. xiii).

Penelope Brown, in an interesting account of speech in Tenejapa, a Mayan community in Mexico, found that the women, overall, used more politeness indicators than the men, and that they had 'characteristically feminine strategies' of politeness (Brown, 1980, p. 129). Brown tries to provide an integrated explanation of women's and men's speech by comparing Lakoff's work with that of Labov and Trudgill (discussed in chapter 3). She relates one of Trudgill's arguments (that women use more high prestige forms of language because of their greater status consciousness) to Lakoff's argument that women use a style of speaking characterized by features indicating hesitancy, tentativeness and politeness: 'it seems reasonable to predict that women in general will speak more formally and more politely, since women are culturally relegated to a secondary status relative to men and since a higher level of politeness is expected from inferiors to superiors' (Brown, 1980, p. 112). Brown's argument has something in common with Preisler's interpretation of women's and men's speech based on women's historical social, and therefore linguistic, insecurity.

In a review of explanations of women's and men's speech, Trudgill (1983b) rejects 'politeness' as an adequate explanation for women's use of more prestige accent and dialect features:

In English the desire to convey an impression of politeness may well often lead to a greater usage of standard linguistic features, but the reverse is not true: the usage of more 'correct' language does not necessarily indicate politeness. It is perfectly possible to employ high status pronunciations and standard grammatical forms together with impolite lexis and other signals of distance and dominance. (1983b, pp. 164–5)

Trudgill makes a similar distinction to that observed in this book – between dialect and accent features, and what he terms 'language use' (conversation management features and indicators of uncertainty and politeness such as those identified by Brown, Lakoff and Preisler). Others have drawn similar distinctions. French and French (1984b) distinguish form-based (accent and dialect) and activity-based (conversation/interaction) studies. They argue that Lakoff's approach is a mistaken attempt to attribute functions (such as the expression of uncertainty) to formally defined features – activity-based studies are required to show how women and men use language in this way.

While French and French's insistence that a definition of form does not provide a definition of function is reasonable, it is clear from our discussion in chapter 3 that accent and dialect are not just 'formal' features: they can convey social meaning, particularly certain things about a speaker (that she is educated) or about an interaction (that it is formal). The argument, then, really relates to how particular forms fulfil particular functions in specific contexts. Here, politeness theory runs the risk of bundling together different types of language usage and appealing to a single, quite specific explanation to account for all differences between women's and men's speech. It is right that a particular function can be fulfilled through a variety of linguistic means, but each linguistic feature may also be performing, simultaneously, a variety of functions.

Conclusion

In this chapter we have shown that the workings of gender are visible in conversational behaviour. At a rudimentary level, certain differences in the speech of women and men may serve as a simple signalling mechanism which makes the sex of each participant immediately apparent in interactions. In this respect, sex differences in conversational habits may perform a similar function to those in voice and accent.

Beyond this elementary level, what is signalled about gender is complex. The studies of conversational practices show many parallels with those of voice and of accent. In particular, the discussion of social network theory in chapter 3 showed how the traditional sexual division of labour has implications for the language varieties used by women and men. This sexual division of labour appears more directly in conversational activity. This is by no means the only way in which gender is manifest in conversation, however. Various conversational features seem associated with power differences between women and men. This introduces a new factor that was less clear in the studies of accent, though it existed, to a certain extent, in studies of voice. Power itself resolves into a variety of components, such as 'expertise', 'status', or 'dominance'. Although these seem closely related, they may be linked with different linguistic mechanisms.

The way in which particular features acquire or are given meanings is also complex. The same linguistic form (such as *you know*) or conversational device (such as interruption) may be given contrary meanings in different contexts. Too many research studies make simplistic claims about the meaning of conversational behaviour.

Specific conversational features such as interruptions, overlaps and minimal responses also contribute to the management and organization of a stretch of talk – to who gets a turn and whose conversational topics are pursued. Not only do they reflect and reaffirm gender and power differences, they are also one of the means by which inequalities between women and men are achieved in talk.

In chapter 5 we continue the theme of gender and linguistic inequality, exploring how women and men are conventionally represented in language.

5

Is Language Sexist?

'Every language reflects the prejudices of the society in which it evolved. Since English, through most of its history, evolved in a white, Anglo-Saxon, patriarchal society, no one should be surprised that its vocabulary and grammar frequently reflect attitudes that exclude or demean women...

A sizeable number of people would like to do something about these inherited linguistic biases. But getting rid of them involves more than just exposing them and suggesting alternatives. It requires change, and linguistic change is no easier to accept than any other kind. It may even be harder.'

(Casey Miller and Kate Swift, *The Handbook of Non-Sexist Writing* (1981))

'[Feminism] is an ideology which, like communism, seeks to abolish history, to abolish human nature, and to abolish every thought which conflicts with its dominant and erroneous idea – the idea of the moral indistinguishability of men and women. Moreover its linguistic imperialism is as great as that of communism. It seeks to appropriate not only vocabulary, but also grammar, and to eliminate gender from a language structured by gender divisions.'

(Roger Scruton, 'How Newspeak leaves us naked', *The Times*, 1.2.83)

Introduction

This chapter represents a change of focus. Up to now we have concentrated on differences in the way women and men use language – and how such differences may be explained. Chapter 5

explores how women and men are *represented* in language: what
truth is there in the claim that language contains a sexist bias? And
if language is sexist, what are the likely effects of this?

There are many definitions of sexism. For the purposes of this
chapter we have in mind a very simple one: sexism is any
discrimination against women or men because of their sex, and
made on irrelevant grounds. So, one might say that a TV programme about breastfeeding that focused on the experiences of
mothers was not sexist, because it is mothers, and not fathers, who
may breastfeed their babies. On the other hand, a programme on
childrearing that excluded fathers might be considered sexist,
because there is no reason why fathers should not be involved in
rearing their children. Although, according to this definition,
discrimination may take place against women or men, in practice
discrimination against women has been seen as more serious, and
has most concerned those who oppose sexism. As our use above of
the word 'might' indicates, this definition allows for disagreements
between people about what is sexist; one may disagree about
whether discrimination has taken place, or about whether it has
been made on relevant grounds. A further point about the definition
is that it applies to sexism in general – to a wide range of social
practices that discriminate against women or men. In this chapter
we ask whether there is a parallel between language and other
forms of social practice. To what extent can language be discrimina-
tory?

Documentation of 'sexist language' is extensive, and our intention
is not simply to repeat the exercise. We shall discuss some of the
more important examples, showing how linguistic inequalities may
be related to social inequalities between women and men. We shall
also try to illustrate some of the problems involved in documenting
sexism in language, and discuss the implications of these problems
for linguistic reform. We shall concentrate on the English language,
as much of the evidence for sexism in language has come from
English, but we shall refer also to work on other languages that show
certain contrasts with English.

There are many differences in the way women and men are
habitually referred to in English – naming conventions being one of
the more obvious examples. Feminists have objected to the convention that, upon marriage, a woman loses her own surname and takes
that of her husband:

Practically it means that women's family names do not count and that there is one more device for making women invisible.

When females have no right to 'surnames', to family names of their own, the concept of women as the property of men is subtly reinforced. (Spender, 1985, pp. 24, 25)

It is not a legal requirement that a married woman adopt her husband's surname, and a minority of women choose to retain their original name upon marriage. Alternatively, one may dispense with patrilineal conventions altogether and follow some other practice, such as using a middle name, or the name of a friend or female relative as a new 'surname'.

There remains the problem of which title to use. *Mr* is the standard title for a man, but women tend still (in Britain) to be distinguished by marital status (*Mrs* versus *Miss*). *Ms* has gained considerable ground, but is not a 'neutral' title for women. In some contexts it seems to have coalesced with Miss (official forms sometimes distinguish only Mrs and Ms). It also has negative connotations for certain speakers, which may inhibit its use:

'Never hand men an easy target. The title Ms gets the politicians going. We have to overcome so many other barriers. It is best to play the system straight down the middle.' (Mrs Dinah Tuck, Britain's only – in 1987 – female Chief Education Officer, addressing a seminar for women. Cited *Times Educational Supplement*, 17. 4. 87. p. 1)

Conventions of usage such as naming conventions are among the more obvious signs of linguistic discrimination against women, but the problem is said to run deeper than this, and to be more systematic. Miller and Swift's argument above is that aspects of the structure of language itself – of its vocabulary and grammar – discriminate against women. Most allegations of this sort of linguistic 'bias' concern the *lexicon* of a language – the stock of words, word forms and meanings made available to its speakers. Before considering this argument it's worth mentioning one or two problems posed by the study of linguistic meaning:

Intuitions: the study of meaning relies on people's intuitions about language: the intuitions of ordinary native speakers, of researchers and of those who compile dictionaries and so on that researchers use as sources. Problems arise because different people's intuitions do not always agree – and because someone's intuitions of how a word or expression should be used do not always coincide with how they actually use it. While there may be disagreements over the meaning of any expression, these are particularly likely to occur with expressions perceived as encoding social values including words that are said to be sexist or to show some other form of social bias. In this chapter we shall try to make it clear when we are relying on our own intuitions, or on those of other researchers and dictionary compilers. We shall also give examples (of language use, of interpretations of language and of prescriptions about language) to support any arguments we make. At the end of the chapter we shall reconsider some of the problems caused by differing interpretations of words and expressions.

Some linguistic distinctions: in discussing the possibility of 'bias' in the structure of a language, we are appealing to the distinction between the *abstract system* of a language (including the lexicon) and *language in use* – what people actually write and speak, which we mentioned in chapter 1. The language system is often thought of as a series of rules that underlie any instance of language use: it is the linguistic knowledge that people draw on to be able to speak or write. But to use language, people need more than linguistic 'rules': they need access to a stock of knowledge about the world (held in common with others in their speech community). In recognition of this, linguists commonly make a further distinction between a speaker's *linguistic knowledge* and *world knowledge*.

The distinctions between system and use, and between linguistic and world knowledge are particularly relevant to the study of meaning. For instance, dictionary compilers need to agree on a definition of terms such as *cat*, or *government*, or *peace* that might be regarded as their 'linguistic meaning'. However the precise interpretation any person places upon such terms when they meet them in a conversation or newspaper article will depend to a large exent on that person's world knowledge. Differences in beliefs about the world may explain certain disagreements about the meaning of expressions.

In discussing examples of sexism we shall make further reference to the conventional distinctions between language system and use, and linguistic and world knowledge. Though convenient, both these distinctions are problematical in ways which have implications for policy decisions on how – or whether – we should encourage 'non-sexist' language.

The Disappearing Woman and the Ascent of Man

two ribbon-tied bonnets in lacy stitches for baby girls ... a snug helmet and jaunty bobble cap for practical chaps. (Paton's knitting pattern)

Girls and boys in our culture receive different names, clothes and toys. They are also responded to differently by adults. There are different expectations of the way girls and boys, and women and men will behave. From birth it is important to know whether someone is female or male, and this need to distinguish between the sexes finds its reflection in the lexicon. English has many terms for people that are distinguished by *gender* (*girl* and *boy*; *man* and *woman*). Gender-neutral terms such as *adult* and *child* are less frequently used of someone whose sex is known. Speakers also need to make a choice between the pronouns *he* and *she* when referring to someone else (a third person). When talking about someone, we normally make their sex explicit. Such gender distinctions cannot themselves be called sexist, but they open the door to certain forms of sexism.

In chapter 3 we mentioned a common bias in the way events have been recorded by linguists, as well as by historians, social scientists etc. This bias has been termed the 'male as norm'. One example of this is that results of academic studies carried out using only male subjects have sometimes been generalized (unreasonably) to the population as a whole. Another example is that women and girls are often 'socially marked': their behaviour is described as though it were an exception to the general rule. Oakley (1981) gives an account of such masculine biases in the social sciences.

There is evidence of a linguistic parallel to the social and historical male-as-norm bias. Two examples are the *linguistic marking* of words for women and the existence of *lexical gaps* – or an absence of words to refer to women's experiences.

The Feminine as a Marked Category

Where pairs of opposites exist in English (such as lion and lioness, and *dog* and *bitch*) one member of the pair often functions as the more 'neutral' term. *Dog* may refer to a male dog, but it is also the general term for a dog whose sex isn't specified. *Bitch*, however refers exclusively to a female dog. 'Neutral' terms such as *lion* and *dog* are sometimes referred to as semantically unmarked whereas their counterparts, *lioness* and *bitch* are *semantically marked*. Sometimes, as in the case of *lioness*, the semantically marked term is also *formally marked* – it is derived from the 'neutral' unmarked term by the addition of a prefix or a suffix. Lyons (1970) gives a more detailed discussion of markedness.

When the lexicon of English distinguishes between masculine and feminine forms of a word for a human being, the masculine form is usually unmarked and the feminine form marked:

actor	actress
manager	manageress
administrator	administratrix*
doctor	doctress†
duke	duchess
mayor	mayoress

(*rare in British English; † no longer in current use)

The terms on the right are formally marked as feminine terms, but they also differ from the masculine terms in other respects:

● The feminine suffix may simply signal that the word refers to a female (as in *actress*) or it may mean 'wife of' (as in *duchess*).

● In cases where formal marking simply signals the feminine form, this is also semantically marked. The unmarked form can refer to men or human beings in general. The marked form is restricted to women.

● The feminine suffix may have additional connotations. *Manageress*, for example, seems to have connotations of lower status: one could be the manageress of a launderette or a cake shop, but probably not of a bank or an international company.

● Feminine suffixes seem to be dying out. *Doctress* has gone, and, though it appears in some dictionaries, we suspect *administratrix* is used by very few people (perhaps more in Scotland than in England). Some people we have questioned about this term even had difficulty working out how to pronounce it! Only when these endings mean something else, such as 'wife of' in *duchess* and *mayoress*, does there seem little immediate danger of this.

Even *actress*, which is still used quite commonly, has come under attack from some members of the profession.

The pattern of formal and semantic marking in English, in which feminine terms are often marked and masculine terms unmarked, is one way in which the lexicon has been said to show a sexist bias – which is why terms such as *actress* have come under attack. Much of the debate about sexist language, however, has focused on the more pervasive words *man* and *he* – on whether these can legitimately be regarded as gender-neutral or 'generic' expressions as well as referring to males. In linguistic terms, this can also be seen as a debate about markedness, showing some similarities with *actor* and *actress*.

SOME 'MAN' ARGUMENTS

By promoting the use of the symbol *man* at the expense of *woman* it is clear that the visibility and primacy of males is supported. We learn to see the male as the worthier, more comprehensive and superior sex and we divide and organize the world along these lines. (Spender, 1985, p. 153)

Using 'man' to mean both the male human and all humans is unnecessarily confusing. The word 'man' should only be applied to males. If some of those who make up the other half of the population are under discussion as well, then the terms 'people', 'humans' or 'humanity' are available and unambiguous. Other alternatives are:

man-hour	work-hour
manpower	workforce
man-made	artificial, synthetic
man-to-man	person-to-person
prehistoric man	prehistoric people
man a post	fill a post

Since very few jobs or roles are exclusive to one sex, work titles incorporating 'man' are inaccurate. Titles should reflect the job being performed (e.g. miner, farmer).

Wanted: a 'female actor' ad printed by Stage

Sir, – For more than a year Pit Prop Theatre has been experiencing some difficulty in placing advertisements for actors in the Stage magazine (cf. Diary, August 26).

The problem appears to be a semantic one. When we wish to define our required acting personnel as female or male actors, our ad is rejected on the basis that the use of expression "female actor" is not "proper use of the Queen's English."

According to the third edition of the Shorter Oxford Dictionary, the word actor is described as being "a stage player 1581", (note that no mention is made of the sex of that player). The word actress is defined as "a female actor. Reply by actor 1712." Obviously the views of John Payne of the Stage's advertising department and those of the editors of the dictionary do not concur.

Previously John Payne had said Pit Prop Theatre could use the term "female actor" provided "acceptance of this term is given in writing from those providing your company with a grant." Both North West Arts and Wigan Education Authority wrote in support of the company and after some questioning, John Payne agreed to accept an advert for "female actor."

However, in the Stage (July 25 and August 8) Pit Prop Theatre which had submitted an ad asking for a "non-white female actor" had one placed which said "non-white female performer." The wording had been altered without prior consultation.

In the same issue of the Stage. Seagull Theatre successfully placed an ad for a "male actor." It is clear that the Stage has no definite policy here: either that, or it is operating a double standard.

For Pit Prop Theatre, and others like us, it is not simply a question of words, but rather of words and their accepted and implied meanings. Historically, the word actress has meant many things to many people. It does not merely say that a woman acts, but that she is of "loose morals," "a prostitute," and a "good-time girl." These are some of the accepted meanings which obviously carry sexist values and judgements.

The English language, both written and spoken, takes liberties with women. We want to redress that. In any case roles have changed. We no longer look for peasants to farm the land. A peasant today has a totally different and derogatory meaning.

Likewise these days more theatre companies find they no longer require someone who can just act. We need people to fill what we call company member roles: ie, who can take a part in the collective decision-making, who can advance policy, who can devise plays. In short we require a "doer." The Oxford Dictionary says an actor is "one who acts, or takes part in any action; a doer 1603." So we feel we are even more justified in using the term actor for our requirements.

We are also a company that employes men and women equally, something that the Equal Opportunities Commission has failed to do nationally. Our policy is to treat women's needs, views and ideas as valid and necessary to our work. We wish to move away from the stereotyped images of women, and the way we advertise is an attempt to reflect that.

English is a living language. It exists as a means of communication. If words cease to communicate what we wish to be heard or known, we change them. We don't serve the English language; the English language is there to serve us, surely?

Pat Winslow
(and eight colleagues),
Pit Prop Theatre,
Atherton, Manchester.

(Letter, *Guardian*, 31.8.83)

statesman	statesperson, politician, leader, diplomat
foreman	supervisor
watchman	guard
fireman	firefighter
milkman	milk deliverer

(National Union of Journalists (NUJ), 1982, pp. 4–5)

Man, used as a kind of suffix, is affected as such elements usually are: it tends to be swallowed up in the larger word ... a word such as *workman* would sound strange with *man* not reduced to *m'n* ... it would appear that the masculinity of the term is more a function of the word as a whole than of the suffix. If *She is the chairman* sounds odd, it is for the same reason that *She is the commissioner* sounds odd – both words refer to posts once held exclusively by men. So it might have been better to leave most of the *man* words alone, trusting to the future feminine occupants of the posts to feminize or neutralize them. (Bolinger, 1980, pp. 97–8)

Pretending, or asserting, that the syllable 'man' signifies males exclusively can lead one into such barbarisms as 'ombudsperson' or 'freshperson' ... 'Man' and 'Mankind' are universally understood to include both men and women. (American academic, cited by Bernard Levin, *The Times*, 19.7.85. p. 2)

Spokespersons of the world – get lost! (Extract from a letter, Guardian, 7.2.83)

The Oxford English Dictionary (OED) suggests that *man* derives from the Indogermanic root *men-* or *mon-* meaning 'to think' (compare the modern word *mind*). Since intelligence was (perhaps still is) felt to be a distinctively human characteristic – in contrast to brutes – the term came to refer to human beings irrespective of age or sex and this was its predominant sense in Old English (spoken from about 450–1100). The term *wer* was used for 'man' and *wif* (the origin of our modern *wife*) for 'woman'. Sometimes *wer* and *wif* occurred as compounds with *man*. The modern term *woman* is derived from the compound *wifman*. *Wer* is no longer found except in compounds such as *werewolf*. As recently as 1752 there is an instance of *man* being used in its original unambiguously generic sense:

There is in all men, both male and female, a desire and power of generation more active than is ever universally exerted. (Hume, 1752, *Political Discourses*)

However, even in the thirteenth century *man* had been used to refer to an adult, male human being. The OED cites a manuscript dating from before 1225 which, in contrasting *man* and *woman*, makes this usage quite clear.

Ert tu so wroð wið mon oðer wið wummon bet...? (*Ancren riwle*, pre 1225)

this has now become the predominant meaning of the term *man*, but it is also found in its 'generic' sense: 'the man in the street', 'Man's religious quest', etc. The objections of feminists to such expressions are that women are effectively hidden behind 'generic' terminology, and also that *man* is not a true generic. People attempting to use it in this way may let slip signs that they are really thinking of males:

As for man, he is no different from the rest. His back aches, he ruptures easily, his women have difficulties in childbirth... (Cited Miller and Swift, 1981, p. 12)

One may contrast the use of *man* with another unmarked term, *dog*:

a The dog is a lot younger than the bitch
b One of the dogs on the farm is a beautiful Golden Retriever bitch
c The dog next door has just given birth to a puppy
d The dog is a mammal

a_1 The man is a lot younger than the woman
b_1 One of the men on the farm is a beautiful French woman
c_1 The man next door has just given birth to a baby
d_1 Man is a mammal

Dog seems acceptable in all these contexts, but the most committed male chauvinist would be unlikely to find b_1 and c_1 acceptable.

There are also problems with d_1 if this is expanded a little (again, compare *dog*):

e The dog is a mammal, i.e. it gives birth to live young which it suckles

e_1 Man is a mammal, i.e. he gives birth to live young which he suckles

It seems that *man* operates as an adult male human being (in contrast to *woman*). It also refers (in some people's speech) to a person irrespective of sex – in this case most frequently, but not exclusively, in the sense of 'Man the species'. However, as soon as the inclusion of *woman* is made explicit *man* sounds awkward – it is as if the 'adult male' sense intervenes and blocks the use of *man* as a generic.

'Generic' *he*, like *man*, has been the subject of much controversy. Writers or speakers do not always know the sex of a person they are referring to, or they may wish to refer to someone regardless of sex. On these occasions, *he* may serve as 'generic' third person pronoun. Justifications for this usage become more half-hearted, or even faintly embarrassed, as time goes on, but nevertheless 'generic' *he* persists.

'GENERIC' HE?

God send every one their heart's desire! (Shakespeare, 1599, *Much Ado About Nothing*, III iv)

The masculine Person answers to the general Name, which comprehends both Male and Female; as Any Person, who knows what he says. (Kirby, 1746, *A New English Grammar*)

RULE V. Pronouns must always agree with their antecedents, and the nouns for which they stand, in gender, number and person; ... Of this rule there are many violations. 'Each of the sexes should keep within its particular bounds, and content themselves with the advantages of their particulr districts.' 'Can anyone, on their entrance into the world, be fully secure that they shall not deceived?' 'on his entrance,' and 'that he shall.' 'Let each esteem others better than themselves;' 'than himself.' (Murray, 1795, *English Grammar*)

they, their, misused for *he, his* as in 'Anyone thinks twice when their life is at stake': read 'his life'. (Partridge, 1947; revised edn 1965, *Usage and Abusage: a guide to good English*)

English has no sex-neutral third person singular pronoun (i.e. one that expresses the common meaning of *he* and *she*), and so the plural pronoun *they* is often used informally (especially in British English), in defiance of number concord, as a substitute for the indefinite pronouns *everyone, everybody, someone, somebody, anyone, anybody, no one, nobody.*

Everyone thinks *they* have the answer (42)

Has *anybody* brought *their* camera? (43)

No one could have blamed *themselves* for that (44)

The plural form is a convenient means of avoiding the dilemma of whether to use the *he* or *she* form.

The use of *they* in sentences like (42–44) is frowned upon in formal English, where the tendency is to use *he* as the 'unmarked' form when the sex of the antecedent is not determined. The formal equivalent of [42] is therefore:

Everyone thinks *he* has the answer (42a)

The same choice is made in referring back to a singular noun phrase with a personal noun of indeterminate gender as head:

Every student has to make up *his* own mind (45)

Although this use of *he* often sounds pedantic, there is no obvious alternative to it, in formal English, except the rather cumbersome device of conjoining both male and female pronouns:

Every student has to make up *his or her* own mind (45a)

> (Quirk et al., 1972, *A Grammar of Contemporary English*, p. 370)

In discussing the 'individual' the author would have preferred to substitute the formulations he/she, him/her for the more usual masculine mode. However, because of the frequency with which this would have occurred the more conventional approach has regretfully been adopted. (Open University, 1981, *Language and Social Reality*)

Ann Bodine (1975) has charted systematic attempts by grammarians since the eighteenth century to institute *he* as the correct sex-indefinite third person singular pronoun (and to stamp out alternatives such as singular *they*). Kirby's 1746 grammar is the first explicit prescription Bodine found for 'generic' *he*, but such prescriptions (along with corresponding proscriptions of singular *they*) have continued into the twentieth century.

The use of 'generic' *he* has, like 'generic' *man*, come under increasing attack from those concerned about sexist language, and numerous writers' and publishers' guidelines, such as those issued by the British National Union of Journalists, recommend alternative forms:

> If the sex of the person being discussed is unknown or could be female or male, use: she or he; she/he; s(he). Alternatively, the plural offers a non-sexist pronoun, or the pronoun may be unnecessary:
>
> Man and his universe   Humans and their universe
>
> Humans and the universe
>
> (NUJ, 1982)

Many people, perhaps because of their traditional grammatical training, feel uneasy about using singular *they* as an alternative to *he*. The NUJ guidelines are not the only ones to omit reference to it; some Open University editors are unwilling to accept it; and its use clearly causes irritation to certain readers:

> Sir, – Even in the interests of anti-sexism I refuse to violate useful grammatical rules. 'Each person should do their duty' ... is a horrid invention... (Letter, *Guardian*, 7.2.83)

Another alternative to 'generic' *he*, used particularly by contemporary feminist writers, is 'generic' *she*:

> Most sex-indefinite and generic referents in this book will be she and her. If there are any men reading who feel uneasy about being excluded, or not addressed, they may care to consider that women get this feeling within minutes of opening the vast majority of books, and to reflect on the effect it has. (Cameron, 1985, preface)

There have also been attempts to construct neutral terms. The novelist Marge Piercey, in writing (in *Women at the Edge of Time*) of a future society without gender distinctions, uses *per* as a third person pronoun. A letter to the *Guardian* (responding to an article on the problems of 'desexing' language) suggests *hes* for *he or she* and *hese* for *his or hers* (7.2.83). Such new constructions have not gained very wide currency – attempts at linguistic engineering seem

to be regarded as rather quirky or eccentric. And some people clearly
regard the whole debate about 'generic' usages as a nonsense:

Sir, – it has been said that having sex on the brain is the wrong place to have
it. The same can be said of sex in the grammar book ... there really is
nothing male about the masculine pronoun, any more than there is anything
female about French water. (Letter, *Guardian*, 7.2.83)

The problems with 'generic' *he* and *man* derive from the fact that we
are in a period of linguistic flux for these items. Language change is
related to social change and neither kind of change occurs at a
steady pace. During periods of linguistic upheaval in the meaning of
any term there is likely to be confusion, dissent and the co-occurr-
ence of a number of different usages. Sometimes this occurs even in
the same sentence: 'If a student came forward with a dissertation
topic that he or she had themselves devised ...'. The usage a speaker
or writer adopts probably reflects a political commitment rather
than any judgement made on linguistic or aesthetic grounds:

Let me briefly recapitulate the powers enjoyed by a majority of new citizens
as I have identified them, here in Britain:
1   He has the vote and hence shares the power to destroy the government of
the day.
2   He enjoys a steadily rising real income ... etc. (Tony Benn, 1970, *The
New Politics*)
Groups of labour MPs may occasionally ask to meet a minister but he or she
is in no sense answerable. (Tony Benn, 1982, article in *New Socialist*)

(In fact, in 1982 Tony Benn's pronoun usage is still variable. Within
the space of a few paragraphs he refers to 'the premier ... his or her'
and the 'Prime Minister ... he'. It is likely that nowadays – late
1980s – he is a more consistent *he or she* user.)

    Man, *actor*, etc. are clearly cases of masculine terms that can have
more general reference, though there are differences. Terms like
actor are generally accepted as unmarked, and formally marked
feminine terms seem to be on the way out. By contrast it is the
unmarked usage of *man* and *he* that is being challenged as linguistic
reformers seek neutral alternatives. But the situation is more complicated than this. It is probably no accident that the Old English *man*
became a masculine term rather than a feminine one. Many apparently neutral terms are used as though they referred to men:

We must somehow become witness to the everyday speech which the informant will use as soon as the door is closed behind us: the style in which he argues with his wife, scolds his children, or passes the time of day with his friends. (Labov, 1966, p. 99)

And when Tony Benn, in the 1970 extract, proceeds to argue that his new citizen 'has access to a mass of information almost entirely denied to his father and grandfather' one begins to wonder how generic the use of *he* actually is.

Some terms such as *nurse* or *model* are conventionally assumed to refer to a woman, but this applies to relatively few words – and mainly those associated with a predominantly female profession. It seems more usual for people to be presumed male until proved female. Perhaps in tacit recognition of this, it is common for writers and speakers to make explicit the sex of someone who is female.

There's a new lady doctor joined the practice. (Street conversation)

A police constable has been allocated to the two villages, in fact a woman police constable, (Local village newsletter, August, 1987)

Miller and Swift (1981) term such usages 'gratuitous modifers' and argue that they frequently diminish a person's prestige, drawing attention to their sex rather than some other, more relevant, characteristic. One can draw a parallel here between references to women and to certain other social groups. Disability is a 'marked' characteristic – newspapers frequently mention a person's disability when this seems irrelevant to the story in which they feature. It has also been common to signal someone's membership of ethnic minority groups. In response to such usages, the NUJ guidelines on race reporting caution journalists:

DON'T say 'black', 'Asian', 'of West Indian origin' or 'immigrant' unless 100% essential to the story. (Macshane, 1978, p. 20)

It is implausible that every gender-neutral word for a human being in English is an unmarked masculine term like *man* and *actor*. Invoking the distinction between linguistic and world knowledge, we could say it is part of our linguistic knowledge that *actor* is an unmarked masculine term whereas *actress* is marked as feminine. On the other hand, the assumption that *citizens* and *informants* are male derives from social and cultural expectations. When the context is appropriate, neutral terms may be taken to refer to females:

Victoria Gillick will be joining us in a studio discussion about the one in 20 teenagers who become mothers each year. (Trailer for BBC Radio 4 *Woman's Hour*)

'Sexist language' is not simply a linguistic problem. The existence of unmarked expressions 'in the language' does not mean these will be used and interpreted in a neutral way. This may lead one to question the value of the linguistic reforms advocated in writers' and publishers' guidelines. The effectiveness of such guidelines is an issue we return to.

Lexical Gaps

Intromission and ejaculation are universal human behaviours. (Scheflen, 1964, article in *Psychiatry*, vol. 27, pp. 316–31)

Trying to articulate the meanings of names which do not exist is a difficult task and yet it is one which feminists are constantly engaged in ... Without ready-made symbols which encode women's meanings, there is no alternative but to use metaphors and similes to suggest what women's meanings might be like. (Spender, 1985, p. 182–3)

The lexicon of a language cannot encode every conceivable concept, but feminists have complained that there are systematic gaps in English which make it difficult to express women's experiences. In a 1978 study of North American English, Julia Stanley and Susan Robbins found a dearth of expressions to refer to women's sexual experience. They note, for instance, that verbs referring to sexual intercourse tend either to be sex neutral (*to have sex*, *to have intercourse*, *to have an orgasm*, *to come*) or to require a male subject (*to screw*, *to penetrate*, *to ejaculate* ... etc.). There is a similar lack of expressions to refer to sexual potency in a woman: English has no direct feminine equivalent of *virility* – and, logically enough, none of *emasculate*.

Despite women's apparent sexual inertia, Stanley (1977) identified (again in North American English) 220 words for a sexually promiscuous woman, but only 20 for a sexually promiscuous man.

Furthermore, virtually all the words for women were pejorative, whereas many words for men had more positive or 'boys will be boys' connotations. In a British study carried out among London school children, Sue Lees and Celia Cowie found an abundance of insult terms used of girls, all related to sexual behaviour. Lees (1983) comments: 'One problem for girls – if the abuse came from boys – is that there aren't equivalent terms they can use against boys' (p. 51). Lees feels the range of insult terms available reflect social attutides towards girls and women: 'The Madonna/whore syndrome is still alive and well today' (p. 53).

There are some signs of change in this, as in other aspects of language. Barbara Risch (1987) found that North American female college students had a rich inventory of 'dirty words' to refer to men – and that these included some terms, such as *bitch*, *whore* and *slut*, normally thought of as feminine. And contemporary feminism, with its insistence on the expression of female experience, has introduced or made more prominent: *sexism*, *male chauvinism*, *androcentrism*, *sisterhood* (in its more modern sense), *sexual harrassment* and a host of other terms.

Woman Scorned

'A fickle thing and changeful is woman always!'
(Virgil, *Aeneid*, c.19BC)

'I have no other but a woman's reason: I think him so, because I think him so.' (Shakespeare, *The Two Gentlemen of Verona*, I ii, 1591)

'What is your sex's earliest, latest care,
Your heart's supreme ambition? – To be fair.'
(George Lyttleton, *Advice to a Lady* before 1773)

That women are not taken entirely seriously is a complaint still heard from many feminists and others concerned about women's condition – and with some reason, for trivializing people is one way of keeping them in their place. It has been common to set a low value on activities associated with women: the low value of women's work is evident in the fact that, in 1985, working women in Britain took home on average 66 per cent of the earnings paid to men

(Central Statistical Office, 1987. For a discussion of systematic social biases against women, see Oakley, 1981). Several differences – and inequalities – between the way women and men are perceived find their reflection in the English lexicon.

Semantic Derogation and the Linguistic Disparagement of Women

Words for women and men are rarely parallel in English. An examination of pairs of words such as *mother* and *father* reveals that these do not differ purely in terms of gender – although some linguists have analysed their meaning as, respectively, 'female parent' and 'male parent'. The different connotations that attach to mother and father can be seen more clearly if we examine their use as verbs:

a   She mothered the children in the village for several years
a_1 He fathered the children in the village for several years
b   It actually was Jane who mothered Harriet's children
b_1 It actually was John who fathered Martin's children
c   Anne really did mother those kittens
c_1 Brian really did father those kittens

Fathering stops, or certainly may stop, at the moment of conception whereas mothering refers (usually) to more continuing nurturance – it can be extended to people other than one's own children and sounds quite reasonable applied to animals. An investigation of North American English speakers (carried out by Salikokos Mufwene) found that these different connotations entered into the meanings of the nouns *father* and *mother* so that *mother* might more properly be defined as:

a female who engenders and/or rears a child, where 'engender' is the less significant function and 'rear' the more significant

Conversely, for these speakers, *father* is:

a male who engenders and/or rears a child, where 'rear' is the less significant function and 'engender' the more significant. (Mufwene, 1983, p. 255. Mufwene expresses these meanings as formulae, which we have translated into ordinary language.)

Clearly these differences in meaning reflect differences in the traditional roles accorded to women and men in our society – and changing roles may stimulate linguistic changes. In some contexts, the more nurturant aspects of fathering are emphasized. In his book entitled *Fathering*, Ross Parke comments: 'a new ideology of fatherhood has begun to make inroads into the old stereotype' (Parke, 1981, p. 12). Miller and Swift discuss these changes in meaning, but seem more sympathetic to the use of *parenting* to convey 'a sense of mutuality and shared responsibility' (Miller and Swift, 1981, p. 79). In Marge Piercey's futuristic gender-free world described in *Woman at the Edge of Time*, children do not have biological parents. The term *comother* is used for those adults (both women and men) assigned to look after a child.

The fact that women's and men's social roles do not have equal value in our culture also has its parallel in language. This can be illustrated by examining two more pairs of words:

governor	governess
master	mistress

Governor and *governess* could at one time be used as roughly equivalent terms: in 1590 Queen Elizabeth I was described as 'the supreame maiestate and gouernesse of all persons'. Now the predominant sense of *governess* is different from that of *governor* – and also lower in status. *Master* and *mistress* can both be used of a person who has control or authority (the OED gives examples of such uses of *master* dating from the eleventh century, and of *mistress* dating from the fourteenth century). However *mistress* has the additional, and nowadays perhaps more common, meaning of 'a woman who illicitly occupies the place of a wife' (examples of this usage date from the fifteenth century). These sexual meanings may lead to the avoidance of *mistress* – and to the consequent extension of *master* to women:

throughout the apprenticeship she set herself, gradually becoming a master of that 'inside voice'. (Review of stories by Katherine Mansfield, *Sunday Telegraph*, 2.6.85)

One or two linguists have documented a more general decline in words referring to women, Muriel Schulz (1975) calls this 'semantic derogation'. She argues that, through history, words referring to women have systematically acquired negative (and often sexual) connotations. *Hussy*, for instance, has the same origin as *housewife* – it once referred to the mistress of a household, or a thrifty woman – but from 1650 the OED gives examples of its use as a 'rude, opprobrious way of addressing a woman'. *Wench* once meant simply 'girl': Shakespeare writes in *Love's Labours Lost* of 'one that was a woman when Queene Guinouer of Brittaine was a little wench'. Semantic derogation is not restricted to words for women, but occurs also in words for other groups with relatively little social power. Leith (1983) documents historical change in the meanings of words associated with social rank or status, including derogation of terms such as *churl* and *villain*.

If one trusts the OED as a source, it does seem that *hussy* and *wench* came into the language with one meaning and that another gradually evolved – but this sort of historical investigation is actually fraught with problems. Any corpus used in the investigation is bound to be highly selective. It is never possible to tell, from a relatively small number of examples, when a particular usage became widespread in a language or for how long two usages overlapped. The necessary reliance of an investigation on written texts also means it is restricted to a particuar kind of language user. Dictionary compilers cannot be sensitive to all the nuances a word has had during its history. It is possible that 'neutral' words for women have always had negative or sexual connotations, at least for certain speakers.

Women, Ladies and Girls

or why don't you get married and have a family? I recommend it. Find yourself some nice girl. No, I'm not allowed to say that, am I? Find yourself a nice lady...

Is it OK working for a lady – sorry, a woman I should say? (BBC Radio 4 interview, 30.7.87)

It sometimes takes a well-tuned ear to make appropriate choices from among the everyday words used for female human beings. One problem is that all these words have psychic overtones: of immaturity and dependence in the case of *girl*; of conformity and decorum in the case of *lady*; of sexuality **and reproduction** in the case of both *female* and *woman*. But all have been invested with other meanings as well, both positive and negative, and no one knows for sure which way any of them is moving – into the mainstream or out. (Miller and Swift, 1981, p. 67)

Accounts of sexism in language have claimed that, so readily does anything associated with femaleness become tainted, that the word *woman* itself has negative connotations. It is certainly possible, in British English, to hear *woman* used as an insult – particularly in the phrase *old woman*:

A: We don't much care for Mr X
B: Why not?
A: He's a bit of an old woman...

Some linguists (notably Robin Lakoff, 1975) have argued that, because of these negative connotations, *woman* requires a euphemism and finds one in *lady*, or occasionally in *girl*. Lakoff argues that *lady* is often used because it seems more 'polite' than *woman*, and that it serves to exalt women (particularly those in low status jobs – hence expressions like *cleaning lady*). It is also devoid of sexual connotations – Lakoff contrasts the two sentences:

a She's only 12, but she's already a woman
b She's only 12, but she's already a lady

Lakoff comments on the 'euphemistic' functions of *lady*:

Besides or possibly because of being explicitly devoid of sexual connotation, *lady* carries with it overtones recalling the age of chivalry: the exalted stature of the person so referred to, her existence above the common sphere. This makes the term seem polite at first, but we must also remember that these implications are perilous: they suggest that a 'lady' is helpless, and cannot do things for herself. In this respect the use of a word like *lady* is parallel to the act of opening doors for women – or ladies. At first blush it is flattering: the object of flattery feels honoured, cherished, and so forth; but by the same token, she is also considered helpless and not in control of her own destiny. (Lakoff, 1975, p. 25)

She argues that *girl*, because of its associations with immaturity, also 'removes the sexual connotations lurking in *woman*'. There are pitfalls in its use, however:

in recalling youth, frivolity and immaturity, girl brings to mind irresponsibility: you don't send a girl to do a woman's errand (or even, for that matter, a boy's errand). (Lakoff, 1975, p. 25)

Lakoff's study was based on her intuitions as a member of her own (white, middle-class, North American) speech community, writing in the early 1970s. Probably not all of her intuitions would be shared by someone living in contemporary (late 1980s) Britain. But the meanings of *lady*, *woman* and *girl* also vary considerably in different contexts.

The meaning of *lady* has changed over the centuries. It is derived from the Old English *hlaefdi*, and at one time its usage was more or less parallel to that of *lord* (derived from *hlaford*): a lady was a mistress in relation to servants, or a woman who ruled over subjects. Whereas *lord* has retained its high status meaning, however, *lady* has been extended gradually so that virtually any woman is now entitled to this designation. Our own intuitions about its contemporary use are that:

● In some contexts, *lady* sounds more polite that *woman*: 'This isn't my stall, love, it belongs to that lady over there' (said by a market trader to a prospective customer), 'Yeah, that's a lady with a hat on' (man to child in a department store). It may also suggest respect: 'She is a lovely lady' (of Princess Michael of Kent).

● However, *lady* is not always devoid of sexual connotations: *lady of easy virtue*, *foxy lady*, 'I saw him out with his new lady last night.'

● *Lady* is used of women when an equivalent 'polite' expression (such as *gentleman*) is not required for men: 'That must place tremendous demands on the ... camera men and make-up ladies.'

● Sometimes *lady* sounds pejorative: 'I was trying to convince someone – a very emotional lady, a rather hysterical lady ...' It has this use in common with *gentleman*, at least in certain contexts: 'a slightly muddled old gentleman' (said of the Archbishop of Canterbury by Lord Bruce Gardyne. The

Archbishop had been critical of Conservative government policies.)

● On other occasions it seems to be virtually interchangeable with
woman: 'If we hadn't had this strong lady – this first woman
Prime Minister' (of Mrs Thatcher).

The use of *girl* refer to an adult woman is also variable. It often
occurs in contexts where one would be unlikely to find a similar
reference to a man as *boy*, such as newspaper reports (particularly
in the British popular press):

a young American girl brings a screen performance to London which
announces her as a glowing new talent for the future (of a 27 year old
woman). (*London Standard*, 17.5.85)

Girl's sex harrassment claim led to assault (Headline referring to a 25 year
old woman). (*Milton Keynes Gazette*, 18.1.1985)

Miller and Swift (1981) mention also examples from the workplace,
such as:

I'll have my girl run off some copies right away

They comment on such usages:

Women in full-time office jobs may be assistants, clerks, secretaries,
executives, book-keepers or managers but, unless their employers are
violating the child labour laws, they are rarely girls. (Miller and Swift, 1981,
p. 68)

Miller and Swift suggest that referring to a woman as *girl* is usually
'patronizing and demeaning', and compare such references with the
once-common habit of referring to men from minority ethnic groups
as *boy* (Miller and Swift, 1981, p. 67).

Girl may also, however, be used with a sense of camaraderie:
'Come on girls, let's go!' (said by a woman to a group of female
colleagues about to go out for lunch together). Here, it seems to have
similar function to 'night out with the boys' if used by men.

One explanation of these different meanings of the terms *girl* (and
boy) used of adults is that if the usage is reciprocal (e.g. when a
group of women call one another *girls*) this indicates familiarity or

friendliness. If the usage is non-reciprocal – when a boss refers to a secretary as *girl* – this may indicate the superior status of the boss. If this explanation is correct, *girl* and *boy* would be functioning as markers either of solidarity or power – in a similar way to terms of address (in English) or the use of 'familiar' or 'polite' pronoun forms in languages such as French (Brown and Gilman, 1972, discuss this use of pronouns).

The selection of examples above is not intended as a complete analysis of the meanings of *lady* and *girl* when used as alternatives to *woman*. The examples do show, however, that *lady* and *girl* sometimes function as euphemisms but that, like any words, their meaning depends, in part, on the context in which they occur. What seems to happen is that connotations produced in many contexts become particularly salient and, for many speakers, begin to 'stick' to a term in other contexts. So, many women now object to the use of *lady* or *girl* because of the connotations of frivolity or immaturity associated with them – and also, perhaps, as a rejection of the notion that the ordinary word for an adult female human being might require a euphemism.

How to Describe a Woman

We have concentrated on allegations that English contains an inbuilt bias, in that words for women either have, or readily acquire negative meanings. But feminists also complain that women are routinely described in a demeaning fashion. The National Union of Journalists' guidelines caution against relying on stereotypes in describing women and men:

There is no reason why girls and women should be generally characterised as emotional, sentimental, dependent, vulnerable, passive, alluring, mysterious, fickle, weak, inferior, neurotic, gentle, muddled, vain, intuitive… Nor is there any reason why boys and men should be assumed to be dominant, strong, aggressive, sensible, superior, randy, decisive, courageous, ambitious, unemotional, logical, independent, ruthless. (NUJ, 1982, p. 6)

Miller and Swift (1981) criticize the way non-parallel terminology is used for women and men, citing examples such as:

Three university students – two girls and a man – were abducted from a research station in Africa.

Of course Miss Doe has help; in this case a large staff of men and maids. (Miller and Swift, 1981, p. 80)

The focus, in many contexts, on a woman's appearance is also criticized:

Emphasis on the physical characteristics of women is offensive in contexts where men are described in terms of business or other achievements. (Miller and Swift, 1981, p. 82)

Some speakers and writers have become conscious of this issue, and try to ensure parallel treatment of the sexes, but many articles in the press still mention women's appearance in contexts where it seems unlikely they would do so for men:

She comes over as something of an enigma. A fussy silk blouse pokes from under a casual striped sweater. Hair, centre-parted, is neat as a doll's house curtains. She's half demure, half bolshie... (Article on Professor Suzanne Romaine, new incumbent of the Merton Chair of English Language at Oxford University, *Guardian*, 28.3.1984)

'Anti-sexist' guidelines also complain about the tendency to describe women, more often than men, in terms of their relation to someone else – particularly in terms of a family relationship such as being someone's mother, wife, grandmother, etc.

The ready availability of pejorative words and expressions may make it easier to describe women (relative to men) in a way that trivializes them or disparages their achievements. But such descriptions do not rely on the existence of gender-typed pejorative expressions in the lexicon. Once again we seem to have gone beyond linguistic meaning, and moved from language system into language use. It seems to be a characteristic of the way people routinely use language that certain stereotyped and demeaning expressions are frequently applied to women and girls. As in the case of 'generic' masculine terms discrimination against women in language has to be regarded as a social issue as much as a linguistic one.

Sexism Abroad

Behind much of the concern about sexism in language lies the concern (not always made explicit) that this is harmful because language has an effect on the way speakers perceive people and events: a language can influence its speakers' thoughts, for good or ill. We shall discuss this point in chapter 6, but clearly all societies have deep-rooted gender divisions, and in most (if not all) women have less power than men. If language is intimately bound up with social structure, we should expect to find these social divisions reflected in other natural languages. If this were not the case, at least some feminists' arguments about sexism in English would be weakened.

There is, unfortunately, little published evidence from other languages. What there is offers support for arguments based upon English – but since other languages differ from English in their structure, the way in which sexism manifests itself is often different. We shall examine evidence from both European and non-European languages.

Sexism in Europe: the 'Natural' versus 'Grammatical' Gender Distinction

Many languages group words together into classes or categories. The basis for this classification varies from one language to another, but in those European languages which have *grammatical gender* (see also chapter 3) nouns may fall into one of two or three categories: masculine and feminine, or masculine, feminine and common/neuter. In French, all nouns must be either masculine or feminine; in German, they must be masculine, feminine or neuter. Usually words referring to females take the feminine gender, and those referring to males are masculine – but there are exceptions. Also, all nouns referring to inanimate objects must have a gender (which may be masculine, feminine or, in the case of languages such as German, neuter). There isn't a one-to-one correspondence between the grammatical categories feminine, masculine and neuter and the biological categories female, male and neutral/inanimate. One can see how this works in German in table 5.1.

These categories affect the structure of the language – they affect the form of the definite article the (it would be grammatically incorrect to write *das Sonne*) and they affect the form of the pronoun used: *er* = he/masculine pronoun; *sie* = she/feminine pronoun; *es* = it/neuter pronoun.

Table 5.1 Grammatical gender in German

Feminine words	Masculine words	Neuter words
die Frau*	der Mann	das Mädchen
(the woman)	(the man)	(the girl)
		das Fräulein
		(the young woman)
die Sonne	der Mond	das Fleisch
(the sun)	(the moon)	(the meat)

Note: all nouns in German begin with a capital letter.

Whereas in English we would write:

The sun ... it shines (or whatever)

In German this would be:

Die Sonne ... sie scheint

There is usually no logical reason for assigning a noun to a particular category (the sun is feminine in German but masculine in French), but sometimes the form of a word will affect which gender grouping it is allocated to. A word ending in *-chen* or *-lein* (suffixes meaning something like 'little', or 'young') is grammatically neuter – and this overrides the physically female properties of a girl (*Mädchen*) or a young woman (Fräulein).

English is a member of the Germanic language family and at one time (during the Old English period) it had grammatical gender. Modern English does not – though it has been said to have *natural gender*: nouns do fall into classes, and this affects which pronoun is selected, but word classes are based on nonlinguistic criteria – *woman* is feminine, *man* masculine, *table* neuter and so on.

We mentioned above a problem in the English 'natural' gender system: when we want to talk about someone whose sex is unknown, we have to decide between *he, he* or *she, s/he, they* etc. One might expect his problem to be avoided in a language which had grammatical gender – a speaker or writer would simply select

whatever pronoun was appropriate to the grammatical gender of
the noun they were using, as in the following examples from French
(in each case we provide a more or less literal translation):

a
... chacun de nos informateurs prend part, qu'il soit homme ou
each of our informants takes part, whether (he) is a man or
femme, jeune ou vieux...
a woman, young or old...
b
... l'énumération des langues ... est évitée par la personne qui mène
... the enumeration of languages ... is avoided by the person conducting
l'enquête. Le dialecte alsacien n'est mentionnè par elle que dans la
the survey. The alsatian dialect is not mentioned by (her) until the
toute dernière partie de l'entretien
final part of the interview...
(Tabouret-Keller and Luckel, 1981)

The French gender system does in fact pose some problems of
interpretation for readers of Tabouret-Keller and Luckel's article.
We know that some of their sociolinguistic interviews were carried
out by a male author, but it is not clear whether any were carried out
by women. In extract (b) above grammatical gender is followed
(*personne* is feminine but may refer to a man or a woman).
Elsewhere there are references to 'collaborators' (*collaborateurs*),
mainly 'teachers' (*instituteurs*). Both *collaborateur* and *instituteur*
are grammatically masculine. They do have feminine forms, but as
in English when words have a masculine and a feminine form the
masculine tends to be used as a generic.

Luise Pusch (1980) has made a study of the gender system in
German, which identifies similar problems. In common with other
languages, German distinguishes between terms referring to males
and females:

die Schwester (sister)	der Bruder (brother)
die Mutter (mother)	der Vater (father)

However, because German has grammatical gender, and because
words for females usually take the feminine gender and words for
males the masculine, a much more systematic distinction is made
between female-referring words and male-referring words than in,

say, English. Some words do not differ in form, but the form of accompanying words such as the definite or indefinite article (*the* or *a*) allows one to see whether the word is referring to a male or a female:

die Abgeordnete (female representative)   der Abegeordnete (male representative)

In other cases, a suffix may be added to the masculine word to produce a femine form:

die Studentin (female student)   der Student (male student)

Pusch found problems with the gender system in German similar to those identified in English. With terms such as *Student(in)* the masculine term is formally unmarked and the feminine is formally marked. (The *-in* suffix in German is more common than suffixes such as *-ess* in English.) The masculine form is also normally semantically unmarked: when a speaker wishes to refer to a student irrespective of sex *der Student* tends to be used. Similarly with terms such as *Abgeordnete*, *der Abgeordnete* tends to be used as both a male referring and a sex-neutral term. For those concerned with linguistic reform, solutions seem harder to find in German than in English, as every noun has to have a gender which is made explicit by the choice of article, pronoun, etc. Pusch sees the feminine *-in* suffix as one of the main targets of reform and suggests that this should simply be dropped, as the distinction between masculine and feminine (or male and female) can be made by the choice of article:

die Student (female student)   der Student (male student)

Since this would still leave the masculine as the semantically unmarked term, Pusch suggests that the neuter gender may be used whenever the sex of the person referred to is unknown or irrelevant. She counters (potential) claims that referring to people as *das* would produce connotations of animals or things with the assertion that this is no worse than women having to live with the feeling that they are permanent exceptions to a male norm.

Feminists have studied other aspects of sexism in German, many of them with clear practical implications (for instance Hellinger, 1980 discusses job titles; and Guentherodt et al., 1980 present

'anti-sexist' guidelines for writers and speakers). The very fact that
such issues can be raised in German suggests that, even in languages
with grammatical gender, 'natural' gender intervenes. It is unlikely
that gender is ever used and interpreted purely as a linguistic
category.

Words for Women and Men – Examples from the Lebanon and Japan

We have spent quite some time on gender distinctions and the
problem of the 'generic' masculine, but there are many ways in
which language embodies gender divisions. Because work on languages other than English has been patchy we cannot yet build up a
comprehensive picture of the relationship between (social) gender
divisions and language. As examples of languages that are unrelated
to English we can look at two studies: one by Nancy Jabbra of a
Lebanese dialect of Arabic, and the other by Motoko Lee of
Japanese. Jabbra (1980) is concerned to show how the Lebanese
dialect reflects the social structure of the community in which it is
spoken. In this community 'marriage makes a much greater difference in the life of a woman – it is her career' (Jabbra, 1980, p. 466).
Jabbra claims that there is a straightforward age progression in
words referring to males:

xutiyaar*	old man
zalamii/rijjaal	man
sabb	youth
sabii	boy

Note: these spellings represent Jabbra's transcription of the dialect

A man's marital status is referred to separately (*zauj* means
'husband') and there is also a separate word for 'son' (*ibn*). For
females, there are some age-specific terms (*sabiyyii* means 'young
lady', corresponding to *sabb*) and *xutiyaara* means 'old woman',
corresponding to *xutiyaar*). The words in common use for females,
are however:

bint	daughter; female child; unmarried girl or woman/ virgin
mara	married woman

These terms are not age-specific – a *mara* may be younger than a *bint*. There are words to refer to other types of woman (for instance *sitt* means 'lady') – in fact, overall, Jabbra claims there are more words for types of woman than for types of man – but for women there is no straightforward age progression as there is for men: the most important distinguishing factor is their marital status.

Gender divisions are very important in the Lebanese community and, as in most societies, men have greater authority: they are the household heads and breadwinners and descent is through the male line. It is also common practice for a wife to move to join her husband on marriage, rather than vice versa. This too is reflected in the language: family names are usually men's names, or are masculine in form; a person may be called by their father's name, but not their mother's (*ibn Joori* is the equivalent of 'George's son', and may be compared with surnames like *Johnson* in English). A married woman may be addressed or referred to in relation to her husband or, sometimes, her eldest son: *mart Joorj*, for instance, or *imm Yuusif* (compare *Mrs Smith* in English). A man is not, however, addressed in relation to his wife or daughter.

Like other varieties of Arabic, the Lebanese dialect studied by Jabbra has grammatical gender. As in German, the masculine form is unmarked: feminine forms are derived from the masculine by the addition of a suffix. Verbs too have feminine and masculine forms in the second and third person singular (the 'you' and 'she/he/it' forms in English). Here also it is the feminine forms which are formally marked.

Lee, like Jabbra, is interested in how language reflects women's and men's social positions. Lee (1976) examines terms used to refer to, and to address married women and men in Japanese. The study shows:

the inventory of terms used for a married woman in Japanese often reflects the woman's subordinate status and role and her confinement to the household. On the other hand, the terms used for a man tend to reflect his superordinate 'master' status and role in relation to his wife or his occupational status and role in his own right. (Lee, 1976, p. 998)

Terms used by a man to refer to his wife include *kanai*, which denotes a person staying inside a house (*ka* = 'house', 'home' or 'family' and *nai* = 'inside'); *uti no yatu* is used in informal speech, with a similar meaning. *Uti no yatu* also has connotations of the wife's low status, since *yatu* is a term normally used of someone of an inferior status. *Gusai*, which means something like 'stupid wife', is now becoming archaic, but is still used in letters by older men as a means of honouring the person they are writing to by lowering their wife's status and therefore their own. Lee notes that 'significantly, there is no term equivalent to "stupid husband" that a Japanese woman can use to refer to her spouse' (Lee, 1976, p. 995). Women commonly refer to their husband as *shujiN* ('master'), and *uti no hito* (roughly 'person of my house') is another popular expression. Lee comments that *hito* means simply a person, and does not have the low status connotations of *yatu*. *Uti no hito*, however, would not be used by a man of his wife.

One or two words for 'husband' and 'wife' have been borrowed from other languages – *waifu* (from English) and *furao* (from German) both mean 'wife' and *hazu* means 'husband'. These terms occur most frequently in the speech of younger women and men. Lee suggests the use of such loan words may be a sign of educatedness and sophistication – and also perhaps of a more egalitarian relationship between husband and wife.

Neutral Languages?

Esperanto

We wish to create a neutral foundation on which the various peoples can communicate with one another in peace and brotherhood without forcing the appurtenances of one people upon others.

Esperanto is 'no one's property', either materially or spiritually. (*Pensaj de Zamenhof*, pp. 17 and 29)

Zamenhof was a doctor who lived in nineteenth-century Poland, in a town beset by racial tensions. He attributed these tensions, in large measure, to the different languages spoken by sectors of the population. Zamenhof set out to devise an auxiliary language that would aid communication between different peoples, and contribute to international harmony. The language had to be not only neutral, but also simple in structure and easy to learn. It became known as *Esperanto*.

There are several respects in which Esperanto is not culturally neutral: its vocabulary is derived mainly from European languages and its structure is also inherently sexist – ironically mainly because of Zamenhof's wish to make it easy to learn. To reduce the learning of vocabulary Zamenhof established a stock of 'root words', from which other words could be derived by the addition of prefixes and suffixes:

bela (beautiful)	malbela (ugly)
rido (laugh)	rideto (smile)

In words referring to people, Zamenhof established the masculine form as unmarked, and added a suffix to obtain the feminine form:

viro (man)	virino (woman)
knabo (boy)	knabino (girl)
patro (father)	patrino (mother)

Zamenhof was also selective in the way he borrowed words from other languages. *Viro* and *virino* are derived from the Latin *vir*, meaning 'man'. *Knabo* and *knabino* have Germanic roots (*Knabe* is German for 'boy' or 'lad'). There is, of course, no logical reason why feminine loan words (such as the Latin *femina* or *mulier* for 'woman') could not have formed some of the basic stock of Esperanto's vocabulary.

Esperanto has three third person singular pronouns: *ŝi* ('she'), *ĝi* ('it') and *li* ('he'). In common with English and several other natural languages, it faces the problem of how to refer to someone whose sex is unknown or irrelevant.

Despite Zamenhof's desire for complete neutrality, sexism seems to be as much a part of Esperanto as of natural languages. Other auxiliary languages, such as *Interlingua* and *Ido* (the latter derived from Esperanto) have dispensed with some of the more extreme examples (for instance they have separate words for *mother* and *father*, *woman* and *man*), but it is still unlikely that they could be called 'neutral' languages.

Speakers of Esperanto, like speakers of natural languages, vary in how they react to accusations of sexism. Some people do not find Esperanto sexist – or at least they see this as a relatively minor issue compared with the problems Esperanto was set up to resolve. On the other hand, there are Esperantists who would like to encourage linguistic reform. The Esperanto magazine *Sekso kaj Egaleco* (*Sex and Equality*) has featured articles and letters concerning the feminine suffix *-in*, the use of third person pronouns, etc. Since Esperanto is a living language, it is likely that it will continue to be subject to pressures for change as social attitudes change.

Turkish

It [feminism] has initiated extraordinary projects [including] the hope that we shall acquire the genderless perception of things which the Turks (famous defenders of the rights of women) have enjoyed for centuries. (Roger Scruton, writing in the *Observer*, 22.5.83)

The official language of modern Turkey is one of the Turkic languages. These languages are spoken in parts of the USSR and Iran, as well as in Turkey itself. The relationship between the Turkic languages and other language groups is still being debated, but Turkish is unrelated to most European languages. Roger Scruton's oblique reference is to the fact that many of the gender distinctions made in English, in several European languages and in Semitic languages like Arabic do not occur in Turkish (nor in other languages – Turkish is only one example). Turkish has only one form of the third person pronoun: *o* (corresponding to *she/he/it* in English and *sie/er/es* in German). Turkish speakers do not need to be explicit about the sex (or even the animacy) of any person they refer to. Turkish does make a distinction between some words for people and (chiefly domestic) animals:

kısrak (mare)	aygır (stallion)
inek (cow)	boğa (bull)
kadın (woman)	erkek (man)
kız (girl)	oğlu (boy)

But these distinctions are not common – and, apart from a few words borrowed from Arabic, Turkish has no equivalent of feminine endings (such as *-ess* etc in English and *-in* in German). Any 'neutral' words for people or animals may be distinguished by sex, by using a term such as *dişi* (female) or *erkek* (male):

dişi ayı (female bear)   erkek ayı (male bear)

One can see the sense in these distinctions – domestic animals have entirely different functions, and the treatment they receive often differs, depending on whether they are female or male. In most cases, however, it is irrelevant whether the animal chasing you through a wood is a female or a male bear.

We should be wary of concluding that Turkish is not sexist. In Turkish, as in English and German, 'neutral' words for an individual may still be assumed to refer to men – and if they are intended to refer to a woman this will need to be marked somehow. (Jean Crocker (1984, cited in Coates, 1984) has made this point in relation to other 'gender-neutral' languages such as Finnish.) There are several respects in which social inequalities may be represented in the structure of a language (so far we know of no systematic studies of this aspect of Turkish), but equally inequalities may be represented in conventions of language use.

Sexism: Some Qualifications

When we talk of the "mastery" of the standard language, we must be conscious of the terrible irony of that word, that the English language itself was the language of the master, the carrier of his arrogance and brutality. Yet, as teachers, we seek to grasp that same language and give it new content, to de-colonise its words, to de-mystify its meaning, and as workers taking over our own factory and giving our machines new lives, making it a vehicle for liberation, consciousness and love, to rip out its class assumptions, its racism and appalling degradation of women, to make it truly common, to recreate it as a weapon for the freedom and understanding of our people.

(C. Searle, *A Common Language* (1983))

Those who argue that a language is sexist seem to make a number of assumptions about language, and how it affects people, that not everyone would agree upon. In the remainder of this chapter, we briefly examine some of these problematical issues.

The Notion of Bias

The debate about sexist bias is premised on the belief that language (both in the sense of an abstract system and of language use) is permeated with society's values. Feminists have claimed that language is biased in favour of men. This notion of linguistic bias is not uncommon – it is shared by people concerned about other forms of social inequality (such as racism) and it is shared by many of those opposed to anti-sexist (or anti-racist etc.) linguist strategies. In the two quotations at the front of this chapter, Miller and Swift mention the 'inherited linguistic biases' of English. Scruton would be unlikely to see the values inherent in English as 'biases', but he does fear distortion of another sort; the 'appropriation' by feminists of the vocabulary and grammar of the language. Both protagonists would agree, therefore, that language is susceptible to distortions of one sort or another.

Although the usage is common in the literature, we ourselves have qualms about expressions such as 'sexist bias' since arguing that language is biased (and therefore in need of reform) suggests the possibility of an unbiased or neutral language. The case of Esperanto showed how a language deliberately constructed as a neutral medium of communication nevertheless embodied certain values in its structure, and we have also seen ways in which language use reproduces social stereotypes. Language is, necessarily, bound up with social values, and campaigners for a non-sexist, non-racist (or whatever) language cannot hope to render it neutral.

Intentionality

Another problem relates to the intentions of a writer or speaker. At the beginning of this chapter we defined sexism as discrimination against women or men on irrelevant grounds, which makes no reference to intention. William Labov, writing in 1966, and Tony Benn in 1972, probably hadn't come across any feminist discussion of sexist language – and it is highly unlikely that they intended to exclude women from their texts. Nevertheless, such non-parallel treatment of women and men is, according to our definition, sexist. This is not to say that listeners or readers do not take into account perceived intentions in their response to a text. We may well react differently to two usages of 'generic' *he*, one encountered in an academic text from the 1960s and the other in a late 1980s text.

Language System versus Language Use

The distinction between language system and language use, although common in linguistics, is not always made by those with a practical concern about language – such as the compilers of anti-sexist guidelines – but we have retained it as a convenient way of organizing our discussion in this chapter. It seems reasonable to distinguish between things that form part of the lexicon of a language (such as the existence of separate terms for *mother* and *father*) and the ways in which people commonly use language (such as focusing on women's appearance or family relationships in newspaper stories).

Though convenient, this distinction is far from straightforward. The boundary between system and use is extremely fuzzy. It is possible to regard the abstract system of a language as a series of generalizations derived from language use, but clearly in this case the two aspects of language are not really separate: what happens when language is used will affect the system – either sustaining it or causing it to change. We can say that the language system makes provision for social inequalities such as sexism, but these need to be sustained (or combatted) through language use.

It would be a mistake to regard language as a single, unified system. No two people will have an identical vocabulary, and no-one will have at their disposal all the words contained in, say, the Oxford English Dictionary. Language is also constantly changing, in terms of the words it possesses and the meanings ascribed to those words. Related to these changes is the fact that, at any moment, different people are unlikely to ascribe identical meanings to a particular word. Disagreements may be particularly likely with terms that are seen to encode social values. The interpretation placed upon such terms will depend upon the values held by a language user. The kind of man who describes himself as 'unashamedly sexist' is unlikely to concur with feminist interpretations of 'generic' *he* or *man*, or words such as *lady* and *girl* used of an adult woman – though he may be perfectly well aware of these interpretations. The language system is perhaps better thought of as a set of (often contradictory) systems, to which any speaker of the language has only partial access. An expression like 'the English language', which seems to gloss over linguistic heterogeneity, is very much an idealization.

World Knowledge and Knowledge of Language

We have suggested that to interpret language in use people need to draw on both their linguistic and world knowledge. This distinction, like that between system and use, is often made for the sake of convenience, but it is equally problematical. It is hard to say where linguistic knowledge ends and world knowledge begins. The fluid and shifting nature of word meaning suggests that one cannot always identify an expression as unambiguously sexist. Meanings vary in different contexts, and depend on the listener's or reader's previous experiences. The context dependency of meanings is important in any discussion of the potential effects of 'sexist' language. This is a general problem of description which we examine more fully in the next chapter.

Man-made Language

Underlying much of the discussion of language and social values is the notion of a dominant social group (male, white, middle class etc.) that is somehow able to impose its meanings on other language users. With respect to sexism Spender writes:

Males, as the dominant group, have produced language, thought and reality. Historically, it has been the structures, the categories and the meanings which have been invented by males – though not of course by *all* males – and they have then been validated by reference to other males. In this process women have played little or no part. It has been male subjectivity which has been the source of those meanings, including the meaning that their own subjectivity is objectivity. (Spender, 1985, p. 143)

To speak of men as the sole inventors and validators of words and meanings is at least an over-simplification. Language, in various ways, reflects the interests of more powerful social groups, and men can be seen to have power relative to women in our society. But gender is only one form of social inequality, and many others cut across it. Women from some social groups are in a relatively powerful position (women from the middle class relative to working-class people; white women relative to Black people etc.). Accepting for the moment the notion of the imposition of meanings by dominant social groups, some women at least would play their part in inventing and validating meanings.

But the whole notion of meanings being 'invented' and 'validated' on high, and then passed down to (presumably passive) recipients is itself problematical. We have seen that language is not a homogeneous system with a single set of approved meanings. In the case of words and expressions associated with women and men the meanings prevalent at any time do seem to serve men's interests (better than women's), but this is unlikely to be due to the actions of an exclusive male cabale.

There is a danger, in the 'man-made language' argument, of confusing codification with the introduction of words and meanings into the language. Men have, until very recently, written the grammars of language. Men have also compiled dictionaries in which certain meanings take precedence over others, and in which citations from (mainly) male authors are used to validate these meanings. Selectivity in codification cannot, however, be responsible for the permeation of our language by sexist values. Deborah Cameron, in a discussion of what she terms 'gatekeepers' of language, acknowledges that dictionaries have only a limited role to play:

people do not learn most words from dictionaries but infer their meanings from hearing them used in particular contexts: we may all differ slightly in our beliefs about what words 'really mean'. If enough people infer from reading the word prevaricate that it means 'stall, play for time' (to take a recent example discussed in the newspapers), that meaning will challenge the one prevaricate is given in dictionaries . It will be no good telling speakers that prevaricate 'really means' 'lie' rather than 'stall', because the meaning of words is ultimately a matter of the way the community uses them in talk. Unless they are compulsive users of dictionaries, this will be determined by contextual inference, and meaning will be inherently unstable. (Cameron, 1985, pp. 81–2)

Despite her reservations about dictionaries, Cameron argues that there are linguistic gatekeepers: public language use in powerful social institutions such as the mass media and the education system helps in the dissemination of words and meanings, and as long as these institutions serve men's interests (more than women's) we can expect them to influence language towards 'male' meanings.

The media and the education system are undoubtedly in a strong position to influence language, but it would be unreasonable to see this influence as operating only in one direction. To be 'in the language', words have to be accepted and used by a language's speakers – and not just those occupying positions of social power. It is likely that the majority of a language's speakers (women as well as men) have helped to sustain 'male' perceptions of the world and their expression in language:

Schools have changed over the years. We don't all go to school in short back and sides no more – it's more freer... (Bradford schoolgirl, speaking on a Channel 4 documentary, 4.5.85)

Language and Thought

We have mentioned at various points in this chapter two other important assumptions underlying the notion of 'sexist language': that a language affects its speakers' perceptions of the world (and so sexist language actually promotes a sexist society as part of the 'natural order' of things); and that linguistic reform (which might lead to a more just society) is both necessary and possible. Neither of these assumptions is unproblematical – but the issues they raise are as relevant to earlier chapters as to this one. We shall, therefore, consider them separately in the final two chapters of this book.

Conclusion

Concern about sexism in language came initially from feminists rather than from linguists – and in fact sexism often operates along the fringes of what has conventionally been analysed as linguistic meaning.

In this chapter we have examined evidence of sexism from English and from some other languages. We have also looked at various attempts consciously to avoid sexist usages. And we have considered some of the assumptions about language that underlie allegations of sexism. While accepting that the notion of sexist 'bias' is in some respects over-simplified, we have tried to show how language is necessarily imbued with society's values – including sexism, in a sexist society. Our belief is that language also helps to reproduce social values, although the reproduction mechanisms are rather complex ones. We consider this issue in some detail in the next chapter.

6

Language, Communication and Consciousness

Introduction

The debate about the relationship between language and gender is less well developed at a theoretical level than might be imagined given the volume of research which has now accumulated. Researchers, however, seem to hold in common an assumption that gendered linguistic behaviour is somehow connected with wider social inequalities. For some, the nature of the connection is more specific: they assume that the various gender differences that we have surveyed in earlier chapters help in some way to create or maintain a social world which is oppressive to women. Many feminist authors, in particular, seem to take the view that language creates rather than reflects social divisions. But there exists no agreed and coherent theoretical framework which clearly and persuasively establishes how linguistic behaviour gives rise to social and economic sexual inequality. Furthermore, the nature of the connection between language and inequality is a controversial one and many writers dispute the idea that language plays any active role.

A variety of existing theories, mainly from linguistics and feminism, have been extended and adapted to explain sex differences in linguistic behaviour. Below, we have tried to organize these theories according to the relationship they suggest exists between language and society, what they see as the source of women's oppression, and what possibilities they see for change. But neat categories are not possible. There are several different ideas, for example, about what counts as 'language', and it is clear that many of the theories which have important ideas to offer have not fully worked out the implications for language and gender.

The balance of serious work in language and gender has focused on detailed empirical investigations whose findings only make proper sense when seen within the context of some larger, as yet poorly developed, theory. In this chapter we review the ideas which are most often mentioned or alluded to in this literature, pointing out which ones could be put together to create a coherent theory of language and gender. We have divided the discussion into the three main approaches which we described in chapter 1.

Language Reflects Social Divisions: A Model of Structure and Agency

The idea that language is a symptom rather than the cause of social inequality is widely held amongst researchers with a training in linguistics. It is not difficult to see how this view has arisen, since there exists a deeply held conviction amongst many linguists that any language (in the sense of an abstract structure) can be used to convey any thought or meaning which humans might wish to communicate. This principle of 'supreme effability' extends to all human languages – none are judged to be less capable than others and meanings which are expressed in one language may be freely translated to another. But, as we saw in the previous chapter, the vocabulary of a language is constantly being added to; new words are made up, old words are given new meanings, words are borrowed from other languages. Hence the traditional linguistic position is that a language can never limit the thoughts of its speakers since linguistic resources can always be found to meet its users' cognitive and social needs: a novel idea can always be expressed and vocabulary can easily be extended where necessary; as certain social groups arise, so their members will be able to signal their allegiance or social distance by accent or other linguistic behaviour. A language will thus come to reflect the social and communicative needs of speakers as they have developed within a particular society.

This view of the relation between language and society largely owes its position in linguistics to anthropological studies of North American Indians conducted in the early twentieth century, from which arose the new discipline of descriptive linguistics. Anthropologists studied languages because they had to communicate with and interview natives, but also because they found they could learn a great deal about a new culture and its members' social preoccupations by studying their language. Franz Boas, one of the first of the anthropological linguists, described the study of language as 'one of the most important branches of ethnological study' in his introduction to *The Handbook of American Indian Languages*.

The development of Boas's ideas by Edward Sapir, whose work on male and female forms in Yana we discussed in chapter 3, was influential on both sides of the Atlantic. In the 1920s he wrote, in a passage which is now well known:

In a sense, the network of cultural patterns of a civilization is indexed in the language which expresses that civilization. It is an illusion to think that we can understand the significant outlines of a culture through sheer observation and without the guide of the linguistic symbolism which makes these outlines significant and intelligible to society... Language is a guide to 'social reality'. (Sapir, 1970, pp. 68, 69)

Insofar as gender inequality can be counted as one of the 'significant outlines' of our culture we can expect this fact to be reflected in the language. Ethel Strainchamps, in a fairly early collection of feminist articles, describes a position broadly similar to Sapir's and continues:

Using such methods an anthropologist from another planet visiting the earth could soon learn from examining human language that the half of the human race bearing offspring is scorned and oppressed by the half doing the impregnating ... the anthropologist could discover that English, one of the most highly evolved of the world's hundreds of languages and the one

spoken in the most thoroughly technological society, retains more vestiges of
the archaic sexual attitudes than any other civilized tongue. (Strainchamps,
1971, p. 348)

The various systematic imbalances in vocabulary, such as the non-
equivalence of words like *manager* and *manageress*, the number of
derogatory words for a woman compared with those for a man, the
historical process whereby many such words have acquired derogatory meanings, these facts all seem to support the social mirror view
of language; that the language has evolved in order to meet the
communicative needs of its speakers. Just as an Eskimo requires
many words to describe different kinds of snow, so members of a
sexist society will require a wide vocabulary with which to denigrate
women.

If the significant outlines of a culture can be seen in the structure
of the language, it can be seen even more clearly in patterns of use.
In chapter 2 we showed how differences in men's and women's
voices corresponded to prevalent ideas of femininity and masculinity. The sociolinguistic studies conducted by William Labov in
New York and Peter Trudgill in Norwich (see chapter 3) show how
important social divisions, of which gender was one along with
social class and ethnicity, are reflected in patterns of pronunciation.
Conversational practices (chapter 4) seem to reflect power inequalities and even the sexual division of labour common in our society.

In brief, it seems that there exists a strong correspondence
between the structure of society and both the structure of the lexicon
and patterns of language use. However, it is insufficient merely to
note that language and social structure possess a similar shape. We
also need a theory which explains how such a situation has arisen, if
only to establish that it is, indeed, language that has been transformed so that it corresponds to society and not the other way
around.

The Role of Individual Speakers

An explanation popular amongst sociolinguistic researchers is that
accents and language styles each have a social meaning or connotation. Certain styles are regarded as 'feminine' or 'masculine', as
'posh' or 'common', as 'powerful' or 'weak'. People are said to adopt
such ways of speaking in order to make statements about them-

selves, to project a particular social image, and in order to signal their group membership and allegiance. Trudgill, for example, spoke of women aligning themselves with the middle-class prestige norm and men identifying with the working-class vernacular. We quoted Le Page and Tabouret-Keller's classic statement of this view:

the individual creates for himself the patterns of his linguistic behaviour so as to resemble those of the group or groups with which from time to time he wishes to be identified, or so as to be unlike those from whom he wishes to be distinguished. (Le Page and Tabouret-Keller, 1985, p. 181)

This is a liberal humanist idea, in the sense that it sees women and men as rational and free agents who are individually responsible for the way they speak. The work by social psychologists (chapter 3), which showed how the use of a particular speech variety led to certain personal costs and benefits seems to rest on a similar assumption, that a speaker will choose a linguistic identity which yields the desired social rewards. Such an idea is simple and attractive, but it can only partially explain many of the differences in the speech of men and women. A moment's reflection will establish that speakers are not wholly free to adopt the style of speech they like in order to become whatever kind of person they like. The simple liberal humanist model fails to acknowledge adequately the constraints which exist on individual freedom, or to explain why women and men apparently aspire to different linguistic identities and why these gendered identities correspond to systematic differences in power and status.

Constraints Arising From Social Structure

In acknowledging that there are limits to an individual speaker's freedom to talk in a particular way, we do not need to undermine the basic idea that Le Page and Tabouret-Keller have proposed but rather add a further dimension. Feminists are probably on more familiar territory than linguists when it comes to understanding the effect of social structure on the freedom of individual men and women. Marxist theory, for example, and its related developments, informs much recent feminist writing and provides a well-worked-out explanation of how social, economic and institutional structures lead to unequal opportunity for individual women and men.

The effect of socioeconomic processes on the speech of men and women is perhaps most apparent in studies of social networks. Lesley Milroy's work in Belfast, for example, shows how the way a woman or man speaks is affected by their position in a social network – whom they speak to, how often and in what capacity. These are patterns of social interaction that reflect both socio-economic structures and the traditional sexual division of labour which, in Marxist theory, is assumed ultimately to serve the interests of capital. Who talks in a 'powerful style' will also reflect the power relations between women and men within institutions. Men more often than women can be found in senior positions; gender inequalities which structure the employment prospects of women will ensure that the majority of mixed-sex interactions at work will be those in which the woman is in a less powerful position than the man. The traditional sexual division of labour is also claimed to create an asymmetric power relation between women and men within nuclear families. Pamela Fishman's research on couples (chapter 4) shows how this division of labour is maintained even in conversations.

Such explanations show how certain ways of speaking acquire social meaning. In terms of the semiotic model we described in chapters 1 and 2, the meaning of speech styles is both 'indexical' and 'symbolic'. It is indexical insofar as a person's biography and social movements lead them to speak in a certain way. But these individual experiences are structured by social processes and hence the way people speak will not only betray their private experience but also their membership of the social group whose members have enjoyed similar social contacts. In this sense, an individual's way of speaking is linked to their group or gender membership by a process of cause and effect. But insofar as the associations between ways of speaking and group membership become socially understood and significant, they are likely also to become symbolic, and individuals will seek to talk in certain ways in order to signal their chosen identity. One way in which speech styles acquire meaning, therefore, is a result of the interaction between the social behaviour of individuals and the constraints imposed on such behaviour by social structure: individuals position themselves in relation to groups created by social processes.

Such a model is one in which social structures set limits on the free agency of individual speakers and is sometimes described as a model of 'structure and agency'. It implies that the intentions and desires of individual speakers will be frustrated by external social processes and it predicts that social conflict will be a normal state of affairs. Why, for example would a rational person choose to talk in an unpowerful manner or meekly accept the social identities permitted by social structure? There are indeed instances where the desire to use a particular language variety leads to political conflict but it is usually a group struggle over a language, such as French and English in Canada, or Welsh and English in Wales, which is the issue rather than the modest differences of language style and accent with which we are concerned here. Such group conflict aside, individual women and men appear to adopt particular accents and speaking styles willingly. The structure and agency model, as we have so far described it, seems to overestimate the degree of conflict and frustration felt by individual speakers.

The Role of Ideology and Institutions

The social theory we are drawing on, however, has a well-established answer to this problem. It proposes that individuals are led to regard certain social behaviour and experiences as 'natural' by the action of *ideology*. In the sense that we are using it, the term *ideology* does not imply any particular political commitment but rather represents a sociological hypothesis which attempts to explain why people can be persuaded to act in ways which are against their own private interests but which ultimately serve the interests of some dominant social group. In the case of gender ideologies, it is assumed that dominant images of femininity and masculinity, which encourage both women and men to seek gratification by conforming to established gender norms, lead ultimately to women's oppression. Ideology is thus put forward as a mechanism to explain how women become complicit in their own oppression.

The concept of ideology adds to our previous explanations of how particular language styles acquire social meaning, and why men and women talk as they do. We have suggested at several points in the book that particular ways of speaking, of voice quality, accent and conversational behaviour, enter into social definitions of masculinity and femininity. These ways of speaking fit with the wider logic of ideas of femininity and masculinity – that women should take up gentle, nurturant roles, for example, whilst men should be dominant and aggressive. Gender ideologies affect people in both diffuse and direct ways. It may be difficult, for example, for a woman to depart from expected norms of female linguistic behaviour without incurring penalties:

I used a couple of harmless little words in a poem about the early definition of sexual roles by the choice of toys. I read this on Radio Wales and there was a mammoth phone-in from offended listeners who hadn't noticed the racialist jokes of the comic just before I went on. Most complained about 'a young girl' saying those awful things. While it was nice to be mistaken for a young girl at 33, I felt somewhat suprised – 'piss' and 'prick' are both to be found in the authorised version of the Bible (prick in a different context, of course). (Fiona Pitt-Kethley, *Independent*, 15.10.88)

Althusser (1970) proposed, in a seminal essay, that ideologies are perpetuated through a variety of 'ideological state apparatuses' (ISAs) such as the Church, the education system, the family, law and so on. One of the functions of such an ideological apparatus is a divisive one – the segregation of individuals into groups in order to give them systematically different treatment. In the original essay, Althusser had in mind a division between the working class and those who ruled and employed them, but similar arguments have been used in connection with gender divisions. Althusser's ideas figure prominently in most feminist accounts of how society works but they have particular implications for language. First, they demonstrate the potential importance of *any* difference in the linguistic behaviour of men and women. Such differences may not lead directly to an inequality, but they may serve the primary ideological role of marking gender as an important social division, of placing individuals clearly into one or another category, so that they can be treated as a woman or as a man and so that their subsequent behaviour can be interpreted according to expected norms of feminine and masculine linguistic conduct. For example, the voice is likely to perform an important ideological role: through its pervasiveness in both public and intimate encounters it constantly establishes a difference between the sexes.

Althusser's emphasis on the role of institutions usefully allows us to see why certain ideas rather than others come to be dominant. Since the majority of the ISAs which Althusser refers to are controlled and run by men rather than women, it follows that the ideas which they promote will serve the interests of men, not because of any conspiracy or malevolent intent, but simply because important decisions about the expected behaviour of women will be taken by men and will reflect men's assumptions and prejudices. Furthermore, it can be expected that any women who attain positions of power in institutions which have historically been controlled by men will be those who have adopted traditional patriarchal values. Again, we have already pointed to a variety of institutions which seem to enforce particular kinds of lingusitic behaviour and to promote certain ideas about feminine and masculine speech. We suggested, in chapter 2, that institutional values within broadcast organizations influenced the uses to which certain male and female voices are put in programming. In chapter 4, we mentioned the role of schools. Teachers often place an emphasis on the 'good' speech and linguistic deportment of girls whilst tolerating rowdy linguistic behaviour from boys and routinely behave differently towards boys and girls in the classroom when soliciting and responding to children's talk. In chapter 5 we discussed the role of 'codifiers' of the language, such as dictionary makers. At the very beginning of this book, we cited extracts from St Paul indicating the past attitude of the Church towards women's speech. The institutions which have influence over language, our attitudes to it, and the way we use it are numerous, and play some role in encouraging the various linguistic differences and inequalities which we have described in earlier chapters. Within a theory of ideology, however, it is the role that institutions play in promoting certain *ideas* as to what constitutes appropriate female and male speech which is important, rather than the temporary, limited role they may play in directly controlling their members' linguistic behaviour. At times in his writing, Althusser seems to equate 'ideology' with language itself, and the two terms are used interchangeably by some authors. In such cases language is being used in the general sense of 'communication' or language use: the way we talk about the world reflects social assumptions and values. The conflation of the two terms reflects the fact that the way most institutions, like individual speakers, communicate ideas is through language. Institutions, however, differ from individuals in that they have recourse to institutional powers with which to enforce their ideologies and ensure public dissemination.

Cameron (1985) has argued that the activities of informal and state institutions ultimately ensure that women's language is given little value. She suggests that the main source of women's linguistic oppression has to do with the way women are prevented from acquiring what she calls 'high registers' of the language (those used in literature, politics, in religious and legal rituals and so on) and quotes from an essay by Cora Kaplan:

The prejudice seems persistent and irrational unless we acknowledge that control of high language is a crucial part of the power of dominant groups, and understand the refusal of access to public language is one of the major forms of the oppression of women within a social class as well as in trans-class situations. (Kaplan, 1986, p. 70)

Cameron builds on this position, documenting aspects of women's denial to such registers and quoting, for example, literacy figures for men and women in developing countries. Literacy, she argues, is required to exercise basic democratic rights and to participate in modernization and innovation. Denial of it to women affects 'both their state of knowledge and their state of consciousness' (Cameron, 1985, p. 148) and is instrumental in their social oppression. In the western and more urban world it is not basic literacy which women are denied, Cameron argues, but the necessary experience to develop the diverse communication skills and appropriate language needed to deal with large institutions and bureaucracies. This leads to a general image of women as 'poor communicators' and a devaluing (by both men and women) of their linguistic competence in other spheres. Whilst the differential literacy figures of women and men in the third world are a significant and worrying aspect of sexual inequality, the idea that institutions play a particular role in constructing women as 'poor communicators' seems to us more difficult to demonstrate. There is probably some truth, however, in the idea that girls' education and upbringing does not give them an equal opportunity to acquire and practice certain language registers which are associated with competitive public debate.

Institutions promote ideologies about language itself, about what sort of thing language is and how it works, as well as those about the linguistic behaviour of men and women. This complex and fascinating area is largely beyond the scope of this discussion, but there is one particularly relevant idea. This is what James and Lesley Milroy (1986) have called a sense of 'authority in language' – the idea that there is a correct and incorrect way to use language, and that those who abuse linguistic expressions should be subject to social sanctions. This deference to linguistic authority, which is promoted through the same institutions that promote other ideas about appropriate language use, is needed to guarantee control of linguistic behaviour and it ensures that certain products of other institutions – dictionaries and manuals of linguistic etiquette such as *Fowler's Modern English Usage* and the meanings of expressions which they list – will be regarded as authoritative.

Although the notion of authority in language is not, in itself, a source of sexual inequality, it is a conservative influence which hinders attempts to introduce non-sexist writing guidelines and to persuade authors to follow them. The use of 'generic' *he* and *man*, and the opposition to 'singular *they*', for example, are often supported by reference to such notions of correctness.

The Structure and Agency Model and Implications for Change

The structure and agency model does not take serious issue with the notion of the Saussurean social contract (see chapter 1), that linguistic expressions and speech styles have agreed and determinate meanings shared by all members of the speech community. What is at issue is how the meanings of linguistic expressions should be determined, whether by prescriptive reference to authorized codifiers and the written texts that have been subject to institutional control, or through a descriptive analysis of the ways in which language is actually used by members of the speech community. In this way, a model which incorporates the notion of ideology fits well with conventional linguistic approaches, although this fact is not always apparent in the writings of linguists and feminists. We have, however, identified a source of confusion in the way the word *language* is used in this literature. When linguists talk of language, they usually have in mind the abstract structure; when sociologists refer to language, they usually have in mind language use, or, more particularly, the set of language practices that have become institutionalized within a community. When this point is clarified, it seems that traditional sociolinguistic accounts of language and gender conflict less than might be supposed with those of many radical feminists. Each has something to offer the other in theoretical terms. Whilst some feminist accounts of language seem facile to linguists, linguists' accounts of society and social processes often demonstrate a lamentable lack of sophistication.

It is possible to take up a range of political positions within a structure and agency model. Liberals, for example, stress the freedom of the individual whilst many left-wing theorists stress the role of structure in determining individual behaviour. Writers range from the belief that social structure imposes little real constraint on the individual to the conviction that nearly all human behaviour is structurally determined. What both political positions share, however, is the idea that any constraints which lead a woman to talk in one way and a man in another result from social processes external to language. In this way, linguistic differences between men and women can be regarded as symptoms of a society which incorporates many gender divisions.

Such a model of language and society suggests that attempts to change the structure of language (by inventing new words, for example, or banning the use of certain existing ones) will not lead to women's emancipation. What must be changed are the ideologies which create and sustain oppressive behaviour, and the social institutions which control and purvey such ideologies. In this sense, a strong and traditional distinction can be maintained between language structure and language use and 'language reform' is only of value if it applies to the latter. Liberals stress the role that individual men and women can play in changing their own linguistic behaviour and in drawing attention to that of others. Radical feminists stress the need for collective action, through consciousness-raising activities which will reveal women's 'true' social condition and free them from the grip of oppressive ideologies, to allow women to acquire more powerful roles in the running of institutions which reproduce such ideologies, and to generate rival ideologies, a project which may require women to maintain a separate space for themselves where new ways of talking and thinking can be worked out.

Language Creates Social Divisions: Models of Linguistic Determinism

The structure and agency model seems able to explain most of the phenomena which we have described in earlier chapters. It fails to engage, however, with a persistent idea that language, far from being an innocent bystander, plays a direct role in the oppression of women by helping construct and maintain sexual inequalities. The idea of linguistic determinism is a popular one, especially in the work of radical feminists. In this next section we will review the more important versions of this thesis.

The Whorfian Hypothesis

We mentioned in chapter 5 the claim that a lack of certain words in a language might prevent its speakers from expressing, or even thinking, certain ideas. When the anthropologist Franz Boas first considered the relationship between language and culture, he briefly entertained the notion that the paucity of words for abstract ideas in tribal languages might prevent their speakers from thinking abstractly, that is to say, he entertained the notion that culture was determined by language rather than vice versa. He came firmly to the conclusion that language did not determine thought:

> It would seem that the obstacles to generalized thought inherent in the form of a language are of minor importance only, and that presumably the language alone would not prevent a people from advancing to more generalized forms of thinking if the general state of their culture should require expression of such thought; that under these conditions the language would be moulded rather by the cultural state. It does not seem likely, therefore, that there is any direct relation between the culture of a tribe and the language they speak, except in so far as the form of the language will be moulded by the state of the culture, but not in so far as a certain state of culture is conditioned by morphological traits of the language. (Boas, ND, pp. 55–6)

Benjamin Lee Whorf, one of Sapir's students, was responsible for developing the contrary proposal that language sets the limits of thought and constructs a speaker's perception of both physical and social reality:

> We dissect nature along the lines laid down by our native language. The categories and types that we isolate from the world of phenomena we do not find there because they stare every observer in the face; on the contrary, the world is presented in a kaleidoscopic flux of impressions which has to be organized by our minds – this means largely by the linguistic systems in our minds. (Whorf, 1956a, p. 213)
>
> Actually, thinking is most mysterious, and by far the greatest light upon it that we have is thrown by the study of language. This study shows that the forms of a person's thoughts are controlled by inexorable laws of pattern of

which he is unconscious. These patterns are the unperceived intricate systematizations of his own language – shown readily enough by a candid comparison and contrast with other languages, especially those of a different linguistic family. (Whorf, 1956b, p. 252)

This idea is sometimes referred to as *linguistic relativity* – that speakers of different languages have different perceptions of nature and hold different views of social reality. Although this proposal is sometimes called the 'Sapir-Whorf' hypothesis the term is misleading, since Sapir's views on the relationship between language and culture were more in line with those of Boas. We use the more accurate term 'Whorfian hypothesis' rather than 'Sapir-Whorf' hypothesis for the claim that language constrains the thinking of individual speakers (a recent discussion of this point can be found in Berthoff, 1988).

Several feminist writers have invoked the Whorfian hypothesis to support claims that the English language (amongst others) is inherently sexist. It forms the main basis of the argument that the lexical biases which we discussed in chapter 5 (markedness, lexical gaps and so on) lead to real social inequalities. For example, we quoted Dale Spender's version of the hypothesis from her book *Man Made Language*:

Human beings cannot impartially describe the universe because in order to describe it they must first have a classification system. But, paradoxically, once they have that classification system, once they have a language, they can see only certain arbitrary things. (Spender, 1985, p. 139)

Hence usages such as 'generic' *man* cause us to perceive women as the inferior sex:

We learn to see the male as the worthier, more comprehensive and superior sex and we divide and organize the world along these lines. (Spender, 1985, p. 153)

Before we examine the evidence supporting such claims, we should admit that the Whorfian hypothesis has had a somewhat chequered history. Although Whorf's work captured the imagination of many researchers in the 1950s, not only in linguistics but in several neighbouring disciplines, early attempts to demonstrate its validity made little headway. The hypothesis soon became unpopular amongst linguists, not just because of lack of evidence, but also because some researchers began to claim that the language of Blacks and the working class was structurally impoverished and, by preventing speakers from complex and creative thought, led to inevitable educational and career failure. The hypothesis lost favour with linguists a decade or so ago.

So although researchers in language and gender inherited a theory which attempted to explain how language use could lead to the oppression of women, it was, ironically, a tainted theory, disreputable in liberal quarters. Its revival nevertheless could be justified. The hypothesis had been put away for reasons that were as much political as scholarly and it was now being called upon for a respectably liberal purpose. Furthermore, the original investigations had come to a somewhat unsatisfactory and inconclusive verdict and the developing study of language and gender provided a new domain in which to test the hypothesis. In the 1970s and early 1980s, empirical investigations in language and gender were daily turning up the kind of detailed evidence that might finally allow the Whorfian hypothesis to be properly tested and validated.

Lexical gaps Many of the early experiments which tested the Whorfian hypothesis examined how speakers of different languages perceived colours. This seemed a promising area for investigation because the colour spectrum could be objectively described as a continuum, although different languages use a variety of colour terms which arbitrarily divide this spectrum into different segments. Lenneberg (1953), for example, concluded that having a name for a particular colour made that colour more easily 'codeable' and this in turn allowed subjects in experiments to remember and recognise instances of named colours more easily than those which did not fit well into one of their colour term categories. The literature on the effects of colour terminology is extensive, although it became later complicated by the discovery that the human perceptual mechanism does in fact 'chunk' the spectrum into a number of focal colours. Nevertheless, some researchers still claim that colour terminology has a weak effect on memory and recognizability.

Such experiments suggest that those distinctively female experiences that lack words – the lexical gaps which we discussed in chapter 5 – may in some way possess reduced cognitive saliency and memorability compared to those for which words exist. There have, however, been few experiments to explore the psychological implications of lexical gaps. 'Reduced codeability' is in any case a rather narrow phenomenon – it does not suggest that people are prevented from enjoying or suffering the experiences which are linguistically uncoded, nor from talking about them to others. This is very apparent in the transcripts of women's conversation which Spender refers to in a discussion of this issue:

M: Often I find there aren't any words that can say what I mean.

J: What's something you want a word for that there isn't a word for now?

M: I'd like a word for the next time I complain about doing the cooking, and my husband says, 'But dear, you're so good at it'. I want a word that describes what he is doing. Getting out of something by flattering me. He wouldn't dare say 'That's women's work', because we have had that one and he knows he can be shown to be unreasonable. So he tries this one instead. But he's doing exactly the same thing. He's still being unreasonable. But this way, I'm the one who appears unreasonable... There's no word to describe that sort of behaviour that puts me down by being so gracious and polite and leaves me in the wrong.   (Spender, 1985, pp. 186–7)

Although lexical gaps do not seem to have a direct effect on thought, this does not necessarily mean that they have no practical consequences. The Whorfian hypothesis suggests only one way in which lexical gaps may lead to women's disadvantage, and we will consider other possibilities below.

Generic males   In contrast to the scarce psychological research into lexical gaps, there have been many recent experiments that have tried to establish whether people tend to think of males rather than females when a writer uses 'generic' *he* or *man*. We showed, in chapter 5, that writers themselves sometimes seem confused over the generic nature of a word, completing a sentence which begins with a generic intention with some phrase which betrays a specifically male reading. There are many such examples to be found which seem to indicate that the use of 'generic' *he* has some effect on a writer's thoughts.

Some book editors argue that when an author uses generic expressions it may lead to general male bias in what they write about that cannot be easily remedied by the rephrasing of sexist linguistic expressions during copy-editing. An internal paper examining 'equality in course material' at the Open University suggested, for example:

Writers also may have male examples in mind when using generic masculine terms. Making what seem to be superficial linguistic changes draws attention to these, and some people have found that having to consider alternatives leads them to approach their topic differently – considering the experiences of women, referring to research on girls etc.

The majority of research on generic expressions has focused on their effects on readers rather than writers. Mackay and Fulkerson (1979) tried to discover whether readers really understood 'generic *he*' as referring to both male or female. As we pointed out in chapter 5, if *he* were genuinely the unmarked pronoun one would expect it to influence our perception of gender no more than when someone asks how tall or old someone is we make an assumption that they are tall or aged. Mackay and Fulkerson found that both men and women rarely judged sentences which contained 'generic' *he* to refer potentially to women. What is more, even sentences which contained a predominantly female antecedent ('a nurse must frequently help his patients get out of bed') were not judged as potentially referring to a female nurse. Moulton, Robinson and Elias (1978) asked a large number of students to write brief stories about people mentioned in stimulus sentences. Some students read about the person in a sentence which used 'generic' *he*, others saw a sex-neutral pronoun (their or *his or her*). The ones who saw the 'generic' *he* much more often wrote about a male subject than the others did. Kidd (1971) had found much the same thing. Silveira (1980) reviews 14 laboratory studies of this kind and found that in every one, generic male terms led to more male-biased responses than neutral wordings did. Martyna (1978) investigated whether college students actually used *he* in a generic sense. She asked subjects to complete sentence fragments that contained people in 'male-oriented roles', 'female-oriented roles' and 'neutral roles', and found little evidence to suggest that college students used *he* in a generic sense, either in writing or speech. Instead, they seemed to imagine a particular gender for the protagonists and use an appropriate sex-specific pronoun.

There have been many experiments of this kind which show, quite conclusively, that 'generic' *he* and *man* are not always understood as generic. Those who use them may insist that the terms are generic, but the evidence indicates otherwise. Even those authors who claim that clarity is the supreme aim in writing (a defence of generic terms often put forward) must accept that they often fail to communicate an author's intentions clearly.

There has also been a number of studies which demonstrate that women and men respond differently to generic expressions. This, in fact, is an implication of the finding that readers imagine a male rather than an indefinite subject when words such as *man* or *he* are used. Whereas men will feel included, women will feel excluded from the reference. It has been suggested that this may lead to a general feeling of alienation amongst women readers and listeners and may lead to unequal opportunity where such generic expressions are used in the representations of job occupations in school text books, career advice given to school children, and job descriptions in adverts. Some discussion of these issues can be found in Briere and Lanktree (1983); Brooks (1983); Dayhoff (1983); and Hyde (1984).

Such experiments, although providing important evidence for authors and publishers, are unfortunately no real test of the Whorfian hypothesis but serve to demonstrate that generic terms are no longer (if they were ever) really generic. If the words *he* and *man* always imply 'male' for a particular reader, then attempts to use the words generically can be expected to fail. This is true even where a subject in an experiment reports to the experimenter that he or she recognizes such generic usages. As we earlier remarked, the intuitions of speakers about their own usage are often faulty and there is evidence that people who deny the permissability of forms like singular *they* will use them in conversational speech. So, in summary, the research on people's understanding of generic pronouns shows clearly that there is a linguistic problem, that they are not always generic in practice, but the results of these experiments do not constitute a proof of the Whorfian hypothesis.

Those experiments which explicitly sought to test the Whorfian hypothesis demonstrate an unfortunate misunderstanding. Whorf was concerned to explore the relationship between the structural patterning of a language – in other words an abstract grammar and vocabulary – and an individual's thought processes. Furthermore, the individual speaker is, on closer inspection of the hypothesis, also an ideal and abstract one. Whorf assumes that all speakers in a speech community will use a shared language in the same way. The idealization he makes is similar to one often made by grammarians – for example, the grammatical competence described by Noam Chomsky is that of an 'ideal speaker-listener, in a completely homogeneous speech-community' (Chomsky, 1965, p. 3). Such a notion is unsatisfactory when the investigation is explicitly concerned with social divisions within a speech community. The fact that the Whorfian hypothesis deals with abstract entities makes it particularly difficult to test experimentally – it is strictly a theory rather than a hypothesis. The experiments described above have investigated the effect of a *particular* utterance on real and individual subjects. The problem is reminiscent of the one that faces researchers trying to discover whether violence on television has an effect on children: no experiment, conducted on a single occasion, can determine the cumulative effect of exposure on an individual, never mind any institutionalized effects in a society or culture.

Cross-cultural studies   What would be useful in the study of television violence would be the discovery of two groups of children, identical in all ways except for exposure to television. Investigators of the Whorfian hypothesis actually have an equivalent possibility – like Whorf, they can make a contrastive study of speakers of different languages. There have been a few cross-cultural studies which have attempted directly to detect a relationship between linguistic structures and gender divisions in society but such as there are have come to doubtful conclusions.

Ervin (1962) constructed artificial words that were morphologically marked as either feminine or masculine gender in Italian. Bilingual speakers of Italian, when asked to rate these words on semantic differential scales, showed a tendency to ascribe different connotations to masculine and feminine words. Guiora and Acton (1979) investigated 'whether grammatical gender in one's native language influences the way in which male or female characteristics are assigned to asexual objects' (Guiora and Acton, 1979, p. 196). They compared speakers of English and Hebrew – a semitic language which has clear gender marking on nouns and which also requires gender agreement on adjectives and other modifiers. The researchers concluded that Hebrew speakers were no more inclined to imbue inanimate objects with feminine or masculine characteristics than English speakers were and they concluded that 'shared human experience is stronger than that of the particular constraints imposed by the structure of native language' (Guiora et al., cited in Clarke et al., 1984, p. 49). Clarke et al. (1981) conducted a similar study to that of Guiora and Acton but with Arabic subjects. Arabic, like Hebrew, has extensive gender marking. They came, however to the tentative conclusion that 'Arabic speakers categorize objects and concepts in a manner which would be predicted by the hypothesis of linguistic relativity' (Clarke et al., 1984, p. 49).

Clarke et al. point out that Whorf's ideas are often simplified, even bowdlerized, by those who attempt to test them. In particular, Whorf carefully distinguished between what he called 'phenotypes' – overtly marked linguistic categories such as gender inflections – and 'cryptotypes' – the less visible but nonetheless systematic grammatical patterning inherent in any language. Cryptotypes, by their very nature, are elusive and difficult to spot but we suggest that the constraints on the gender of the grammatical subject in words describing the sexual act (which we discussed in chapter 5), or the asymmetry between the verbs *father* and *mother* may be regarded as cryptotypical. In a little quoted article, Whorf tackles the problem of gender in English, calling it a 'covert class' – which appears to be somewhere between a phenotype and a cryptotype in its influence over subconscious thought. It is worth quoting his discussion fully:

Gender in English is a system of relations that has an almost minimal outward representation in morphemes. Its only motor reactions [i.e. utterable words] are the two pronouns 'he' and 'she'... The gender nouns, such as boy, girl, father, wife, uncle, woman, lady, including thousands of given names like George, Fred, Mary, Charlie, Isabel, Isadore, Jane, John, Alice, Aloysius, Esther, Lester bear no distinguishing mark of gender like the Latin -us or -a within each motor process; but nevertheless each of these thousands of words has an invariable linkage-bond connecting it with absolute precision either to the word 'he' or the word 'she'... These thousands of linkage processes rallying around the common point of the pronoun and ramifying to all the thousands of nouns of one gender form a sort of psychic complex belonging to (1) the nonmotor and nonactualized realm, (2) the thinking function in Jung's definition, (3) the linguistic and cultural order.

There is no reason why such a complex should not enter into various functional relations with other material thought without necessarily requiring the activation of any of the individual words or class marks with which it is connected. We can be thinking of, say, the division of labor between the sexes in a certain culture without having to think of the rather bookish words 'female' and 'male' and to refer continually to them in our meditations upon such a subject. What we more probably do as we run over such a question in our minds is sift the facts in terms of a sort of habitual consciousness of two sex classes as a standing classificatory fact in our thought world, something which is quite different from sex as a concept or sex as a feeling-value. The basis of this shadowy, abstract, and wordless adumbration of a sex classification is not a word like 'sex' or 'female' or 'woman'; it is a linguistic RAPPORT as distinguished from a linguistic UTTERANCE. In English it is probably a rising toward fuller consciousness of the two great complexes of linkage bonds pertaining to the linguistic sex-gender system ... But in a language without sex gender, like Chinese or Hopi, any thinking in terms of a sex classification could not be of this nature; it would presumably operate around a word, or a feeling, or a sexual image, or a symbol, or something else. (Whorf, 1956c, pp. 68–9)

Whorf's suggestion fits well with the Saussurean notion of a system of words which are set in opposition with each other, except in this case an opposition between two sets of words occurs because of their potential to enter into different grammatical patterns. According to Whorf, then, the English language will have a greater influence on its speakers' subconscious attitudes to gender than either a language with overt gender marking (such as French or Italian) or one without any grammatical gender system (such as Chinese or Turkish). In this case the findings reported by Ervin and Clarke et al. seem to conflict with, rather than support, Whorf's hypothesis.

In summary, there are many problems with the Whorfian hypothesis. What has become known as its 'strong' form – that language 'determines' rather than 'influences' thought, is surely discredited. But despite many attempts, even a weak influence of language structure on an individual speaker's thought has eluded satisfactory demonstration. Nevertheless, our review of the Whorfian hypothesis has turned up important evidence of a gap between the authoritative accounts of what 'generic' masculine terms mean and how they are used and understood in practice. This is not just interesting as a possible example of 'false consciousness' brought about by prescriptive ideologies of language use, but also establishes that, importantly, there is some kind of link between the way language is used and the way people will think and react. What has not been proved is the idea that the abstract structure of language constrains the thoughts if its speakers.

The Semiotic Approach

There is an alternative reason which can be put forward to explain why the influence of language on thought has proved so difficult to pin down: the effect of language may be lost amongst competing determining mechanisms. We communicate in many ways besides verbal language, with body gesture, graphic images, with repertoires of actions such as etiquette or diplomacy. Semiotics, imperialist tradition that it is, has already shown us how these can be treated as 'languages', albeit rough and ready ones compared with verbal language, but fragmentary languages nonetheless. If language systems have a determinant effect on thought, then these non-verbal systems must also be taken into account.

Traditional sociolinguistics goes some way towards a semiotic analysis where speech styles or accents are described as having social 'meanings'. Semiotic analysis can be extended much further, however, to include the repertoire of voice qualities, conversational practices, and so on, that comprise the aspects of language use which we have discussed in previous chapters. We can take 'interruptions' as an example. Just as a word or phrase can be regarded as a 'signifier' in semiotic terms which stands in contrast to others, so an interruption can also be regarded as a 'signifier' which belongs to a repertoire, or system, of conversational practices. Its meaning arises partly from its contrast with other possible actions such as silence or some supportive gesture such as a head nod. Furthermore, interruptions appear to have some kind of syntax or syntagmatic structure – the meaning of interruption is partly indicated by its positioning in an utterance. An interruption may thus be heard to be supportive rather than hostile, and so on.

Such an approach has not, as far as we are aware, been worked out in relation to language and gender. But it suggests that part of the problem in assessing the linguistic determinacy thesis is that we do not fully understand what language systems are operating – what systems of symbolic signs our culture has developed and with which we exchange meanings. Semiotic analysis does not stop at suggesting various conversational practices and paralinguistic phenomena can be viewed as 'languages'. What is proposed is an integrative framework which recruits all cultural practices as potential languages, which are used to communicate using precisely the same principles as are involved in verbal language. This implies that any test of the hypothesis that 'language determines thought' must take into account not only verbal language but also all those systems of ideas which are conveyed through other cultural practices. Furthermore, any similarity between language structure and culture ceases to be of interest, for the semiotic project seeks to abolish the distinction between language and culture. They turn out to be varieties of the same thing.

Virtually all the phenomena we have described so far can thus be theorized in terms of abstract language structure. Semiotic analyses of this kind, although they include a surprising range of non-linguistic behaviour which we are unaccustomed to think of as 'language', are nevertheless structuralist analyses which build on the original Saussurean concepts. This may appear to abolish the distinction between 'language structure' and 'language use', but not necessarily so. As we will now go on to show, there is a more recent development of 'structuralism' which allows us to establish a rather different distinction between 'structure' and 'use'.

The Poststructuralist Model

What has become known as the *poststructuralist* theory of language and gender is especially associated with feminists working within a European tradition rather than the Anglo-American one that includes Whorf. It is a theory which draws both on psychiatric accounts (from Freud and the French psychiatrist Jaques Lacan) of early sexual development and the structure of the unconscious and on proposals by the French philosopher and historian Michel Foucault about the relationship between language and power. Poststructuralism builds on the structuralist ideas we have described above, incorporating them into a wider theoretical framework. Two principal features of the theory are of interest to us here. The first is the emphasis it places on the role of context in determining the meaning of utterances and texts. The second is the powerful role it gives language in determining a speaker's thoughts and consciousness. Unfortunately, the literature on poststructuralism is a difficult and forbidding one in which, alas, a reader's struggle to grasp ideas is not always well rewarded. Below we can only outline some of the relevant features of the theory.

Context and meaning Communication has traditionally been seen as a process which involves encoding the ideas in the mind of a speaker (or writer), transmitting them through some medium (speech or writing) and subsequent decoding in the mind of a listener (or reader). In its essentials it is a view which has been around for a couple of millenniums at least. It has, however, been criticized by poststructuralists and others as an inaccurate model of how human communication actually works. Harris (1981), for example, suggests it incorporates two fallacies: the fallacy of 'telementation' – the idea that communication consists of transferring ideas from one mind to another, and the fallacy of the fixed code – the idea that words and sentences have fixed and stable meanings.

According to the fixed code fallacy the meaning of a word or utterance can be decoded by the application of a set of linguistic rules which form the individual speaker's knowledge of language. Words or utterances may, of course, be ambiguous, but such ambiguities will themselves be marked as possibilities during the decoding process. If a listener arrives at a different understanding from that intended by a speaker then, according to this principle the reason must lie either in some noise or distortion affecting the reception of the message, or in the speaker and listener using different algorithms for encoding and decoding meaning – in other words they speak different languages. Words, according to this view, may change their meanings through time – but at any one moment in linguistic history the current meaning (or meanings in the case of ambiguous words) can be specified.

The poststructuralist approach to meaning draws on both semiotics and literary theory, and also fits well with recent theories of communication developed in philosophy and cognitive psychology. In the former fields it enjoys a somewhat radical reputation, whilst in the latter it forms something of an orthodoxy. At its extreme this view suggests that meaning is not fixed by language but is dependent entirely on context. Cameron (1985) for example, refers approvingly to the Soviet linguist Volosinov, and to more recent writing by the French poststructuralist, Julia Kristeva:

Both these writers point out that all meaning is in the end contextual, and that it is impossible in principle to determine once and for all the meaning of any expression. Determinacy either of form or of meaning is a myth, shored up by the pointless abstractions of structural linguistics. (Cameron, 1984, p. 15)

Volosinov's book, *Marxism and the Philosophy of Language* was written in the late 1920s by an obscure figure and remained almost wholly hidden from history until it first appeared in English translation in the early 1970s. Several currently fashionable ideas in semiotics and linguistics were prefigured in Volosinov's work and many scholars have taken intellectual delight in rediscovering them. Volosinov's basic thesis was that the 'abstract objectivism' of traditional linguistics misled scholars into thinking that meaning existed independently of its use in concrete circumstances: 'Language acquires life and historically evolves precisely here, in concrete verbal communication, and not in the abstract linguistic system of language forms, nor in the individual psyche of speakers' (Volosinov, 1973, p. 95). Put like this, it may sound like a commonplace notion. Indeed, structural linguistics has devised a number of techniques for explaining how context adds to or embellishes the meaning of sentences but these techniques support, rather than threaten, the idea that words have 'core' or 'literal' meanings which can be listed in dictionaries. Volosinov went further, however. He proposed that it was impossible to distinguish between those aspects of a word's meaning that derive from the context of utterance and those which a linguist might traditionally call the 'literal meaning'.

This idea corresponds to a more recent debate in linguistics over the definition of word meanings. To take one example, how much of our knowledge of what a kitten is like can legitimately be said to form part of the meaning of the term *kitten*? It has been argued (by, for instance, Umberto Eco, 1984) that each word has a range of potential associations, which will vary to some extent for each speaker depending on their previous experiences. On any occasion (when the word is encountered in context) some of these associations are emphasized, or 'blown up'; others remain untapped (in Eco's terms, they are 'narcoticized'). In the sentence 'The kitten caught me with its paw, leaving four little beads of blood on my knuckles', 'claw-bearing' seems an important aspect of the meaning of *kitten*. Elsewhere ('The kitten cried piteously at the door') 'claw-bearing' seems less relevant, at least for most speakers.

In poststructuralist theory, however, the notion of 'context' has as much to do with the social and political relations in which speakers and listeners find themselves, as with the linguistic context created by neighbouring words. For example, in chapter 5 we remarked on the different meanings which the word *girl* seemed to have, depending on whether it was used by a woman of equal status or by someone (male or female) of higher rank. Here, the power relation between speaker and hearer needs to be understood before the meaning of *girl* can be understood. Such context dependency extends also to the interpretation of other signifiers, such as voice quality, accent or conversational practices. For example, we saw in chapter 2 that in a pre-pubescent boy a high pitch is associated with masculine characteristics (it conveys a sense of higher muscular activity and forcefulness) but in adult males, high pitch usually connotes effeminacy. Again, the structure and agency model we described above suggests that individuals are, to a degree limited by social structure, able to negotiate their own social identity by adopting a certain style of speaking that possessed a particular social meaning. However, ideologies of gender may ensure that a given style has a different meaning if used by a woman rather than a man. For example, a high status pronunciation may be heard as 'polite' if used by a woman, but 'educated' if used by a man. An interruption may be heard as normal, assertive masculine behaviour and pass unremarked but a woman who tries to use this style in order to gain interactional power may be heard as aggressive and 'difficult'. The contextual theory of meaning applies equally to all cultural signifying practices. It explains, for example, why the 'meaning' of trousers or a tie is different when they are worn by a woman rather than a man.

The idea that social context is an important aspect of meaning is a simple one but it nevertheless has some far-reaching implications. It suggests that speech styles (or other discourse practices) do not have absolute meanings that transcend their context of use, but must be understood by reference to particular gender ideologies and power relations between the sexes. First, by proposing that similar behaviour in men and women may be given different social meaning, it focuses attention on the role of gender ideology rather on sex differences in language use as the source of gender inequality. Nevertheless, it puts an emphasis on the need for the sex of a speaker to be easily apparent in interactions, for a speaker's use of language can only be properly interpreted if her or his sex is known. Second, ideology and the nature of institutionalized power relations may ensure that the linguistic strategies which enable men to maintain their status and position are rendered impotent when used by women.

Such a contextual view of meaning leads to a rather different notion of language which is concerned not so much with the Saussurean, and abstract, structure of a language system but rather on particular utterances and texts set in social contexts. Theories of how social contexts are structured become an essential component of any theory of meaning. Language which is rendered meaningful by being situated in this way is usually referred to as 'discourse' in the poststructuralist literature. Hence, if women are oppressed in any way by language it is not the language structure which can be held responsible but rather specific discourses which necessarily imply particular power relations and particular ideologies.

Linguistic determinism Cameron (1985) points out that if one rejects the notion of determinacy of meaning, then one must reject the radical feminists' position that language can determine thought:

Linguistic determinism is a myth. Where there is no determinacy, there can be no determinism... Male control over meaning is an impossibility. No group has it in their power to fix what expressions of a language will mean, because meanings cannot be fixed. (Cameron, 1985, p. 143)

This contextual view of meaning seems at odds with the notion of linguistic determinism, but it has, in fact, given rise to a new and more extreme form of the determinacy thesis.

Meanings do not exist prior to their articulation in language and language is not an abstract system, but is always socially and historically located in discourses. Discourses represent political interests and in consequence are constantly vying for status and power. The site of this battle for power is the subjectivity of the individual and it is a battle in which the individual is an active but not sovereign protagonist. (Weedon, 1987, p. 41)

The idea, then, is that individual speakers are exposed to the ideological effects of 'discourses' rather than 'language'; that these, unlike abstract language structures, embody particular meanings and values. Just as, in the Whorfian hypothesis, the language structure was claimed to constrain a speaker's conscious and unconscious thought, so in poststructuralism, such discourses construct a person's unconscious and conscious self, referred to as their *subjectivity*.

How we live our lives as conscious thinking subjects, and how we give meaning to the material social relations under which we live and which structure our everyday lives, depends on the range and social power of existing discourses, our access to them and the political strength of the interests which they represent. (Weedon, 1987, p. 26)

The notion of how and why discourse has such a tyrannical grip on the individual is one of the more difficult and obscure aspects of poststructuralism. Briefly, it is supposed, as in classic Freudian theory, that the unconscious is structured by early sensual experi-ence – an experience which is directly given by the innate sensory perceptual system and not yet mediated by mental or psychic structures. This organic sensuality becomes genitalized and sexual as the child matures. As in Freud, the psychic self is structured according to early sexual development and is determined by the child's anatomical identity and relation to mother and father. The difference is that the structures of the unconscious are seen as a 'symbolic order' of a Saussurean and linguistic kind. Girls and boys enter this symbolic order in different ways, determined by the sexual anatomy. An individual's consciousness of self (subjectivity) de-velops from these early unconscious structures. A subject adopts certain ways of talking before she or he becomes fully aware of the significance of such behaviour and of the power relations and ideologies which they inevitably imply. We enunciate the words of history, of others, before we make them our own. We appropriate the thoughts, beliefs and meanings of others before us, and so we are turned into such people as went before us, and eventually come to evaluate and experience the world in similar ways.

Rather as in Whorfian determinism, it is supposed that only those subject positions which are conveyed through discourse are avail-able to individuals. Furthermore, this process is disguised by liberal discourses in the western world which encourage an individual to take up the position of a rational subject:

The crucial point for the moment is that in taking on a subject position, the individual assumes that she is the author of the ideology or discourse which she is speaking. She speaks or thinks as if she were in control of meaning. She 'imagines' that she is indeed the type of subject which humanism proposes – rational, unified, the source rather than the effect of language. (Weedon, 1987, p. 31)

In these respects, the poststructuralist approach is reminiscent of the Marxist notion of 'false consciousness'. The difference is that there is no real or 'true' consciousness which lies below the false one. Discourse is an ideological process which is described as constructing all aspects of consciousness and self.

One of the problems with the poststructuralist approach to language and gender revolves around the definition of 'language' and 'discourse'. Although we have presented a particular concept of 'discourse' here, it is not clear in the literature that this is always what is to be understood by the term. Sometimes a structuralist and Saussurean view of discourse is also appealed to – as when discourse is used to mean a particular set of ideas which form a system of oppositions. This seems, for example, to be the sense used by Chris Weedon, above, in the phrase 'liberal discourse'. When used like this, the term 'discourse' becomes almost indistinguishable from the term 'ideology', just as 'language' and 'ideology' became synonymous in Althusser's writing. This confusion is reflected in a debate over the extent to which subjectivity is determined by language as opposed to social structures and ideological processes of a more familiar kind. Cameron (1985) despite being sympathetic to a broadly Lacanian, and anti-humanist, view of the 'gendered speaking subject' suggests that the role of language is overestimated:

I agree with the semiologists and with all anti-humanists that our 'personalities', our desires, our needs, our ways of behaving, are constructed in our interactions with the world... What I cannot accept, however, is the privileged status accorded language in this process of construction. Of course it plays some part – it cannot be just a reflection of other things, for it is basic to much of our experience – but other things are important too: perhaps even more important, for they happen earlier in our lives and are less able than language to become objects of reflection and interpretation in their own right. I am thinking of socio-familial relations; of the division of labour and economic organisation that regulates societies; of the physical environment; of individual genetic make-up. (Cameron, 1985, pp. 169–70)

The problem is that for poststructuralists it is impossible to separate discourse from the other 'interactions with the world' which Cameron mentions. First, this is because within poststructuralist theory it is difficult to maintain a principled distinction between verbal language and other signifying practices. Second, because the meanings of discourses are grounded in perceived and institutionalized power relations and gender ideologies.

Possibilities for Change

There is a moral problem associated with attempts to change the social order when one adopts the anti-humanist approach. If a person's wants, desires, experiences – all that makes up her or his 'subjectivity' – are constructed through discourse, then how ethical is it to attempt to thwart these desires and assault the 'self'. Within the humanist model all that is created, by language and ISAs, is a veneer of false consciousness, which can be stripped away in order to reunite women and men with their alienated selves. With the anti-humanist position there is no 'true' self to be revealed or to be reunited with; what is constructed by ideology is all that exists.

Poststructuralists escape this dilemma by pointing to the unstable nature of subjectivity. Just as there exist competing discourses, so there exist in each of us internal contradictions which the individual subject can exploit through consciousness raising activity. The individual's subjectivity is not a homogeneous structure but is rather fractionated and contradictory. Different discourses play upon this and invite the speaking, listening subject to respond in a variety of contradictory ways. The emphasis on discourse as the site of struggle means that social relations, which provide the context for discourses, must be changed rather than 'language' in order to change meanings:

To see subjectivity as a process open to change is not to imply that the material structures such as the family, education and the whole process which constitute and discipline our sense of ourselves both conscious and unconscious, can be changed merely at the level of language.

Discursive practices are embedded in material power relations which also require transformation for change to be realised. (Macdonnell, 1986, p. 106)

In several respects, then, there is little to choose between the 'structure and agency' model and the poststructuralist one when it comes to programmes of political action. Both place an emphasis on changing social structures, institutions and ideologies rather than on linguistic reform. This may seem to suggest that the only argument in favour of making changes at the level of language is the discredited Whorfian hypothesis. This is not, in fact, the case. In the last section of this chapter we move on to examine the potential role of individual speakers in reproducing social relations and ideologies through discourse and the potential political contribution that they can make.

The Dialectical Position: A Linguistic Model of Discourse

It may seem strange to some readers that this section is headed 'The Dialectical Position' since we have, in our earlier account of the 'structure and agency' model described a classic Marxist dialectical model. The dialectic there, however, concerned the relationship between the individual and social structure. There are three players, so to speak, in the present game: language, society and the individual speaker, and in this section we explore the possibilities of a synthetic view in which language both helps construct sexual inequality and reflects its existence in society.

Such a synthesis builds upon the poststructuralist insight that it is discourse, rather than abstract language structure, which is the 'site of struggle' and a cause of oppression, but we have two main dissatisfactions with the poststructuralist account of discourse as we described it above. First, it takes what seems to us an unnecessarily determinist position. Such a position is not supported by any empirical research and it cannot be easily reconciled with traditional liberal and humanist views of the speaking subject. Neither of these are criticisms which would be accepted by poststructuralists, and they undoubtedly reflect the values of our own linguistic tradition. Nevertheless, we consider that poststructuralism leaves obscure the vital mechanism by which discourse oppresses the individual speaker.

We believe that it is possible, by taking the view that language comprehension and production require an active role by a reasoning speaker or hearer, to take a position which fits more easily with a liberal, humanist view of the individual speaker. By drawing on work in pragmatics (the linguistic description of language use) and psycholinguistics (the linguistic approach to mental processes involved in language comprehension and production) we can see more clearly the ways in which discourse embodies particular world views and belief systems and how it may be oppressive to women. These mechanisms turn out to be far from mysterious.

Propositional Structure

Imagine that a man says to his wife and a visiting neighbour:

I see you two women have stopped gossiping.

Rather like the classic question 'Have you stopped beating your wife?', this utterance incorporates certain *presuppositions*. In particular, it presupposes that the women's activity can properly be referred to as 'gossiping'. The relevant characteristic of a presupposition is that it cannot easily be denied. Making the sentence negative, for example, leaves the presupposition intact:

> I see you two women have not stopped gossiping.

For the same reason, whether the women were to reply 'Yes' or 'No', they could not deny the charge of gossiping. The incorporation of contentious material into the presuppositional rather than the propositional part of utterances or texts is a well-known ploy of propagandists and advertisers. Presuppositions can, in principle, be taken up by listeners, but pragmatic constraints on discourse make this difficult. Attempts to deny presuppositions are, for example, usually heard as hostile acts (since it suggests that the speaker's assumptions are in error) and may be a difficult activity for a speaker in a subordinate position. In informal conversation each speaker can usually only deal with a single topic in a turn before the conversation passes to another participant and to take up a presupposition may mean that the main proposition remains unaddressed. There is usually pressure to respond quickly in spoken interaction (partly because the maxim of 'first in gets the floor' usually applies) and this means that not all implications and presuppositions in an utterance are necessarily immediately apparent to a hearer. Ideological biases in texts and discourse can be made manifest when analysed at leisure, but may be accepted unproblematically when processed 'on-line' by a hearer or reader working at speed.

The recognition that implicit values and beliefs may be located in presuppositional structures allows us to review the potential consequences of lexical gaps in the language. The dialogue which we reproduced from Dale Spender's book *Man Made Language*, showed that the lack of a word did not prevent a particular idea from being thought and discussed. Nevertheless, lexicalization may bring important pragmatic benefits. Where there is no existing word or short phrase it is difficult to incorporate the idea in the presuppositional part of a sentence. M (in the transcript above) needs, in other words, to be able to say to her husband something like 'Please stop squigging me', without having to enter a tedious explanation and argument as to the meaning of the word 'squig'. Hence lexical gaps will restrict the ways in which an idea can be introduced into discourse and talked about.

This is not the only benefit of lexicalization. In public discourse, there is usually competition for time (or space) and things which cannot be said succinctly often cannot be said at all; conventions of public speaking and writing are such that personal narratives are often seen as irrelevant digressions; the existence of a word seems to give social legitimacy to a concept. These are some of the arguments, quite distinct from the Whorfian hypothesis, which have contributed to the idea that, because of systematic lexical bias in the language, women are a 'muted group' and that 'language silences women'. Looked at from the point of view of pragmatics, rather than the Whorfian hypothesis, this is a claim with some substance.

Discourse and Social Reality

One problem with the poststructuralist account as we describe it above is that it left obscure the process by which context endowed words with a particular sense in discourse. A linguistic approach to this problem involves the notion of redundancy. Redundancy will occur when some aspect of meaning that is given in the definition of one word is repeated as part of another word's meaning. So, in the sentence:

> The woman drank up her champagne.

we can argue that both *woman* and the possessive pronoun *she* are marked for 'female': the information is given twice in the sentence. The notion of redundancy is thus a powerful mechanism in language which allows participants in discourse to use words in rather different ways yet remain understood. It is, moreover, a fairly mechanical procedure as far as the hearer is concerned – it can described in terms of a fixed code view of meaning. However, the following utterance creates a complication:

> A nurse should always carry her watch.

If we already 'knew' that nurses were female, this sentence would also include redundancy, but this redundancy would be filled in from world knowledge rather than from the linguistic definition of *nurse*. On the other hand, even if we knew that there were both male and female nurses, a discourse which used such an expression would convey to us the expectation that a nurse will be female. The word has shifted from its possible 'male or female' denotative scope in the language to being specifically female in this utterance. But such an utterance may be heard to imply that the word *nurse* is female not just here but generally so: the fact that particular meanings are sustained only by the linguistic context is not always apparent. If someone heard the word *nurse* for the first time, it is likely that 'female' would be heard as being part of its literal meaning.

　　Discourses, however, usually involve sequences of sentences. Let us now examine a longer example:

> Jane began to look white and left the room. The woman drank up her champagne

Here we have provided some more context for our earlier sentence. Strictly speaking, the pronoun *her* is now ambiguous – it may now refer to *Jane* or as before to *woman*. But most readers (particularly if they had not been faced with the earlier example) would probably opt for Jane. The reasons for this are rather complex. When two sentences, or utterances, are placed together readers will usually try to construe a relationship between them and turn them into a coherent text. One method is to construct a little story: 'Jane was feeling rather ill, perhaps through overdoing the champagne, so she left the room. Perhaps she was going to be sick – certainly she didn't want what was left of her drink.' Such stories are things we mundanely produce when making sense of texts or discourse. What is interesting is that they again appeal to a knowledge of 'how the world is' in order to provide coherence. Such knowledge has nothing to do with the language – our knowledge of things like the effects of alcohol, what people do when they feel sick and so on are hardly coded in the words that appear in the sentences above. Umberto Eco (Eco, 1979) has described a range of ways in which the reader, in order to make sense of a text, must take many 'inferential walks' outside the text to collect further information and evidence. The reader is portrayed as a kind of Sherlock Holmes, who travels through a text (or spoken discourse) looking all the while for clues and building hypotheses about meaning which may be proved or disproved by later evidence.

The alternative to the 'fixed code' view of the communication process is, then, one in which less emphasis is placed on the structure of language and more on the encyclopedic knowledge of the language user. Meanings arise, in this model, from an interaction between language and cultural knowledge; the communication process is one which requires reasoning processes. This model of language processing is now a familiar one in artificial intelligence and cognitive psychology where the inferences we have described are referred to as 'bridging inferences'. It has been shown, moreover, that readers and hearers are very poor at distinguishing between information that was strictly given in a message and information that they had to infer. (See Green, 1987, for an introductory account of such processes.)

It may be the case that a hearer or reader arrives at the same understanding as that intended by the speaker or writer, but if so that is not so much a demonstration of telementation as that both participants are orienting towards the same background assumptions and world knowledge. Such a model of communication puts an onus on a speaker or writer to take into account the state of knowledge of the hearer/reader, and hence predict how a hearer might take an utterance. In other words, it requires a speaker to recognize the world view of the hearer and produce an utterance that makes sense within that framework. But we have also noted that it is often possible for a reader or listener to reconstruct the world view which is needed to make sense of a discourse: language may be used to construct a possible social reality, this need not always be known in advance.

We can now note that the kind of knowledge required to make sense of discourse is often that of a sexist world. According to this theory, a hearer or reader will constantly be required to make sexist assumptions in order to make sense of discourse. Look, for example, at the text of the following advert:

What Do You Get When You Fall In Love?

You may get a diamond ring as big as the Ritz. You may get a red rose every day. You may lose your appetite. Eventually, you will get: twice as much washing up; twice as much ironing; twice as much underwear drying on the radiators; twice as much cooking to do; less than half the duvet in the middle of the night. What else can you look forward to? Endow your loved one with the Electrolux vac with the hose at the back (the 610 or 612 for those less romantic among you) and you'll whizz through the chore of cleaning in no time. Bless your union with an Electrolux WD1039 washer/dryer and, even if you can't swing a cat in your kitchen, you'll be able to wash and dry everything in a space no bigger than a fridge. Then, live happily ever after with an Electrolux dishwasher and neither one of you will waste any candle-lit evening up to your elbows in mild, green, bubbly substances. Come the patter of tiny expectations, and you'll find all these a god-send.

(Electrolux Domestic Appliances 1988 'Lifestyle' advertising,
Guardian, 21.3.1988)

Here, a reading of the advert requires a complex social knowledge. The reader needs to understand a stereotypical heterosexual living arrangement which involves a certain division of household labour, and which will lead ultimately to children. It is an appeal not only to a romantic ideology of marriage but also to lived experience. It would be possible to elaborate at length upon the world view that this advert assumes. But, in fact, the advert is not a straightforward one. It ambiguously hails the reader; the social experience which underpin a man's understanding may be different from that used by a woman to reach her reading. The reader needs to adopt a particular gendered 'subject position' in order to understand how the advert is meant to apply to them.

Sally McConnell-Ginet (1984) has also used a framework which draws on both pragmatics and psycholinguistic theory to argue that discourse conveys a sexist world view. She draws on a theory of meaning proposed by Paul Grice (1957). Grice proposed that there is a kind of social contract that binds individuals in discourse. The contract provides a certain guarantee of co-operativeness on the part of participants. Speakers will not, for example, confuse hearers as to their intentions by including irrelevant detail: they will be as precisely informative as is required. McConnell-Ginet argued, however, that the kind of evidence which we presented in chapter 4 shows that men and women have been socialized into different attitudes towards conversation: women see it as essentially a co-operative activity whilst men see it as competitive. Hence in any communication between a man and woman, the woman is unlikely to challenge the belief system that is needed to make sense of the man's discourse (whether these are known in advance or inferred at the time). When talking herself, however, the co-operative woman will adopt the man's world view in order to frame utterances. This is an asymmetrical relationship, McConnell-Ginet argues, since the man will never frame his talk in terms of the women's value system. If there is a difference between the man's world view and experience and those of the woman, then it is the man's that directs the entire discourse. Eventually all instances of a word's use will reflect the man's value system rather than the woman's. This model does not necessarily imply that the woman actually changes her world view, however, only that the woman's experience and values never appear as assumptions in mixed sex discourse; that her world view is never the one in which the coherence of the discourse is grounded.

Like Malz and Borker (whose work we discussed in chapter 4) McConnell-Ginet regards these differences in conversational behaviour as due to differences in 'gender roles' learned in childhood, but it is also possible to regard them as a feature of power asymmetry in discourse. It is well known from social-psychological studies in language behaviour that there is a general tendency towards convergence – that is, there is a co-operative principle in talk that causes people to move towards an interlocutor's speech style. In unequal relationships, however, it has been observed that it is the less powerful speaker who moves most towards the style of the more powerful (see, for example, Thakerar et al., 1982). This suggests that discourse in contexts where there exists an asymmetric power relation will orient to and reflect the assumptions and world view of the more powerful participant.

Thus we can begin to see how belief systems and conceptual frameworks, experience about the world and so on are exchanged and distributed unequally in discourse according to existing power and gender relations. The model puts less emphasis on the 'coded' nature of words and structures and more on the role of context, experience and reasoning in the hearer/reader. We do not dispense altogether with a conventional 'meaning' for words that transcends occasions of actual use; the model still assumes that words have some kind of 'literal' meaning that all speakers know of and which ultimately constrains the way that word can be used in discourse.

But it is inevitable, McConnell-Ginet argues, that the man's view ultimately becomes seen as a part of the 'literal' meaning of the word rather than a situated or emergent meaning. One reason for this is that if women's world views are invisible in discourse, then children learning the language will not perceive the conflict between male and female world views – they will hear only an instantiation of a male view. But another is that if women always talk as if they adopt a male world view, then eventually they will come to adopt it. There is, in fact, a widely held view that the repetition of an act leads to its appearing natural and hence to its eventual acceptance. If one lives in conformity with some ideology, one is eventually likely to come to believe it.

Conclusion

In this chapter we have tried to demonstrate that language may play a role in reproducing and constructing ideologies which are oppressive to women, but that the process whereby this is accomplished is often misunderstood. The model we have proposed suggests that social realities are not 'encoded' in language in the sense of an abstract structure but are embedded in particular discourses and are necessarily activated during acts of comprehension and production. Hence we are right to locate the struggle over realities in discursive practices. This is what lies behind the quotation from Trevor Pateman with which we began this chapter, that every action either 'reproduces or subverts a social institution'. This view of the linkage between language and ideology places equal emphasis on the role of traditional ideological apparata, institutions and the role of the individual speaker. In this respect it represents a shift of emphasis from an exclusive interest in social processes and institutions. It demonstrates how much of the real and endless business of ideo-logical reproduction and renewal takes place in daily spoken interac-tion; that individuals help recreate the social world in ordinary everyday encounters; that they do not just reaffirm it for themselves and reassure themselves that the world is still 'normal' but that what they do ultimately helps reproduce social structure and the gender inequalities which that implies.

Although we have discussed many different ideas as to how language is implicated in sexual oppression, we have discovered that there are fewer conflicts between theoretical approaches than has sometimes been supposed. Many conflicts are more illusory than real and rest on the different ways in which the distinction between language structure and language use is drawn. One of the few ideas that we have been able to dispose of is the strong version of the Whorfian hypothesis – that the verbal language system determines thought. The mechanisms which link language and social processes are both more complex and subtle.

One problem with such a complex model is that it produces no clear recipe for remedial action. Rather, action seems to be required on all fronts simultaneously. On the other hand, such a model suggests that many proposals for social action, including the institutional reform of linguistic practices, are individually of some value. If they hold out a false hope, it is only when they suggest there is a single linguistic panacea for the problems of sexual inequality. We have tried to demonstrate that linguists have, at times, been guilty of underestimating the role of language in producing and maintaining such inequalities, partly through their rather narrow definition of what constitutes 'language' and partly through an unnecessary fear that to accept that language plays a role may lead them to a position they would find theoretically untenable and illiberal. Drawing upon notions in pragmatics and cognitive psychology, however, we have argued that there remains a place for the idea that when people talk to each other they are engaged in an important political activity, in which existing power relations dictate the way in which social reality is renegotiated amongst participants.

7

Linguistic Intervention

'The first non-sexist Bible to be published in Britain was launched yesterday. The revisers have systematically changed expressions such as "any man" to "anyone", but have kept the masculine, especially for God, on the grounds that this is faithful to the original.'

(*Guardian*, 4.10.85)

'Starting this September, this nine week course will help you discover whether you've got what it takes to be a Firefighter.'

(Advertisement to recruit women to the London Fire Brigade, *Time Out*, 29. 6. 88–6. 7. 88)

'Has there been discussion or formulation of a school policy on written and spoken language? Is a conscious effort made to use language which promotes a positive self-image of pupils and staff, black and white, female and male? Is gender stereotyped language avoided e.g. "strong lads", "giggly girls"? Are pupils addressed similarly regardless of sex in terms of praise, compliments, reprimands, assessment?'

(*Implementing the ILEA's Anti-Sexist Policy*, ILEA, 1985)

'I'm trying to learn to behave differently myself, with only I must say the most limited of success. And I'm trying to watch out and remind the men tactfully – it's like water dripping on a stone.'

(Managing Director of firm trying to introduce 'feminine' styles of management)

'Excuse me, but I didn't interrupt you. Would you mind letting me finish?'

(Woman to male colleague in a mixed discussion group)

Introduction

Our discussion in earlier chapters shows that many of the extensive gender differences in language which we documented constitute a social problem for many people. Our review of social theory in the previous chapter, however, shows how difficult it is to explain the precise role played by language in creating and maintaining sexual inequality. This suggests that the task facing those who attempt to reform social relations between the sexes using linguistic strategies will be a delicate one. The practical implications of such 'linguistic engineering' are the focus of this chapter: is it necessary, or desirable, consciously to 'police' one's own language or that of others? Can changes to language produce concomitant social change? Can they affect how women and men are perceived and how they perceive themselves?

Intervention and Change: Some Case Studies

Below are four case studies which illustrate how changes in language behaviour may arise in a variety of contexts associated with equal opportunities. The first, on computer conferencing, shows how the introduction of a novel medium of communication obliged people to adopt new communication strategies and led to a change in the traditional pattern of contributions from female and male participants. The other case studies all concern more deliberate attempts to equalize opportunities between women and men or girls and boys. They include industrial training schemes, classroom teaching and equality guidelines for writers of course materials.

Case Study 1: Computer Conferencing at the Open University

In mid-1986 the United Kingdom's Open University (OU) installed a computer conferencing system on its central mainframe computer to augment its already various methods of distance teaching. The idea behind computer conferencing is that students, distributed around the country and abroad, and equipped with personal computers and modems, can dial up the university's central computer, read the written contributions sent in by other students and staff, and respond to any items of interest by drafting a contribution of their own and transmitting it via the telephone line to the computer. As a number of participants comment and respond to each others' contributions, so a discussion builds up. A single continuous line of discussion is referred to as a 'conference' and the system supports several hundred. This discussion has rather different discourse characteristics from either a spoken conversation or an exchange of letters, but combines certain qualities of each: it is an informal, turn-taking system but responses to contributions take an indeterminate time to arrive – from a few seconds to several weeks. Topics are taken up, changed or dropped according to the interests of participants in much the same way as in a conversation.

For the first year the system was tested by members of staff at the Open University, who came from a wide range of status and occupational backgrounds. After a while it became apparent that certain characteristics of the system seemed to encourage the participation of junior and marginal members of staff:

● There was no internal system of status hierarchies (as might occur at a meeting when certain speakers have roles that give them special rights to talk). Each conference had a 'moderator' (rather like a committee chair), but this person did not select contributors. Any person could join any conference, make contributions when they wished to, and could, if they wanted, set up their own conference and become a moderator.

● External status remained largely hidden. Participants were identified by 'usernames', and many were unknown to one another outside the system. Usernames even concealed the participants' sex (though this could usually be discovered by looking their name up in the system directory).

● Several accompaniments to spoken conversation that might support status differentials were absent from the conferencing system. In particular, there were no non-verbal signals such as seating position, clothing, posture, gesture, accent and tone of voice.

● The public nature of the discourse seemed to prevent high status participants ignoring comments from junior colleagues – other participants could draw attention to such silences and request a response.

● The system also affected conversation management: contributions were inserted in strict chronological sequence, and there could be no equivalent of an interruption. Even the order of responses gave them no special status, since participants entering the conference could scan the full range of previous contributions and respond to those that seemed most interesting. The system could handle several topics at once, and participants could respond to any number of these.

● A normal conversation is ephemeral. Participants build up a shared knowledge which is not available to anyone who joins later, and which is only partly available to those who leave periodically to deal with other tasks. The conferencing system allowed any new participant to wade through the past history of a conference and see how it evolved. When they started participating, it was with exactly the same knowledge and experience as any other member.

The ability of the system to handle several topics at once was frequently used in the early days by women to make substantive comments on a previous topic and also remonstrate with male colleagues over their use of 'sexist' language. Such metalinguistic comments could be made, and responded to, without disrupting the flow of the discussion. After a while, it seemed that a new communicative culture was developing in the system in which participants generally monitored their own and others' contributions in this respect.

Furthermore, discourse on the conferencing system did not seem to show the kinds of gender imbalances which are typical of face to face interaction. Women's participation rate (in terms of the number of messages they left) was roughly equivalent to that of men, and their contributions were taken up as often for discussion. Unfortunately, several of these features failed to survive when the system was first used by students in 1988. 1,300 students of a course on Information Technology were enrolled on the conferencing system, of whom only 358 were women. Women's contributions to one of the conferences monitored were slightly less than proportional to their numbers; the conference became increasingly dominated by the activities of a small number of students, though these were not all men; the self-imposed anti-sexist policies were completely lost.

Many factors may explain this. For instance, the system became more status oriented, partly because students seemed to feel themselves in a less powerful position relative to staff (usernames immediately distinguished students from staff, though not women from men). To save space, the computer department began to delete large or old conferences from the system – this meant that new participants could not quickly become familiar with the conference culture. Also, access was more difficult for students working from home than for university staff with terminals on their desks. It may also be that men, more often than women, were able to overcome various technical difficulties, and that they could find more time to play with the system in the evenings and at weekends, when cheap rate telephone calls could be made.

Nevertheless, the medium shows promise. Women's contributions may have been higher on other conferences that were not monitored. One conference on the role of women in science and engineering was clearly dominated by women, and although one or two of the more active men made contributions these rarely determined the flow of conversation.

Case Study 2: Equal Opportunities in Training: Three Examples From Industry

Some 18 years after the Equal Pay Act of 1970, and 13 years after the 1975 Sex Discrimination Act, women still have a long way to go before they gain equality with men in the workplace. However, many companies do now have an equal opportunities policy and some make special provision to encourage women into jobs traditionally occupied by men.

A formal policy – Esso UK: Esso has a formal equal opportunities policy dating from 1984. This aims 'to ensure that no job applicant or employee receives less favourable treatment on the grounds of race, colour, sex, marital status, religion, ethnic or national origin'. (A separate policy deals with disability.) Towards the end of 1985 the Board of Esso decided to take positive action to ensure the policy was more effectively implemented. To date, implementation of the policy has included:

● 'Awareness training' seminars for all employees. The purpose of these seminars was to explain the company's policy and demonstrate senior management support for it; to encourage employees to explore what they saw as the 'real issues' surrounding equality of opportunity in the company; to provide information on the distribution of female and male employees within the company (information on other social categories, such as the number of employees from ethnic minority groups, was not available when the seminars were held); and to plan strategies for follow-up action.

● Encouragement of women to apply for jobs in Esso – for instance the company supported the Women Into Science and Engineering campaign; they produce a brochure entitled 'Women in Esso'; and there is an equal opportunities component in training courses for interviewers (covering, for instance, appropriate questions to ask of applicants during job interviews).

● Apart from those relating to interviewing, there are no training courses dealing specifically with equal opportunities, but the company tries to integrate equal opportunities into its normal programmes. All training programmes are open to men and women.

● There is a sexual and racial harassment procedure – although this does not seem to have been invoked, at least during the last 18 months.

Female and male employees of Esso are still largely distributed along traditional lines: most of the highly paid managers are men, and 70 per cent of women employees are in 'support functions' (secretarial and administrative jobs). However, there are some changes: female graduate recruits have increased from 13 per cent of total recruits in 1984 to 40 per cent in 1988; some women have broken through to senior management positions; and there is a slowly increasing number of women (albeit still a tiny minority) employed in non-traditional 'blue collar' and 'blue collar interface' jobs.

Language use and communication between the sexes have not been targeted as specific issues in Esso's equal opportunities policy – although they seem to be incidental to many of the general training programmes. External consultants who provide courses on 'leadership training' are asked about their approach to equal opportunities; in other courses touching upon communication skills, such as

'working as a member of a team' or 'making a presentation', a
training manager would ensure a consultant's approach on equal
opportunities was consistent with company policy.

Robin Schneider, Head of Staff Relations (and with special
responsibility for equal opportunities), mentioned one complaint
from women at the Awareness Training seminars: 'I can make a
point in a meeting and it'll be listened to and then forgotten, and
then the same point will be made by a man and – "Oh yea, we'd
better do something about that!" ' On the whole, however, he felt
communication between the sexes wasn't a problem, not because it
had been tackled as an issue but because of the general climate
obtaining in the company: 'We're a relatively informal company,
and if somebody finds somebody calling them "Love" objectionable,
for instance, they tend to say it and are supported by their colleagues
around them'; 'One of the things about the company is that we do
quite a lot of work in small groups – that's the way our training
works. And because of this we do put quite a lot of emphasis on
listening and supporting other people, which means that although
the degree of tolerance isn't immensely high it would be considered
bad form to talk over anybody, whether it be male or female;' '. . . of
course, you get people who go on in meetings, but I think it's as likely to
be the women as the men . . . I think because we have high recruitment
standards and we haven't gone in for tokenism then any woman who's
in the job reckons they're in the job because they can do it and they've
been selected on that basis; and hence they've got as much right to
say whatever they want as anyone else.' These statements clearly
represent Robin Schneider's view of the situation – they do not arise
from any formal analysis of female and male communication.

Robin Schneider's perception is that the company's equal opportunities policy has made some improvement in the working environment: 'In order to co-operate together [as a team] you need to get
the skills that each individual has used effectively by the team. So,
one theme that does seem to emerge there is that there is an
advantage to having a much more mixed working environment than
we did, because that tends to give you a greater diversity of skills
and input. So when you're problem-solving, which is a lot of what
we do, then you've actually got a better seed-bed of ideas that you
can move forward from.'

'Feminine' management styles – Stuart Crystal: the glass-making

company Stuart Crystal does not have a formal equal opportunities policy, but the managing director, Roger Pauli, has been concerned to introduce more 'feminine' styles into management. Feminine styles are characterized as 'organizing processes' whereas masculine styles are concerned with 'taking command of people and processes'. Roger Pauli explained: 'If I were to appoint a man to a job, I would expect his first questions to be – "What's my title? Who am I in charge of? Who do I report to? How much authority have I got?" If I appoint a woman to a job, I expect that she would say – "What have I got to do? What do people need from me? What am I going to be responsible for? How will I know whether I've done it right? Who do I work with?"'

The encouragement of women into management positions is seen not as an end in itself but as a way of promoting a more feminine style of management for both women and men. As a way of encouraging women, the company took part in a two year training project, initially in collaboration with Aston University, and part funded by the government through the (then) Manpower Services Commission (MSC). The project was coordinated by Marion Butler, who is also Roger Pauli's personal assistant. It involved providing courses for women in general management skills, to enable them to compete with men for management positions. A condition of the MSC funding was that the courses had to be for women only. Many courses covered aspects of communication, for instance 'assertiveness training', 'confidence building', 'initiative taking', 'negotiating skills', etc.

At the end of the two year project the company continued to provide training courses on these topics, but with the exception of assertiveness, where they feel women might be intimidated by men, courses are now open to men and women. The courses have enjoyed some success in that they have been popular with employees and some women taking them have found the confidence to apply for and obtain more senior positions.

Of the company's eight highest paid managers, four are women and four men – though other areas of management are still dominated by men. But Roger Pauli and Marion Butler felt that women in management positions faced problems – and in some cases these were increasing. Men were often patronizing to women, and tended to dominate meetings. Roger Pauli gave an example: 'I had a meeting with a [female] sales manager and three of my [male]

directors once ... it took about two hours. She only spoke once and
one of my fellow directors cut across her and said: "What A is trying
to say, Roger ..." and I think that about sums it up. He knew better
than A what she was trying to say, and she never got anything said.'
There are no formal training programmes to encourage men to
adopt more feminine styles of management. This operates by
example and at a 'subliminal' level. Roger Pauli feels anything more
formal would be counter-productive.

Stuart Crystal was the subject of a recent (1988) television
programme on women and management – but this programme
produced a number of adverse reactions. Whereas the original
training project had been carried out quietly and unobtrusively, the
television programme put women in the public eye and caused
considerable resentment amongst male employees. The company's
approach has now returned to being more 'low key'.

Training schemes organized by a freelance consultant: many companies, like Esso UK, contract out training to external consultants.
Diane Taylor is one such training consultant. She provides courses
for managers and supervisors in industry and commerce and for
trainers on schemes such as the government sponsored Youth
Training Scheme (YTS) for school leavers, and the Employment
Training scheme (ET) for the unemployed. Her courses cover a
variety of topics, including: grievance and disciplinary procedures,
staff appraisal, effective communication, managing organizational
change, recruitment and selection procedures. She also runs courses
specifically on equal opportunities – but she feels that this issue is an
inherent part of all the training she offers.

Language is an important focus for Diane Taylor's equal opportunities work. For instance, in a management development course on
communication she might ask course participants to consider how
women in their company, with management potential, are 'giving
away power' in language. On the basis of research (such as some of
that considered earlier in this book) she believes women use less
direct speech than men; more tag-questions and hedges; more rising
intonations at the end of statements; and more adjectives such as
'awfully', 'sweetly', and 'nicely'. In discussion the men on her
courses tend to agree that women's language differs from that of men
in these respects.

Diane Taylor hopes to convince participants on her management courses that female employees need their support. She also believes that women need to change their language – that they will present themselves more effectively and have more power to influence others if they use more direct speech. This is particularly important in contexts such as meetings, where the impression one makes is important and where women are disadvantaged to begin with by making fewer contributions than men. As well as conveying this message to managers and trainers she runs some 'women into management' courses. Here she is 'far harder' and 'more direct' in training women to be more assertive in their language.

In connection with the equal opportunities courses she runs for trainers on YTS and ET, Diane Taylor encourages trainers to look at the whole structure of equal opportunities, including stereotyping and language. She suggests resources for trainers on these topics – such as an examination of linguistic biases (many of which we discussed in chapter 5). Young people, for instance, might examine stereotypes of women and men through such exercises as looking up in a dictionary the number of words used to describe a sexually active female, or comparing the connotations of non-parallel terms like *bachelor* and *spinster*.

In courses on equal opportunities she meets with some hostility, both from men (particularly in traditional areas of employment) and from women who think she is trying to turn them into 'surrogate males'. Hostility tends not to survive to the end of a course, 'because hopefully you've raised people's awareness to such an extent that they can see the need for change.'

Using language as a focus for equal opportunities forms only a small part of Diane Taylor's work. But she hopes that these activities, along with her other work, will help to promote a more supportive working environment for women, and one where changes in communication patterns can take place. She clearly hopes that at least some of these changes will spill over into other aspects of social life: 'My personal agenda is to try and create change for women.'

Diane Taylor receives feedback on her work from former course participants who are undertaking certificated courses (in which they need to demonstrate 'competence' in equal opportunities). One YTS trainer, for instance, went on to change the language and style of all her training materials. Feedback from courses run for private companies is more spasmodic – though she knows some people at least do change both their own, and their companies' practices. The actual effects on employees or trainees (e.g. whether changes in communication styles, and in the attitudes that underlie them, actually take place) are harder to monitor. Diane Taylor acknowledges that she cannot systematically evaluate this aspect of her work.

Case Study 3: Equality in the Classroom

Jackie Hughes was, until recently, Deputy Head of Jervoise Junior and Infant School in Birmingham. The Head of the school, Frank Jewitt, was keen to promote equal opportunities – and various strategies were employed by teachers to challenge racist and sexist stereotypes. There was no formal (written) equal opportunities policy but several whole school projects (including one on dance and another on toys) provided the focus for equal opportunities work. There were also continuing attempts to develop anti-sexist and anti-racist approaches to classroom language, organization and 'ethos'.

In the autumn term of 1987 Jackie Hughes began a cross-curricular project on 'Images' with her class of third and fourth year juniors. A broad aim of the project was to foster equal opportunities and reduce prejudice. More specific aims were worked out in considerable detail. They included:

- to develop/extend the language awareness of all pupils and foster an understanding of the range of functions all language can have
- to develop/extend pupils' knowledge and awareness of other cultural groups within British society and how and why people have settled here
- to develop/extend pupils' knowledge and awareness of the diversity of cultures and traditions that have shaped and are shaping 'British culture'
- to encourage/develop an understanding among pupils of the dynamic nature of 'culture' – to appreciate and understand the contribution of women as well as men, Black as well as white, in developing and shaping this culture
- to extend/develop pupils' existing abilities in skills of reading comprehension, recording and analysis of the information they acquire

- to enable pupils to acquire information from a variety of sources and using a variety of methods

- to correct misinformation and bias by developing/extending skills of observing, analysing, interpreting, judging, etc.

- to develop an understanding among pupils of the need to classify information while fostering an awareness of how classification can lead to stereotyping

- to acquaint pupils fully with the principles of democracy and with the legitimate processes that may be used to protect the civil liberties of all groups in society

- to encourage/develop the formulation of questions and hypotheses, the posing of problems and the thinking through and testing of possible solutions

- to enable pupils thus to recognize the existence of prejudice, discrimination and power and their economic, social, group and individual effects

- to foster an awareness and understanding of the interdependency of humanity and the world we live in

- to enable pupils to feel comfortable with their own identity and culture within the classroom/school environment

- to facilitate the ability to interrelate with those from other cultures/of the other sex

- to appreciate the unique value of each human being and the social/cultural groups to which they belong

- to develop a moral commitment to the philosophy of equality of opportunity

- to encourage the development of a repertoire of response strategies to cope with group and individual manifestations of prejudice and discrimination

- to nurture and encourage non-racist/non-sexist verbal behaviour among staff and pupils

- to facilitate respectful and creative interaction, therefore, between pupils and staff

These aims are clearly very wide ranging: the project was concerned with the development of pupils' knowledge and skills, but it was also meant to affect attitudes and behaviour. The promotion of equal opportunities was the main explicit aim of the project, and some of the work focusing on gender won an award for positive action in education sponsored by the Fawcett Society (an organization that campaigns for equality between women and men).

As part of their work, pupils were encouraged to examine images they held of themselves and other people. Gender images were included in this examination, as were images of other social groups: young and old people; people from different ethnic groups and different religious groups; disabled and able-bodied people. Pupils were encouraged to think critically about the sources of positive and negative images and to challenge popular stereotypes. Language was an important focus for this work, but many other forms of representation (music, pictures, clothing, etc.) were also examined.

In their examination of linguistic images, the pupils thought about the language used to describe other people (including terms of abuse). They collected and analysed written texts such as newspapers, magazines, comics and textbooks, and developed a checklist to detect bias and 'perpetuation of stereotypes that lead to prejudice and discrimination'. They 'brainstormed' their own stereotypes about women and Black people to produce words often used to classify them (gentle, aggressive, sexy, lazy, etc.). They also looked at books that challenged stereotypes – including non- or anti-sexist stories for children. Both boys and girls responded favourably to books providing positive images of girls. One outcome of this aspect of the pupils' work was the production of the *Equal Opportunities Express*, with a 'small ads' section advertising for a 'lady builder', 'male nanny' etc.

Jackie Hughes also noticed there were some inequalities in classroom talk. Boys were more eager to talk than girls. In whole class discussions they became impatient and called out if they didn't get a turn quickly enough. Girls, on the other hand, tended to 'obey the rules', putting their hands up and waiting to be called upon to contribute. In such a situation, it was hard not to reinforce boys' behaviour. Jackie Hughes found that in small discussion groups it was relatively easy to intervene: the composition of groups could be chosen so that they weren't dominated by more talkative pupils; it was also possible to discuss with small groups why some pupils might find it more difficult to contribute. Whole class discussion was more difficult to change, but again involving the pupils themselves in a discussion of classroom talk seemed to make them more sensitive and aware of others' needs.

In an attempt to evaluate her work, Jackie Hughes consulted other teachers, the pupils, a parent governor and an adviser. She felt this collection of 'evaluative audiences' would provide a useful picture of the effectiveness or otherwise of the project in 'teaching for the reduction of prejudice'. Responses from these audiences were favourable, leading Jackie Hughes to conclude that the project had been successful. She concedes that a more formal evaluation would have been impossible: 'How do you evaluate attitudes and values being developed?'

Case Study 4: Equality Guidelines for Course Materials

The Open University of the United Kingdom is a major publisher and producer of educational materials. In 1983 the School of Education at the Open University established an Equality Working Group, whose terms of reference were to review:

- course materials
- employment patterns
- representation issues

in the light of the School's commitment to an equal opportunities policy. As part of its brief, and after consultation with course teams and editors in the School of Education, the Equality Working Group drew up a set of guidelines for 'Equality in Course Material'. These were approved by the School Board and are now School of Education policy. They tended to focus on the Open University's printed study texts, but were followed shortly by a set of guidelines covering broadcast materials. One of us (J.S.) was involved in the production of the guidelines.

As the title suggests the guidelines are concerned not just with gender but also with the representation of certain minority groups in course material. They also go far beyond language in its conventional sense. The guidelines give suggestions for: adequate representation of the experiences of women and minority groups in course materials (including the avoidance of stereotypical portrayals); discussion of social inequalities where this is relevant to course materials; ensuring a wide range of contributors are able to make an input to courses; and avoiding sexism in language. An appendix drafted by an editor, John Pettit, suggests alternatives to 'sexist' language similar to those discussed in chapter 5 above.

Although language use was only part of an overall strategy for ensuring better representation of women and minority groups, there was a fear that course team activity would focus more on this than on other aspects of the recommendations. It's easier to effect change at the linguistic level than in some other respects suggested in the guidelines. Changing a draft text to include more examples of women, or to draw on a wider range of academic sources, requires considerable work and may be quite contentious. Inequality of treatment may also be hard to spot by those unfamiliar with the field. But an editor can usually suggest acceptable rephrasings that obviate the need for 'generic' *he* and *man*.

As it turned out, the language recommendations attracted considerable attention – most supportive but some antagonistic. There were letters to the Equality Working Group; an interview on the BBC/OU radio programme *Open Forum*; an article in the OU's staff newspaper *Open House*; and a debate in *Sesame*, the OU's student newspaper, sparked off by an article suggesting (amongst other things) that the linguistic guidelines represented an attempt at 'thought control'.

There has been no survey of School of Education courses since the guidelines were introduced, but the view of course editors is that these have been useful. Course teams tend nowadays to avoid 'sexist' language. If any examples persist, editors are able to weed these out. Because the guidelines are known to represent school policy, such intervention meets with few protests.

Whether any changes can be directly attributed to the equality guidelines is, of course, another matter. The climate of opinion has changed in the OU, as in other institutions, so that it is now simply less acceptable to use 'sexist' language. The adoption of the guidelines – and even the creation of the Equality Working Group itself – can be seen as symptomatic of this changing climate as well as, perhaps, contributing to it.

The case studies demonstrate that language use and social change are closely linked in practice as well as in theory. They also illustrate some of the problems we face in trying to discover whether language intervention is a useful way of changing or challenging social relations. We shall consider these issues below.

Language and Social Change

The first case study, on computer conferencing, indicates that a change in language practices and in the relationships between language users may arise as a by-product of an unrelated techno- logical innovation and change in communicative context. This is a useful reminder that language changes historically without deliber- ate intervention in either the linguistic or social arena. From the point of view of the historical linguist, language seems inherently variable and subject to change. Some of the work we discussed in chapter 3 – Nichols (1978), Gal (1978) and Milroy (1980) – found differences in the degree and type of sex differentiation that occurred in the language varieties used by younger and older speakers. Trudgill (1972) notes that the 'covert prestige' attached to vernacu- lar forms of language in his Norwich study is associated with the age as well as the sex of speakers: younger women are much less likely than older women to over-report their use of high status pronuncia- tion features – they tend more often to be accurate, or to under- report such usages. Trudgill comments: 'Whether this is a feature which is repeated in every generation of female speakers, or whether it reflects a genuine and recent change in ideology it is not possible at this stage to say' (Trudgill, 1972, p. 192). Beattie's (1981) study of university tutorials (discussed in chapter 4) may also suggest that under some circumstances young women use interactional features hitherto thought to be commoner in men.

Such linguistic variation and change is unlikely to result from a conscious, politically motivated decision on the part of speakers to change their language habits. It is more likely to be related to social factors such as personal aspirations, changes in lifestyle within a community, or encounters with new contexts of communication. Although all linguistic change is ultimately linked with social pro- cesses, these may not themselves represent social change – in fact lan- guage and language behaviour may alter more rapidly than the social structures which they mark. For example, new ways of talking 'macho' or of sounding feminine can emerge without a significant change in social definitions of masculinity and femininity. In the case of com- puter conferencing, linguistic behaviour and discourse structure must reflect the constraints of the new medium of communication – but it will be interesting to monitor the extent to which new discourse mechan- isms for maintaining traditional power relations emerge in the system.

In the majority of cases, linguistic change reported in the literature is linked with social processes but not with any deliberate
attempt either at linguistic or social intervention. In practical equal
opportunities measures, however, there is an intentional intervention, and the question arises whether attempts to change people's
language are an effective means of changing attitudes and social
behaviour, and reforming social structures.

Strategies for Intervention

Many institutions now have policies designed to promote equality of
opportunity, or equality of treatment, between women and men.
While such policies can benefit either sex they are normally designed
to open up opportunities for women. The motivations for such
policies may be overtly feminist – but not necessarily so. In industry,
for instance, there may be concern about the 'wastage of talent' of a
considerable proportion of the workforce, or potential workforce.
Similarly, the goals of different policies vary – from changing
attitudes or opening up new opportunities amongst a particular set
of people to effecting a more general and profound social change.

Although we have used the term 'policy', strategies for intervention vary in their level of formality – not all could be said to
constitute a formal policy. The promotion of change may derive
from a personal attempt to affect the perceptions or the behaviour of
others – as when an adult trainer tries to encourage women to be
more assertive, or a teacher consciously directs more questions
towards the girls in her class. The case studies show examples of
both formal and informal intervention. Anti-sexist guidelines are
normally carefully worked out and issued as a matter of policy to
writers, editors or members of professional organizations. When
produced by and for institutions, they have the weight of being seen
as institutional policy. In the 'conferencing' case study, intervention
(in the form of monitoring 'sexist' language) occurred initially
informally and at an individual level, when women began to
comment on men's use of language. The status of the intervention
changed as it became part of the culture of the conference to monitor
(sexist) language use, but it never achieved the status of a formal
institutional policy and seemed to be lost when the membership of
the conferencing system expanded.

The extent to which language is the target of change also varies. Many initiatives, such as the equal opportunities policy in operation at Esso, do not have language use as an explicit focus: language seems, in fact, to be rather tangential to the work being done. Nevertheless, if Robin Schneider is to be believed, the way people communicate is affected by the general climate in an institution, even if not specifically targeted by any policy. There appears to be an assumption here that language reflects rather than creates unequal relationships between women and men.

In other cases, language plays a more central role: Diane Taylor explicitly drew attention to what she saw as linguistic inequalities in her industrial training courses; the images conveyed in language, and the nature of classroom discourse, were an important part of the equality project at Jervoise School; and the OU equality guidelines, like many other writers' guidelines mentioned in chapter 5, outlined strategies for avoiding linguistic 'sexism' – the use of words or phrases felt to discriminate against women.

When people do specifically target language like this, they are not concerned with promoting linguistic change *per se*. Diane Taylor and Jackie Hughes discussed linguistic inequalities and linguistic 'bias' in an attempt to raise peoples' awareness of stereotyping and social inequalities. Their main aim here seems to have been to use awareness of language as a vehicle to promote social change – with any (subsequent) changes to peoples' own language habits arising as a consequence of this. In such cases, there again appears to be a tacit assumption that language reflects, rather than creates, social inequality.

Other kinds of linguistic intervention seek to promote linguistic change in the belief that new language practices will themselves contribute towards a change in the relations between women and men. Sometimes this may be at a local level (providing a better opportunity for girls to talk in class, or women employees to contribute more effectively in meetings) – but interventions may be more ambitious, aiming to effect a more general social change. People who oppose such linguistic intervention sometimes invoke arguments based on notions of 'correct grammar', 'logic' or 'aesthetic' values – all of which rest on ideological assumptions, such as the doctrine of correctness in language which we discussed in chapter 6. But many opponents quite explicitly acknowledge that they see 'feminist tampering' with the language as a more serious threat.

Both supporters of linguistic change and those who complain about it routinely make assumptions about the nature of language and the way it constrains the thoughts and beliefs of language users.

It is not too difficult to see how conscious interventions, at these various levels, may be premised on assumptions about 'women's language' which we questioned in earlier chapters (particularly chapter 4). They may also be motivated by theories of language and consciousness which we found to be unsatisfactory when we reviewed them in chapter 6. This serves as a reminder that the ideological struggle in which reformists are engaged is one that includes popular notions about language and how it works, as well as about gender. Nevertheless, a more satisfactory justification for linguistic intervention can be found, and the model of discourse which we set out in chapter 6 can be applied successfully to many language policies. If our beliefs and expectations are supported by the continuous reinforcement of day to day discourse, then any change in this, anything that challenged our expectations might be expected to be disruptive. Attempts at linguistic intervention should not be dismissed on the grounds that some of the justifications put forward by those who promote them are open to question. The value of intervention should be assessed according to the best available theory.

In chapter 6 we argued that institutions have a crucial role to play in the reproduction and transmission of ideologies. But the so-called 'gatekeepers' of language, such as publishers' editors, are, as we have seen, also in a position to promote change. While by no means all institutionally motivated interventions are successful, they might seem to stand a better chance than personal interventions. If the weight of the institution could be brought to bear on recalcitrant authors, so that they all followed publishing guidelines, then alternative representations of women and men would reach large audiences. And if schools were effective in encouraging their pupils to be critical of linguistic (and other) stereotypes, this might go some way towards countering stereotyped images available elsewhere. But individual actions too would be expected to have an effect – however slight. If a large enough, and consistent enough disruption occurred from different sources, one might predict that our expectations (and our beliefs and attitudes) would change. In practice, we can note that the introduction of an institutional policy is often dependent on the behaviour of one or two key people. Successful change seems to require activity at both the personal and institutional level.

Is It Worth Promoting Linguistic Change?

The promotion of linguistic change has been described as a decidedly prescriptive activity and as such is abhorred by some linguists. Linguists, nevertheless, have been involved in prescriptive activities for decades – such as language planning in developing countries, the selection of varieties for foreign language teaching, and so on. It is clear that there are occasions where language guidelines are appropriate.

There is an important difference between the kind of prescriptivism which proscribes certain usages as ungrammatical, thus supporting an illiberal linguistic ideology that grammar is an absolute matter properly under the guardianship of an elite, and the kind of prescriptivism that lays down ethical guidelines, such as 'anti-sexist' guidelines. The import of the word 'ought' in 'you ought to say *everybody should watch his language*, and that in 'you ought to say *everybody should watch their language*, is quite different. Hence, where there are good grounds for believing some language usage to be sexist, it should be avoided in the same way as any other sexist behaviour.

Linguists are not the only ones to have qualms about linguistic intervention. The popular notion that language determines an individual's thoughts introduces a moral dimension to attempts at intervention, which become seen as attempts at 'thought control'. Arguments about this frequently become rather muddled. Even if one believes that changing the language will allow you, in any simple way, to re-engineer a person's thoughts then you are hardly taking away a freedom, since such a speaker is already somehow the victim of their language.

Such moral questions apart, there remains the important issue of whether, on pragmatic grounds, it is worth attempting linguistic intervention; whether a change in linguistic behaviour will, in practice, bring about desired social change. Our discussion in chapters 5 and 6, along with evidence from some of the case studies in this chapter, suggests that patterns of cause and effect are not so straightforward as implied by many linguistic intervention programmes. For instance:

● attempts to prove the effects of a language on its users are fraught with problems. It is possible to design 'laboratory' experiments to measure the effect of a particular usage in a particular context on a particular set of language users, but such experiments are somewhat divorced from real life. On the other hand, the gradual but continuous transmission of cultural values through a variety of media and a whole set of social practices, both linguistic and nonlinguistic, is not amenable to similar empirical investigation. Our case studies illustrate how linguistic interventions are usually carried out in a context of wider social and organizational changes. It is very difficult to find real-life examples where a language policy has been the only kind of intervention.

If it is difficult to measure the effects of current linguistic practices it is equally difficult to measure the effects of change. It is notable that none of the interventions we discussed had been systematically evaluated in terms of its immediate impact on language use, let alone any subsequent effect on beliefs and attitudes.

● sociolinguistic studies often suggest that change occurs in the opposite direction – that linguistic change is motivated by changes in the social/cultural environment. Our case studies contained examples of this sort of change.

If, as we suggested in chapter 6, language functions as part of a larger system of social practices, one can argue that changes to particular components in the system (linguistic or nonlinguistic) will affect other components. In this case, we can say that linguistic changes tend to accompany other social or cultural changes; they may play a part in motivating such changes; but they are not a prerequisite for other forms of social change.

● people attempting to challenge, and change, society's values often talk about one set of values being 'dominant' at any one time. But societies are not homogeneous (and so the transmission of whatever are the dominant values is not totally successful). Just as language can be regarded as a system of systems with many internal conflicts and contradictions, social values can be thought of as networks of values, some in conflict and some mutually contradictory. This arrangement militates against total indoctrination – a potential for challenge and change is built into society and into an individual's personality, beliefs and behaviour. For feminists and others concerned with promoting social change the idea must be, not so much to 'free' people from total oppression as to take one's stand in an ideological struggle – to replace one set of dominant values by another.

Conclusion

When translating from an effectively grammatical gender language such as French: either one produces a text in which the masculine reference predominates or one specifies the feminine equally at every point (*he/she*, *him-or-herself*, etc.). The effect of the latter strategy – the signified determination to move against linguistic sexism – could only be an addition by the translator to Barthes writing in French; for this reason alone, it has not been adopted here (translator's note to Barthes, 1977).

When compared with larger social and ideological struggles, linguistic reform may seem quite a trivial concern. A preoccupation with women's economic, social and physical oppression is one thing. A concern to replace *fireman* with *firefighter* can all too easily bring on ridicule – terms such as *personhole cover* are part of the stock armoury of those opposed to this sort of linguistic intervention. There is also the danger that effective change at this level is mistaken for real social change. One may feel that a battle has been won when an institution adopts the word *chair* rather than *chairman* even though all 'chairs' remain male.

It is clear that linguistic intervention on its own would be most unlikely to have any effect – other than making the interventionists appear slightly eccentric. But most current attempts at intervention are occurring in a context of social change. It is futile to speculate whether they are symptomatic or causal: they are an integral part of a whole set of social processes enlisted to effect changes in the relations between women and men. The reason why they arouse opposition may be precisely because they are seen as easy targets in the enemy ranks.

There is no neutral ground for the language user. It's true that some writers continue to use 'generic' *he*, say, while expressing regret at the absence of a 'neutral' third person singular pronoun in English. But the issue of linguistic sexism has been so well aired for the past ten to 15 years, and the different usages so firmly tied to ideological positions, that it would seem impossible to use a generic form or other common example of 'sexist language' in a neutral way.

References

Abbot, P. and Sapsford, R. (1987) *Women and Social Class*, London, Tavistock Publications.

Althusser, L. (1971) 'Ideology and ideological state apparatuses' in *Lenin and Philosophy and Other Essays*, London, New Left Books.

Apple, W., Streeter, L. A. and Krauss, R. M. (1979) 'Effects of pitch and speech rate on personal attributions', *Journal of Personality and Social Psychology*, 37:715–27.

Atkinson, M. (1984) *Our Masters' Voices: the language and body language of politics*, London, Methuen.

Bales, R. (1970) *Personality and Interpersonal Behaviour*, New York, Holt, Rinehart and Winston.

Barthes, R. (1977) *Image – Music – Text*, London, Fontana.

Baumann, M. (1979) 'Two features of "Women's Speech"?' in Dubois, B. L. and Crouch, I. (eds) *The Sociology of the Languages of American Women*, Papers in Southwest English IV, San Antonio, Trinity University.

Beattie, G. W. (1981) 'Interruption in conversational interaction, and its relation to the sex and status of interactants', *Linguistics*, 19:15–35.

Beattie, G. W. (1983) *Talk: an analysis of speech and non-verbal behaviour in conversation*, Milton Keynes, The Open University Press.

Beauvoir, S. de (1953) *The Second Sex*, London, Jonathan Cape.

Bem, S. (1974) 'The measurement of psychological androgyny', *Journal of Consulting and Clinical Psychology*, 42:155–62.

Bernard, J. (1972) *The Sex Game*, New York, Atheneum.

Berthoff, A. E. (1988) 'Sapir and the two tasks of language,' *Semiotica*, 71:1–47.

Bickerton, D. (1980) 'What happens when we switch?', *York Papers in Linguistics*, 9:41–56.

Boas, F. (ND) *Introduction to the Handbook of American Indian Languages*, Washington, Georgetown University Press.

Bodine, A. (1975) 'Androcentrism in prescriptive grammar: singular "they", sex-indefinite "he", and "he or she"', *Language in Society*, 4:129–46.

Bornstein, D. (1978) 'As meek as a maid: a historical perspective on language for women in courtesy books from the Middle Ages to Seventeen Magazine' in Butturf, D. and Epstein, E. L. (eds) *Women's Language and Style*, Dept. of English, University of Akron.

Brend, R. (1975) 'Male-female intonation patterns in American English', in B. Thorne and N. Henley (eds) *Language and Sex: difference and dominance*, Rowley, Mass., Newbury House.

Brown, B. L., Strong, W. J. and Rencher, A. C. (1973) 'Perceptions of personality from speech: effects of manipulations of acoustical parameters', *Journal of the Acoustical Society of America*, 54:29–35.

Brown, B. L., Strong, W. J. and Rencher, A. C. (1975) 'Acoustic determinants of perceptions of personality from speech', *International Journal of the Sociology of Language*, 6:11–32.

Brown, P. (1980) 'How and why are women more polite: some evidence from a Mayan community' in McConnell-Ginet, S., Borker, R. and Furman, N. (eds) *Women and Language in Literature and Society*, New York, Praeger.

Brown, R. and Gilman, A. (1972) 'The pronouns of power and solidarity' in Giglioli, P. P. (ed). *Language and Social Context*, Harmondsworth, Penguin.

Cameron, D. (1984) 'Sexism and semantics', *Radical Philosophy*, 36, 14–16.

Cameron, D. (1985) *Feminism and Linguistic Theory*, London, Macmillan.

Cameron, D. and Coates, J. (1985) 'Some problems in the sociolinguistic explanations of sex differences', *Language and Communication*, 5, 3:143–51.

Carleton, M. and Ohala, J. J. (1980) 'The effect of pitch of voice on perceived personality traits', Meeting of Kroeber Anthropological Society, Berkeley.

Central Statistical Office (1987) *Social Trends*, 17, HMSO.

Cheshire, J. (1982) *Variation in an English Dialect*, Cambridge, Cambridge University Press.

Chomsky, N. (1965) *Aspects of the Theory of Syntax*, Cambridge, Mass., MIT Press.

Clarke, M. A., Losoff, A., McCracken, M. D. and Rood, D. S. (1984) 'Linguistic relativity and sex/gender studies: epistemological and methodological considerations', *Language Learning*, 34:47–67.

Clarke, M. A., Losoff, A., McCracken, M. D. and Still, J. (1981) 'Gender perception in Arabic and English', *Language Learning*, 31:159–69.

Clarricoates, K. (1983) 'Classroom interaction' in Whyld, J. (ed.) *Sexism in the Secondary Curriculum*, New York, Harper and Row.

Clench, M. (1978) 'Tracheal elongation in birds-of-paradise', *Condor*, 80:423–30.

Coates, J. (1984) 'Language and sexism', Committee for Linguistics in Education (CLIE) working paper no. 5.

Coates, J. (1986) *Women, Men and Language*, London, Longman.

Coleman, R.O. (1973) 'A comparison of the contributions of two vocal characteristics to the perception of maleness and femaleness in the voice', *STL–QPSR*, 2–3:13–22.

Damste, P.H. (1964) 'Virilization of the voice due to anabolic steroids', *Folia Phoniatrica*, 16:10–18.

Damste, P.H. (1967) 'Voice change in adult women caused by virilizing agents', *Journal of Speech and Hearing Disorders*, 32:126–32.

Darwin, C. (1874) *The Descent of Man and Selection in Relation to Sex*, Detroit, Gale Research Company.

Drummond, H. (1899) *The Ascent of Man*, London, Hodder and Stoughton.

Dubois, B.L. and Crouch, I. (1975) 'The question of tag questions in women's speech: they don't really use more of them, do they?', *Language in Society*, 4:289–94.

Eakins, B. and Eakins, G. (1976) 'Verbal turn-taking and exchanges in faculty dialogue' in Dubois, B.L. and Crouch, I. (eds) (1978) *The Sociology of the Languages of American Women*, Papers in Southwest English IV, San Antonio, Trinity University.

Eco, U. (1979) *The Role of the Reader*, London, Hutchinson.

Eco, U. (1984) *Semiotics and the Philosophy of Language*, London, Macmillan.

Edelsky, C. (1979) 'Question intonation and sex roles', *Language in Society*, 8:15–32.

Edelsky, C. (1981) 'Who's got the floor?' *Language in Society*, 10:383–421.

Edwards, J.R. (1979) 'Social class differences and the identification of sex in children's speech', *Journal of Child Language*, 6:121–7.

Edwards, V. (1986) *Language in a Black Community*, Clevedon, Avon, Multilingual Matters.

Elliott, J. (1974) 'Sex role constraints on freedom of discussion: a neglected reality of the classroom', *The New Era*, 55, (6).

Ellis, H. (1896) *Man and Woman*, London, Walter Scott.

Elyan, O., Smith, P., Giles, H. and Bourhis, R. (1978) 'RP-accented speech: the voice of perceived androgyny?', in Trudgill, P. (ed.) *Sociolinguistic Patterns in British English*, London, Edward Arnold.

Ervin, S. (1962) 'The connotations of gender,' *Word*, 18:249–61.

Esposito, A. (1979) 'Sex differences in children's conversation', *Language and Speech*, 22, (3):213–20.

Fairbanks, G. (1942) 'An acoustical study of the pitch of infant hunger wails', *Child Development*, 13:227–32.

Fairchild, L. (1976) 'Thermo-regulation of pitch of croak in Fowlers toads', *Science*, 212:950.

Fischer, J.L. (1958) 'Social influences on the choice of a linguistic variant',

Word, 14:47–59. Reprinted in Hymes, D. (ed.) (1964) *Language in Culture and Society*, New York, Harper and Row.

Fishman, P. M. (1978a) 'What do couples talk about when they're alone?' in Butturf, D. and Epstein, E. L. (eds) *Women's Language and Style*, Department of English, University of Akron.

Fishman, P. M. (1978b) 'Interaction: the work women do', *Social Problems* 25, (4):397–406.

Fishman, P. M. (1983) 'Interaction: the work women do' in Thorne, B., Kramarae, C. and Henley, N. (eds) *Language, Gender and Society*, Rowley, Mass., Newbury House.

Flach, M., Schwickardi, H. and Simon, R. (1968) 'Welchen Einfluss haben Menstruation und Swangerschaft auf die ausgebildete Gesangsstimme?', *Folia Phoniatrica*, 16:67–74.

French, J. and French, P. (1984a) 'Gender imbalance in the primary classroom: an interactional account', *Educational Research, 26*, (2).

French, J. and French, P. (1984b) 'Sociolingustics and gender divisions' in Acker, S. et al. (eds) *World Yearbook of Education 1984: women and education*, London, Kogan Page.

Furfey, P. H. (1944) 'Men's and women's language', *The American Catholic Sociological Review* 5:218–23.

Gal, S. (1978) 'Peasant men can't get wives: language change and sex roles in a bilingual community', *Language in Society*, 7:1–16.

Gal, S. (1979) *Language Shift: social determinants of linguistic change in bilingual Austria*, London, Academic Press.

Gedda, L., Fiori-Ratti, L. and Bruno, G. (1960) 'La voix chez les jumeaux monozygotiques', *Folia Phoniatrica*, 12:81–94.

Gibb, G. D. (1869) 'The character of the voice in the nations of Asia and Africa contrasted with that of the nations of Europe', *Journal of the Anthropological Society*, April:244–59.

Giles, H. (1973) 'Accent mobility: a model and some data', *Anthropological Linguistics*, 15:87–105.

Giles, H. (1980) 'Accommodation theory: some new directions', *York Papers in Linguistics*, 9:105–35.

Giles, H. and Powesland, P. F. (1975) *Speech Style and Social Evaluation*, London, Academic Press.

Giles, H., Taylor, D. M. and Bourhis, R. Y. (1973) 'Towards a theory of interpersonal accommodation through speech: some Canadian data', *Language in Society*, 2:177–92.

Goodwin, M. H. (1980) 'Directive-response speech sequences in girls' and boys' task activities', in McConnell-Ginet, S., Borker, R. and Furman, M. (eds) *Women and Language in Literature and Society*, New York, Praeger.

Graddol, D. J. (1983) 'Three experiments in the perception of speaking fundamental frequency', paper given to Institute of Acoustics Speech Group, Nottingham.

Graddol, D. J. (1986) 'Discourse specific pitch behaviour', in Johns-Lewis, C. (ed.) *Intonation in Discourse*, London, Croom Helm.

Graddol, D. J. and Swann, J. (1983) 'Speaking fundamental frequency: some social and physical correlates', *Language and Speech*, 26:351–66.

Green, J. (1987) *Memory, Thinking and Language*, London, Methuen.

Green, M. C. L. (1980) *The Voice and its Disorders*, Tunbridge Wells, Pitman Medical.

Grice, P. (1957) 'Meaning', *Philosophical Review*, 66:377–88.

Guentherodt, I., Hellinger, M., Pusch, L. F. and Tromel-Plotz, S. (1980) 'Richtlinien zur Vermeldung sexistischen Sprachgebrauchs', *Linguistisches Berichte*, 69:15–21.

Guiora, A. Z. and Acton, W. R. (1979) 'Personality and language behavior: a restatement', *Language Learning*, 29:193–206.

Gumperz, J. J. (1987) 'Preface' in Brown, P. and Levinson, S. C. *Politeness: some universals of language use*, Cambridge, Cambridge University Press.

Haas, M. R. (1944) 'Men's and women's speech in Koasati', *Language*, 20:142–9. Reprinted in Hymes, D. (ed.) (1964) *Language in Culture and Society*, New York, Harper and Row.

Harris, R. (1981) *The Language Myth*, London, Duckworth.

Hellinger, M. (1980) 'Zum Gebrauch weiblicher Berufsbezeichnungen im Deutschen–Variabilitat als Ausdruck aussersprachlicher Machtstrukturen', *Linguistische Berichte*, 69:37–57.

Henton, C. G. and Bladon, A. W. (1985) 'Breathiness in normal female speech: inefficiency versus desirability', *Language and Communication*, 5:221–7.

Hirshman, L. (1974) 'Analysis of supportive and assertive behaviour in conversations', paper presented at a meeting of the Linguistic Society of America, July, 1973. See summary in Thorne, B. and Henley, N. (1975) *Language and Sex: difference and dominance*, Rowley, Mass., Newbury House.

Holmes, J. (1986) 'Functions of *you know* in women's and men's speech', *Language in Society* 15:1–22.

Jabbra, N. W. (1980) 'Sex roles and language in Lebanon', *Ethnology*, 19, 4:459–74.

Jespersen, O. (1922) *Language: its nature, development and origins*, London, Allen and Unwin.

Kalcik, S. (1975) ' "… like Ann's gynecologist or the time I was almost raped": personal narratives in women's rap groups', *Journal of American Folklore*, 88:3–11.

Kaplan, C. (1986) *Sea Changes: culture and feminism*, London, Verso.

Kidd, V. (1971) 'A study of images produced through the use of a male pronoun as the generic', *Movements: Contemporary Rhetoric and Communication*, Fall (1):25–30.

Kingston, M. H. (1976) *The Woman Warrior*, Harmondsworth, Penguin.

Kramer, C. (1977) 'Perceptions of male and female speech', *Language and Speech*, 20:151–61.

Labov, W. (1966) *The Social Stratification of English in New York City*, Washington DC, Center for Applied Linguistics.

Labov, W. (1972a) *Sociolinguistic Patterns*, Philadelphia, University of Pennsylvania Press. Also published (1978) Oxford, Basil Blackwell.

Labov, W. (1972b) *Language in Inner City: studies in the Black English Vernacular*, Philadelphia, University of Pennyslvania Press.

Lakoff, R. (1975) *Language and Woman's Place*, New York, Harper and Row.

Laver, J. (1968) 'Voice quality and indexical information', *British Journal of Disorders of Communication*, 3:43–54.

Laver, J. (1975) 'Individual features in voice quality', PhD dissertation, University of Edinburgh.

Laver, J. (1980) *The Phonetic Description of Voice Quality*, Cambridge, Cambridge University Press.

Laver, J. and Trudgill, P. (1979) 'Phonetic and linguistic markers in speech' in Scherer, K. R. and Giles, H. (eds) *Social Markers in Speech*, Cambridge, Cambridge University Press.

Lecroy, M. (1981) 'The genus paradisaea – display and evolution', *American Museum Novitates*, 2714.

Le Page, R. B. and Tabouret-Keller, A. (1985) *Acts of Identity: Creole-based approaches to language and ethnicity*, Cambridge, Cambridge University Press.

Lee, M. Y. (1976) 'The married woman's status and role in Japanese: an exploratory sociolinguistic study', *Signs* 1, 4:991–9.

Lees, S. (1983) 'How boys slag off girls', *New Society*, 13th October.

Leet-Pellegrini, H. M. (1980) 'Conversational dominance as a function of gender and expertise' in Giles, H., Robinson, W. P. and Smith, P. M. *Language: social psychological perspectives*, Oxford, Pergamon.

Leith, D. (1983) *A Social History of English*, London, Routledge and Kegan Paul.

Lenneberg, E. H. (1953) 'Cognition in ethnologinustics' *Language*, 29:463–71.

Lieberman, P. (1967) *Intonation, Perception and Language*, Cambridge, Mass., MIT Press.

Loveday, L. (1981) 'Pitch, politeness and sexual role: an exploratory investigation', *Language and Speech*, 24:71–88.

Luchsinger, R. and Arnold, G. E. (1965) *Voice-Speech-Language*, Belmont, Wadsworth Publishing Company.

Lyons, J. (1977) *Semantics*, I, Cambridge, Cambridge University Press.

Macaulay, R.K.S. (1978) 'Variation and consistency in Glaswegian English' in Trudgill, P. (ed.) *Sociolinguistic Patterns in British English*, London, Edward Arnold.

Macdonnell, D. (1986) *Theories of Discourse*, Oxford, Basil Blackwell.

Mackay, D. and Fulkerson, D. (1979) 'On the comprehension and production of pronouns', *Journal of Verbal Learning and Verbal Behaviour*, 18:661–73.

Macshane, D. (1978) *Black and Front: journalists and race reporting*, London, National Union of Journalists.

Majewski, W., Hollien, H. and Zalewski, J. (1972) 'Speaking fundamental frequencies of Polish adult males', *Phonetica*, 25:119–25.

Maltz, D.N. and Borker, R.A. (1982) 'A cultural approach to male-female miscommunication' in Gumperz, J.J. (ed.) *Language and Social Identity*, Cambridge, Cambridge University Press.

Marland, M. (1977) *Language Across the Curriculum*, London, Heinemann.

Martin, F.M. (1954) 'Some subjective aspects of social stratification', in Glass, D.V. (ed.) *Social Mobility in Britain*, London, Routledge and Kegan Paul.

Martyna, W. (1978) 'What does *he* mean – use of the generic masculine', *Journal of Communication*, 28:131–8.

McConnell-Ginet, S. (1983) 'Intonation in a man's world' in Thorne, B., Kramarae, C. and Henley, N. (eds) *Language, Gender and Society*, Rowley, Mass., Newbury House.

McConnell-Ginet, S. (1984) 'The origins of sexist language in discourse', *Annals of the New York Academy of Sciences*, 433:123–35.

Miller, C. and Swift, K. (1981, British edn) *The Handbook of Non-Sexist Writing for Writers, Editors and Speakers*, London, The Women's Press.

Milroy, J. and Milroy, L. (1986) *Language and Authority*, Oxford, Basil Blackwell.

Milroy, L. (1980) *Language and Social Networks*, Oxford, Basil Blackwell.

Milroy, L. (1988) 'Gender as a speaker variable: the interesting case of the glottalised stops in Tyneside', paper presented at *Sociolinguistics Symposium 7*, University of York, April, 1988.

Moulton, J., Robinson, G.M. and Elias, C. (1978) 'Sex bias in language use: "neutral" pronouns that aren't', *American Psychologist*, 33:1032–6.

Mufwene, S. (1983) 'Investigating what the words "father" and "mother" mean', *Language and Communication*, 3, 3:245–69.

Nichols, P. (1979) 'Black women in the rural south: conservative and innovative', in Dubois, B.L. and Crouch, I. (eds) *The Sociology of the Languages of American Women*, Papers in Southwest English IV, San Antonio, Trinity University.

NUJ (1982) *Non-Sexist Code of Practice for Book Publishing*, London, National Union of Journalists.

O'Barr, W. M. and Atkins, B. K. (1980) ' "Women's language" or "powerless language"?' in McConnell-Ginet, S., Borker, R. and Furman, N. (eds) *Women and Language in Literature and Society*, New York, Praeger.

Oakley, A. (1981) *Subject Women*, Oxford, Martin Robertson.

Oakley, A. and Oakley, R. (1979) 'Sexism in official statistics' in Irvine, J., Miles, I. and Evans, J. (eds) *Demystifying Social Statistics*, London. Pluto Press.

Ohala, J. J. (1983) 'Cross-language use of pitch: an ethological view', *Phonetica*, 40:1–18.

Ohala, J. J. (1984) 'An ethological perspective on common cross-language utilization of F_0 of voice', *Phonetica*, 41:1–16.

Parke, R. (1981) *Fathering*, London, Fontana Open Books.

Pateman, T. (1975) *Language Truth and Politics*, published by Jean Stroud and Trevor Pateman.

Pedersen, M. F., Munk, E., Bennet, P. and Moller, S. (1984) 'The change of voice during puberty in choir singers', in Van den Broeke, M. P. R. and Cohen, A. (eds) *Proceedings of the X International Congress of Phonetic Sciences*, Dordrecht, Foris Publications.

Perello, J. (1962) 'Le disfonia premenstruel', *Acta Oto-Rino-Laryngologica Ibero-Americana*, 23:561–3.

Phillipsen, G. (1975) 'Speaking like a man in Teamsterville: culture patterns of role enactment in an urban neighbourhood', *The Quarterly Journal of Speech*, 61:13–22.

Preisler, B. (1986) *Linguistic Sex Roles in Conversation: social variation in the expression of tentativeness in English*, Berlin, Mouton de Gruyter.

Pusch, L. F. (1980) 'Das Deutsche als Mannersprache – Diagnose und Therapievorsclage', *Linguistische Berichte*, 69:59–74.

Risch, B. (1987) 'Women's derogatory terms for men: that's right, "dirty" words', *Language in Society*, 16, 3:353–8.

Runciman, W. G. (1964) 'Embourgeoisement, self-rated class and party preference', *Sociological Review*, 12:137–54.

Sachs, J., Lieberman, P. and Erickson, D. (1973) 'Anatomical and cultural determinants of male and female speech', in Shuy, R. W. and Fasold, R. W. (eds) *Language Attitudes: Current Trends and Prospects*, Washington, Georgetown University Press.

Sachs, H., Schegloff, E. and Jefferson, G. (1974) 'A simplest systematics for the organisation of turn-taking for conversation', *Language*, 50:696–735.

Sadker, M. and Sadker, D. (1985) 'Sexism in the schoolroom of the '80s', *Psychology Today*, March, 1985:54–7.

Sapir, E. (1929) 'Male and female forms of speech in Yana' in Teeuwen, St W. J. (ed.) *Donum Natalicium Schrijnen*, Nijmegan-Utrecht. Reprinted in

Mandelbaum, D. G. (ed.) (1949) *Selected Writings of Edward Sapir in Language, Culture and Personality*, Berkley and Los Angeles, University of California Press and London, Cambridge University Press.

Sapir, E. (1970) 'Linguistics as a science' in D. G. Mandelbaum (ed.) *Edward Sapir: culture, language and personality, selected essays*, Berkley, University of California Press.

Schegloff, E. (1972) 'Sequencing in conversational openings' in Gumperz, J. and Hymes, D. (eds) *Directions in Sociolinguistics: the ethnography of communication*, New York, Holt, Rinehart and Winston.

Schegloff, E. and Sacks, H. (1974) 'Opening up closings' in Turner, R. (ed.) *Ethnomethodology*, Harmondsworth, Penguin.

Schultz, M. (1975) 'The semantic derogation of women' in Thorne, B. and Henley, N. (eds) *Language and Sex: difference and dominance*, Rowley, Mass., Newbury House.

Searle, C. (1983) 'A Common Language', *Race and Class*, xxv, 2:65–74.

Shuy, R. (1970) 'Sociolinguistic research at the Center for Applied Linguistics: the correlation of language and sex' in *International Days of Sociolinguistics*, Rome, Instituto Luigi Sturzo.

Silveira, J. (1980) 'Generic masculine words and thinking', *Women's Studies International Quarterly*, 3:165–78.

Smith, P. M. (1985) *Language, The Sexes and Society*, Oxford, Basil Blackwell.

Soskin, W. F. and John, V. P. (1963) 'The study of spontaneous talk' in Barker, R. (ed.) *The Stream of Behaviour*, New York, Appleton-Century-Crofts.

Spender, D. (1978) 'The right way to talk: sex differences in language', *Times Educational Supplement*, 3 November:19.

Spender, D. (1982) *Invisible Women: the schooling scandal*, London, Writers and Readers Publishing Co-operative.

Spender, D. (1985 2nd edn; 1st published 1980) *Man Made Language*, London, Routledge and Kegan Paul.

Stanley, J. P. (1977) 'Paradigmatic woman: the prostitute', in Shores, D. L. and Hines, C. P. (eds) *Papers in Language Variation*, University of Alabama Press.

Stanley, J. P. and Robbins, S. W. (1978) 'Sex-marked pedicates in English', *Papers in Linguistics*, 11, 3/4:487–516.

Stanworth, M. (1981) *Gender and Schooling: a study of gender divisions in the classroom*, London, Women's Research and Resources Centre.

Strainchamps, E. (1971) 'Our sexist language' in V. Gornick and B. K. Moran (eds) *Women in sexist society: studies in power and powerlessness*, New York, Mentor Books.

Sturrock, J. (1980) *Structuralism and Since*, Oxford, Oxford University Press.

Swacker, M. (1975) 'The sex of the speaker as a sociolinguistic variable' in Thorne, B. and Henley, N. (eds) *Language and Sex: difference and dominance*, Rowley, Mass., Newbury House.

Swann, J. and Graddol, D. (1988) 'Gender inequalities in classroom talk', *English in Education*, 22, (1):48–65.

Tabouret-Keller, A. and Luckel, F. (1981) *International Journal of the Sociology of Language*, 29:51–66.

Thakerar, J. N., Giles, H. and Cheshire, J. (1982) 'Psychological and linguistic parameters of speech accommodation theory' in Fraser, C. and Scherer, K. (eds) *Advances in the Social Psychology of Language*, Cambridge, Cambridge University Press.

Thorne, B., Kramarae, C. and Henley, N. (1983) (eds) *Language, Gender and Society*, Rowley, Mass., Newbury House.

Trudgill, P. (1972) 'Sex, covert prestige and linguistic change in the urban British English of Norwich', *Language in Society*, 1:179–95.

Trudgill, P. (1974) *The Social Differentiation of English in Norwich*, Cambridge, Cambridge University Press.

Trudgill, P. (1983a, 2nd edn; 1st published 1974) *Sociolinguistics*, Harmondsworth, Penguin.

Trudgill, P. (1983b) *On Dialect: social and geographical perspectives*, Oxford, Basil Blackwell.

Valentine, C. A. and St Damian, B. (1988) 'Gender and culture as determinants of the ideal voice', *Semiotica*, 71:285–303.

Volosinov, V. N. (1973) *Marxism and the philosophy of language*, New York, Seminar Press (trans. L. Matejka and I. R. Titunik).

Vuorenkoski, V., Lenko, H. L., Tjernlund, P. and Vuorenkoski, L. (1978) 'Fundamental voice frequency during normal and abnormal growth and after androgen treatment', *Archives of Disease in Childhood*, 53:201–9.

Weedon, C. (1987) *Feminist practice and poststructuralist theory*, Oxford, Basil Blackwell.

West, C. (1984) 'When the doctor is a lady', *Symbolic Interaction*, 7, (1):87–106.

West, C. and Zimmerman, D. H. (1983) 'Small insults: a study of interruptions in cross-sex conversations between unacquainted persons' in Thorne, B., Kramarae, C. and Henley, N. (eds) *Language, Gender and Society*, Rowley, Mass. Newbury House.

Whorf, B. L. (1956a) 'A linguistic consideration of thinking in primitive communities' in J. B. Carroll (ed.) *Language, Thought and Reality*, Cambridge, Mass., MIT Press.

Whorf, B. L. (1956b) 'Science and linguistics' in J. B. Carroll (ed.) *Language, Thought and Reality*, Cambridge, Mass., MIT Press.

Whorf, B. L. (1956c) 'Language, mind and reality' in J. B. Carroll (ed.) *Language, Thought and Reality*, Cambridge, Mass., MIT Press.

Whyte, J. (1986) *Girls Into Science and Technology: the story of a project*, London, Routledge and Kegan Paul.

Wolfram, W. (1969) *A Sociolinguistic Description of Detroit Negro Speech*, Washington DC, Center for Applied Linguistics.

Zimmerman, D. H. and West, C. (1975) 'Sex roles, interruptions and silences in conversation' in Thorne, B. and Henley, N. (eds) *Language and Sex: difference and dominance*, Rowley, Mass., Newbury House.

Index